Prose of the World

Saikat Majumdar

Prose of the World

MODERNISM AND THE BANALITY OF EMPIRE

COLUMBIA UNIVERSITY PRESS   NEW YORK

Columbia University Press
Publishers Since 1893
New York   Chichester, West Sussex

Copyright © 2013 Columbia University Press
Paperback edition, 2015
All rights reserved

Library of Congress Cataloging-in-Publication Data
Majumdar, Saikat.
Prose of the world : modernism and the banality of empire /
Saikat Majumdar.
   p. cm.
Includes bibliographical references and index.
ISBN 978-0-231-15694-3 (cloth)—ISBN 978-0-231-15695-0 (pbk.)—ISBN 978-0-231-52767-5 (e-book)
1. Commonwealth fiction (English)—20th century—History and criticism.
2. Banality (Philosophy) in literature. 3. Place (Philosophy) in literature.
4. Narration (Rhetoric). 5. Literature and society—Commonwealth countries—
History—20th century.   I. Title.

PR9080.5.M35   2013
823'.909—dc23   2012014234

Cover design: Lisa Hamm   Cover image: ©plainpicture/Arcaid

For Subho

Every native everywhere lives a life of overwhelming and crushing banality and boredom and desperation and depression, and every deed, good and bad, is an attempt to forget this. Every native would like to find a way out, every native would like a rest, every native would like a tour. But some natives—most natives in the world—cannot go anywhere. They are too poor. They are too poor to go anywhere. They are too poor to escape the reality of their lives . . . so when the natives see you, they envy your ability to leave your own banality and boredom, they envy your ability to turn their own banality and boredom into a source of pleasure for yourself.

—Jamaica Kincaid, *A Small Place*

Contents

Introduction: Poetics of the Prosaic 1

1. James Joyce and the Banality of Refusal 37

2. Katherine Mansfield and the Fragility of Pākehā Boredom 71

3. The Dailiness of Trauma and Liberation in Zoë Wicomb 101

4. Amit Chaudhuri and the Materiality of the Mundane 135

Epilogue: The Uneventful 169

Acknowledgments 181

Notes 185

Bibliography 209

Index 221

Prose of the World

INTRODUCTION
Poetics of the Prosaic

Just about two years before the December made famous by Virginia Woolf as the time of momentous change for "human character,"[1] her fellow Bloomsbury writer, Katherine Mansfield, wrote the following in her diary on December 21, 1908:

> I should like to write a life much in the style of Walter Pater's 'Child in the House'. About a girl in Wellington; the singular charm and barrenness of that place, with climatic effects—wind, rain, spring, night, the sea, the cloud pageantry. And then to leave the place and go to Europe, to live there a dual existence—to go back and be utterly disillusioned, to find out the truth of all, to return to London, to live there an existence so full and strange that Life itself seemed to greet her, and, ill to the point of death, return to W. and die there. A story, no, it would be a sketch, hardly that, more a psychological study of the most erudite character. I should fill it with climatic disturbance, & also of the strange longing for the artificial. I should call it 'Strife', and the child I should call—Ah, I have it—I'd make her a half caste Māori & call her Maata. Bring into it Warbrick the guide.[2]

Mansfield wrote this from Beauchamp Lodge in Paddington, not far from the Grafton Galleries, where Roger Fry curated the first exhibition of "postimpressionist" painting that was to inspire Woolf's famous comment. Inhabiting a moment just two years before that December, however, Mansfield proposed to write a work set half a globe to the south, in her native New Zealand, a place she had left just five months earlier, scarcely knowing, at the time of writing these lines, that she was never again to see her country of birth. In the Wellington of her childhood, she proposed to create a character taken from the indigenous tribes of the colony, with whom the British settlers had a history of violence. "Strife," as far as we know, was never written; what we have instead is the abandoned draft of a novel titled *Maata*, based on her Māori school friend and lover from Wellington, Maata or Martha Grace Mahapuku. The etchings of strife in the diary entry, however, have hardly anything to do with the violent conflicts between the white settlers and the Māori that culminated in the Treaty of Waitangi of 1840. The strife, instead, is quintessentially Mansfield: a psychological conflict between "the singular charm and barrenness" of Wellington and the "full and strange" life in Europe. It is a conflict that promises to account for at least some of the restless energy behind Maata's movement between Wellington on one hand and England and continental Europe on the other, a movement that defines much of Mansfield's own life as well.

Katherine Mansfield is one of those writers whose work and personal life are usually imagined in a clear mutual relationship. Claims about the way her stories echo, develop, or fulfill material contained in her notebooks, diaries, and letters—which have been resurrected relatively recently—are by now fairly standard. However, I want to place an importance on this diary entry that goes beyond its resonance with individual stories in her oeuvre, even beyond the story imagined but unwritten, and beyond the abandoned novel that comes closest to the aspiration contained in these lines. The tension between the "barrenness" and "fullness" of life etched in these lines, in fact, provides the narrative context for most of her work. This tension articulates itself through a minute preoccupation with the ordinary reality of everyday life, where the infertile banality of immediate existence is placed in a teasing relationship with the promise of the exciting fullness that life is capable of offering.

Capable, yes, but only at a distance. That fullness is not realizable *here*, "here" being a trope that is in equal measure spatial and cognitive. The fullness will always exist out *there*. This is the narrative already delivered in the yearning lines of the diary entry, in the diarist's conception of charm and barrenness as aesthetic affects that are enabled by a longing for Europe or, more specifically, London, the metropolitan center of empire. It is a longing that will shape the trajectory of movement for the protagonist whose life originates in the colonial backwaters. London will not only promise but help the protagonist realize a fullness of life that will, in the end, overpower her in its intensity. The climatic cycles that shape life in suburban New Zealand also define the colonial periphery as a place of natural idyll that is too far removed from the epicenter of culture where momentous cultural events can "change" human nature, where charm itself is a kind of barrenness. Nothing happens here; life is empty, uneventful, on the margins of human history. Temporality here is mired purely in the rhythms of the natural environment, which is iterative, unregenerative, and, in the end, banalizing, next to the imagined and subsequently realized fullness of life at the center of imperial culture. Yet the life of the protagonist must be rooted in this barrenness, if only for the sake of a promise of fullness from a distance.

The oppressive banalization of everyday life on the margins of empire is an ineluctable experience of colonial modernity. If Mansfield's 1908 diary entry historicizes a colonial yearning for the excitement and eventfulness of the metropolis that was to rise to a high point in the Woolfian imagination of December 1910, just as interesting is the diary of Virginia Woolf's (at that time) future husband, Leonard, beginning November 10, 1908, a period during which he served as a bureaucrat in a distant outpost of empire. A single word, "Routine," is repeated as the only entry "for four days straight . . . during his three-year appointment as assistant government agent of the Hambantota district in Ceylon."[3] The iterative banality of colonial life is infective; it is a malaise that ails the agents of imperial administration, too. However, while the boredom of imperial bureaucrats captures a significant experiential dimension of everyday life on the colonial periphery, it is radically different, in its affective structure and political meaning, from the way large groups of colonized people etch their self-image through a sense of the banality of their individual and collective lives against the magnetic epicenter of historical, social, and cultural phenomena represented in the metropolitan center of empire.

This book is an attempt to understand the most significant literary articulation of this hierarchical structure of colonial modernity. It is driven by the belief that modernity in the colony, which is well encapsulated in colonial and postcolonial Anglophone fiction, follows the disrupted and uneven globalization of European modernity, an ideal to which local modernities are held in a fractured and subordinated relation. The banalization of everyday life provides aesthetic form to this fracture. But this aesthetic also gets radically reinvented as a narrative impulse in Anglophone fiction produced in the colonies. This narrative impulse is the central subject of this book. Banality and its often-attendant emotion boredom need to be understood as key motifs for colonial and postcolonial literary criticism as they help to aestheticize the relation between the imperial metropolis and the colonial periphery.

As a form of negative aesthetic, banality has an oppositional relationship with literature. The oppositionality is structured by a failure to fulfill the usual promise of literature to engage and entertain its audience. But if the expected pleasures of the text remain rooted within its construction and production of readerly desire, banality emerges as a failing of a specific kind: the failure to produce the new, the original, and, by implication, the engaging. The structure of this failure remains more or less the same outside the domain of the literary text as it is within it. The dread of banality, therefore, is rooted in an inability to transcend the immediate conditions of life surrounding the experiencing subject. The banal is precisely what thwarts the spatial transcendence of the immediate and the temporal transcendence of the everyday. It is the absolute tyranny of the immanent and the inescapable, the denial of the possibility of the excess that is the core of aesthetic pleasure. Boredom is usually understood as the psychic affect that arises in response to the banalization of one's existence, involving the lack of excitement, novelty, activity. As an aesthetic failure, banality exists in an antithetical relation to the intuitive function of literature; a valorization of the banal within narrative parameters can therefore only embody a contrarian aesthetic mode.

Precisely because of their antithetical relation to the traditional goal of literature to engage and entertain, the motifs of banality and boredom deserve to become central concerns for the project of literary criticism when they are articulated as aesthetic motifs in their own right. Sianne Ngai has significantly described marginal emotions like envy, irritation, boredom, anxiety, and paranoia as "noncathartic" affects[4]—in the sense that they resist the obvious cathartic impact of socially recognized and aesthetically canonized emotions like pity, fear, love, or anger. I would suggest that one of the most radical distinctions between classical and modern literature is the degree to which such "noncathartic" affects gain centrality in the literature of the modern or post-Enlightenment period. Banality and boredom, I argue, are among the most radically noncathartic of such affects that mark the conditions of this modernity. Moreover, they help to aestheticize the relation between the dominant and subordinated models of modernity, sharply illustrated in the affective politics of colonialism and its aftermath. As aesthetically oppositional tropes, banality and boredom enter the literature of modernism as markers of radical innovation, yet a full understanding of the genesis and afterlives of these motifs requires an analysis of the political relation between the colonial center and periphery that is deeply linked with yet distinct from the idiosyncratic aesthetic impulses of experimental modernism.

This book identifies the way the banality of everyday life and the boredom that often accompanies it paradoxically shape a narrative instinct along the margins of the global British Empire from late colonial modernism to the present day, as revealed in the fiction of four writers: James Joyce from Ireland, Katherine Mansfield from New Zealand, Zoë Wicomb from South Africa, and Amit Chaudhuri from India. This is a body of English-language fiction in which the banality of everyday life comes to define a globally mappable narrative impulse that has mostly been understood in a linear continuity with the formal innovations of metropolitan modernism. Instead, I propose a reading in which this impulse narrativizes a colonial problematic that significantly shapes the innovative aesthetics of literary modernism. If narrative is triggered by the tremor, velocity, and eventually the excitement of the event, the temporal and affective lack embodied in the banal in these late colonial and postcolonial fictions comes to shape a narrative impulse that is aesthetically oppositional. It is this oppositionality that has primarily been interpreted in terms of literary modernism's radical aesthetic. Rather than being driven predominantly by the subjective idiosyncrasy of formal experimentation, I suggest that the narrative energization of banality is just as significantly rooted in the social experience of colonial modernity.

Gathering momentum in the troubled late colonial decades of the global British Empire, literary modernism is a movement deeply embedded in the cultural, historical, and political tensions and anxieties between the metropolis and the periphery. If an ethnographic exploration of quotidian reality comes to shape English narrative realism since the late eighteenth century, the modernist fragmentation of the empirical archive of the everyday into the affective aesthetics of the banal is driven by desire and longing flowing from the colonial margins toward the heart of empire. As a subtly ideological marker of political marginalization, the aesthetics of banality represents the intimate, micropolitical consequences of colonialism, anticolonial resistance, and postcolonial identity formation, but at a distance from the public space where history is enacted as a grand spectacle of struggle and nation building. Banality and boredom make up evaluative and affective names for an introspective aesthetic whose apparent isolation from the tremors of public history is more symptomatic than conclusive.

This urgent confluence of modernist innovation and colonial anxiety in the hands of key literary modernists of late colonial origin is this book's point of departure. Subsequently, the book explores the contested aesthetic and political legacies of this late colonial modernism as they spread beyond the Anglo-European canon and resonate with Anglophone cultures in the global South at various points of anticolonial resistance and postcolonial development. If the noncathartic motifs at the heart of this study gain literary centrality at a point of entanglement of an aesthetic modernity and a political crisis, these motifs also offer a significant way to read an archive of Anglophone fiction where this modernity as well as its crisis reaches its global expanse. However, the late colonial context of modernism is especially important as a point of departure of this affective relation, as this period sets off in earnest a process of cultural globalization wherein the planetary expansion of Anglophone literature becomes accelerated on a scale not seen before.[5] Imagined as "an array of discrete yet interconnected localities," as John Marx has argued, the late colonial and subsequently postcolonial production of English-language fiction is driven by a disruptive conflict with the imperial hierarchies of culture. In the historical backdrop of literary modernism, this conflict becomes invested with an immediacy unimaginable before.[6]

Katherine Mansfield, whose career charts an emotionally afflicted journey from the antipodean peripheries of empire to its cultural center in Bloomsbury, is an author whose work intricately reveals the manner in which the banal is aestheticized as an index of the relation between the empire and the colony. In her writing, the infertile banality of everyday life is a sensual, felt experience that points to the cultural politics of colonialism only by implication, through its imagination of a fuller life at the heart of empire. In the diary entry, her embodiment of this imagination in the figure of a half-caste Māori woman modeled on a character personally significant to her is, at the same time, an implicit indication of colonial desire, which is for the most part more effectively overshadowed in her stories. Rarely if ever does subjectivity belong to an indigenous figure in her work, which revolves, to a far greater degree, around settler colonial life. The banality of this settler life is a covert assertion of the removal of this life from the spectacle of public history that stages the dramatic conflicts of colonialism. The spectacular conflicts of colonial history, in such a life, are ironized in the private affliction of banality and boredom defining the sensibility that looks toward the imperial center.

Like Mansfield, other writers in this archive also deploy the motifs of banality and boredom as constituents of aesthetic experience, in which the interplay of desire, longing, and fulfillment signals the dynamics of colonial history, but at a subtle and idiosyncratic distance from the grand spectacle of historical events. Banality, for these writers, is a lack that indicates colonial disempowerment by implication, a lack that becomes a radical narrative drive in these fictions. Despite its being a negative value, the banal, in these texts, energizes a form of narrative aesthetic. As it seeks to explore this apparent paradox, this book asks a variety of related questions: How does the aesthetic celebration of banality relate to the empirical representation of the everyday? How significantly would this relationship mark the continuities and disjunctures between the realism of the early English novel, nineteenth-century naturalism, the stream-of-consciousness narration of early-twentieth-century modernism, and Anglophone narratives from decolonizing and decolonized cultures in the late-twentieth- and early-twenty-first-century global South—narratives that, in turn, engage in a critical relationship with the literary institutions of Western modernity such as the novel and realism? Similarly, what are the differences between the functional detail that shapes setting and context in realism and the symbolic detail in modernism that invites the epiphany? Does the valorization of banality and boredom hinder affective engagement? If narrative is driven by the spectacle of the event, how does the banality of eventlessness enable a narrative impulse? Does banality stall narrative, or does it transform it? In the final measure, does such a narrative indicate an aesthetic failure or a radically innovative aesthetic? Similarly, if boredom signals an affective failure or a frustration of the need for engagement or excitement, how does such a failure turn into a subject of aesthetic representation?

Once again, Mansfield's complex location between the metropolitan center of British modernism and the distant margin of empire provides some revealing insights behind the narrative energization of banality. These insights, moreover, have a unique resonance with the scope and objective of this book. The narrative centralization of banality and its affective counterpart, boredom, enables a complex interaction between the sociocultural consequences of colonialism and the experimental aesthetic of literary modernism. The radical life breathed into the banal, I suggest, defines an aesthetic unique to modernism that both extends and troubles the tenets of narrative realism of the nascent English novel that emerged in the culture of the late Enlightenment. To illustrate this claim and to understand how the fate of the banal stages an ambiguous conflict between the aesthetic principles of Enlightenment modernity and those of experimental modernism, I would like to turn to what is perhaps the most famous polemic in early-twentieth-century British fiction.

Desire from the Shores of Pleasure

In her essay "Mr. Bennett and Mrs. Brown," Virginia Woolf accuses Arnold Bennett of being a novelist of a drudging, bureaucratic mode. This essay is usually considered the clearest articulation of experimental modernism's ideological difference from its close contemporary, the Edwardian fictional tradition, as represented by Bennett, John Galsworthy, and H. G. Wells. Writing of Bennett's novel *Hilda Lessways*, Woolf objects to the plenitude of everyday details that she sees as used merely to create a context and produce the setting: "One line of insight would have done more than all those lines of description; but let them pass as the necessary drudgery of the novelist."[7] Hilda's voice, the contours of her mind and character, Woolf feels, are forever pushed off the narrative's horizon by an array of trivial things—the flour mill opposite Hilda's window, the bricked path extending from the flour mill, the log of rents and freeholds and copyholds and fines—all of which, according to Woolf, merely indicate the tedium of unregenerative novelistic labor that keeps the author away from the spirit and soul of his characters. The Edwardian novelist, according to Woolf, is too often like a government bureaucrat nose deep in a sea of biographical and circumstantial details, most of which are incidental to the inner life of the characters: the Holy Grail for the modernist avant-garde. About H. G. Wells, her response assumes a similar tone of regret: "He is a materialist from sheer goodness of heart, taking upon his shoulders the work that ought to have been discharged by Government officials, and in the plethora of his ideas and facts scarcely having leisure to realize, or forgetting to think important, the crudity and coarseness of his human beings."[8] His commitment to producing a world replete with every possible everyday detail makes Wells, for Woolf, a "materialist," while a writer like Joyce, in spite of the latter's interest in all things scatological that initially earned her distaste, is, in the end, "spiritual." Indulgence in the methods of Edwardian realism, to which she admits having felt "strongly tempted," can, on the other hand, only produce stories that are "the most dreary, irrelevant, humbugging affairs in the world."[9] A refusal to celebrate "the crudity and coarseness of human beings" turns the Edwardians into soulless bureaucrats, taking upon themselves the details of rents, wages, calico, and copyhold estates at the expense of the "astonishing disorder" of the human sensibility.

Woolf here holds the Edwardians guilty of an excessive preoccupation with physical details, which stifles the fiction's transcendence beyond the material. The Edwardian writers produce prose that is truly prosaic, in the sense Hegel implied in the phrase "the prose of the world," all those quotidian circumstances and obstacles that limit individual expression and prevent aesthetic transcendence.[10] The "quotidian" or the everyday, by preventing transcendence beyond the immediate, can only reproduce a world that is psychologically or aesthetically sterile. "The whole thing," Hegel says, "appears only as a mass of individual details";[11] the tyranny of external details obfuscates the uniqueness of subjective vision, which is the core of aesthetic beauty. While the quotidian can perform a range of functions and satisfy a variety of needs (including those of comfort, stability, and empathy), constriction into the realm of the quotidian, with no avenues of transcendence beyond it, transforms the quotidian into the banal. What was merely descriptive now becomes a value—or, as a negativity, an antivalue. Alternatively, cast into a temporal scheme, the predictable iterations of the everyday become banal.

The relationship of the quotidian with the banal has a curious parallel within the principles of narrative fiction. Quotidian details are often essential to flesh out the world of the novel and to produce the tangible immediacy without which realist narration, at least, cannot take shape. But when such quotidian details define the limits of this fictional world, preventing aesthetic, psychic, or symbolic transcendence, that world, as Woolf implies, becomes dreary, predictable, and banal. That is when the narrative becomes prosaic in the Hegelian sense. The evaluative and the generic implications of the term "prosaic" have coexisted simultaneously in literary history. In the context of Woolf's polemic, however, the evaluative meaning of the term comes to the surface and coincides with the image of bureaucratic labor. Such labor provides socially and economically valuable knowledge but can only be a banalizing model for the art of narrative fiction—"the necessary drudgery of the novelist." In the realm of the state and the economy, the methods and institutions of bureaucracy reinforce a nontranscendental organization of the everyday, and, in fact, the affinities between the bureaucratic systematization of factual information and the banality of realist fiction observed here by Woolf go considerably beyond the metaphor. The institution of bureaucracy, as Max Weber has reminded us, represents the logic of rationalism that marks the modern state and the institutions of capitalism.[12] All the conditions for the successful functioning of Weberian bureaucracy—the "iron cage" of rationality, in Weber's terms[13]—notably the methodical performance of specific duties, the structure of strict hierarchy, and the preservation of factual records, embody the spirit of rational capitalism that for Weber is the most important dynamic of transformation for European modernity in the seventeenth and eighteenth centuries. The worldview of narrative realism, especially within the early English novel, is also an epistemic legacy of this modernity. It seems clear that "rational capitalism," as Weber has characterized it,[14] and the epistemic mode of narrative realism are at least partially traceable to the same political and intellectual climate. In this light, Woolf's allusion to bureaucratic labor in her criticism of what she sees as the drudging meticulousness of narrative realism reveals more than is first apparent.

The stream-of-consciousness method of fiction, in contrast, seeks a radical disruption of what we might call the mode of bureaucratic realism. This disruption reflects experimental literary modernism's unease with the rationalist model of political and philosophical modernity ushered in by the European Enlightenment. As Woolf would put it, this disruption hinges on "the spasmodic, the obscure, the fragmentary."[15] It is significant that she uses adjectives rather than nouns to articulate the difference between the Edwardian and the experimental-modernist modes of fiction, which share the physical atmosphere of the ordinary everyday but differ radically in the *way* they approach the material. The fragmentary details of quotidian city life, for instance, flood a characteristically Woolfian moment of *jouissance* on an ordinary June day, through the stream of consciousness that represents Clarissa Dalloway's mind. Indeed, some of the finest moments of Woolf's own fiction are constituted through the often aimless exploration of not only the general texture of everyday life but in fact through that of objects, moments, and situations that appear as the most banal and marginal elements of the social and aesthetic construction of the everyday. As Woolf identifies the banalization of the Edwardian narration of the everyday, she introduces a certain question of value—if only through its lack—as the point of departure of the modernist literary polemic. If the production of an ordinary, everyday world played a key role in the formation of the traditional realism essential to the rise of the novel, the physical and factual confinement within the details of this everyday world also came to appear as aesthetically oppressive to the modernist innovators in the early twentieth century.

How does high modernism respond to this problem? One could do worse than to say "epiphany," probably the most concentrated instance of modernist elevation of the banal onto a plane of aesthetic transcendence, but a fuller answer is more complex than merely the successful epiphanization of everyday objects and situations in modernist fiction. Such an answer would take us back to the opening moment of this discussion—to the way Katherine Mansfield's writings promise to transform the motif of banality into a narrative instinct. Lars Svendsen has provided a map of the affective entropy contained in boredom, an emotion that often follows or surrounds the aesthetic of banality. Quoting Roland Barthes's suggestion that "Boredom is . . . desire seen from the shores of pleasure," Svendsen argues that desire here implies "going beyond the 'same', that which is outside—transcendence."[16] Svendsen argues that "boredom is immanence in its purest form" and reaches the seemingly hopeless conclusion that boredom not only embodies immanence but the final and definite impossibility of transcendence of any kind. It is an accurate analysis within the cognitive framework of boredom as a malaise of the metropolitan West. However, if banality can be imagined as an aesthetic that is comparable to boredom as an affect, I would point out that the life of these motifs as the aesthetic and affective consequences of colonial modernity corresponds more accurately to the kind of desire that, for Barthes, constitutes boredom.

Modernity in the colony, I argue, is marked by a desire whose object can only be perceived from a distance. It is a desire whose very affective force depends on the spatial difference between the desiring and the desired. At this distance lies the final object of colonial desire, the metropolitan center of empire, a venue where events unfold and history happens with all its excitement. The banal, in the colonial and postcolonial fiction that gives it shape, is immanence forever haunted by the lure of transcendence but never fulfilled by it. As an aesthetic condition of colonial modernity, banality embodies a fractured relation to metropolitan modernity; at the same time, it remains perpetually animated by a desire to heal the fracture, to inhabit the transcendence that the center holds out as a promise. Through a play between desire and fulfillment, the imagined and the real, the immediate and the distant, the banal becomes a force that drives narrative. This narrative is shaped through the tension between the banality of everyday life and the promise of transcendence that is variously fulfilled, deferred, and frustrated in fiction produced by the colonial architects of literary modernism.

The narrative innovations of modernism draw a kind of conscious attention to banality as a value, and often, concurrently, to boredom as an affect. This involves a radical shift from the merely functional use of everyday details for the empirical production of setting and context, as seen in more traditional forms of realism. This is the ironic context of Woolf's quarrel with Bennett, a context that remains unstated in her polemic. The radical modernist response to this problem is neither to abandon the everyday, nor to bring the dramatic and the spectacular to cause a rupture in its texture (as magic realism would do later in the century), but to invest fragments of this ordinary life with the libidinal energy of the banal haunted by the unfulfilled promise of transcendence. Through this narrative innovation, the banal, in a radical turn of cultural history, becomes an affirmative narrative force. Such is the paradox of narrative movement embodied in the empty, unfulfilled, and stifling lives of Mansfield's settler colonial women in the New Zealand countryside or in the lives of Joyce's "paralyzed" Dubliners; the banality of the immediate, for all of them, is energized by the possibility of a full and enriching life existing out of their reach but not their sensory imagination. Even the actual event of the epiphany, whether it is fulfilled or frustrated, is structured through desire for a transcendence of the banality of everyday life far from the metropolitan center. The unfulfilled or deflated epiphany that abounds in Joyce's fiction at some level reflects the frustrated desire to move beyond the banality of the local that is teasingly touched by the lure of a magical transformation but is denied the reality of such a transformation.

The key question with which we are left might look like this: does the banal *remain* banal? Or does it get transformed, even fragmentarily, through the longing for fullness or transcendence? While there is a significant narrative shift from an objective description of the physical world to the idiosyncrasy of subjective consciousness in literary modernism, a number of contradictory impulses are also potentially at work within the shift itself. Liesl Olson, in her recent exploration of the modernist preoccupation with the ordinary, would have us pause longer over the complex relationship between the Edwardian representation of the ordinary everyday and that of Woolf, its archmodernist critic. According to Olson, critical attention to the "aesthetic of self-conscious interiority" in modernist literature has diverted us from its firm mooring in the ordinary materialism of the shared external world of the everyday,[17] which such interiority never transcends or transforms fully. Not only does modernism share with Edwardian fiction a similar world of the ordinary, but it also foregrounds the manner in which this ordinary world resists aesthetic transcendence, which it does just as often as it celebrates such transcendence in heightened moments such as those of the epiphany. Olson's example is, significantly, that of Woolf, who remains positioned in a perpetual ambivalence between the prosaic materialism of the external world—which is ordinary precisely because it belongs to a realm of common experience—and the poetic interiority of the unique, subjective sensibility, where the ordinary is transformed into the luminous index of inner lives.[18] Not giving in fully to either impulse is the peculiar triumph of modernist fiction. Woolf's disdain for Bennett's methods in her essay is therefore partially deceptive, as in her own fiction she draws upon this world of banal, external materialism more than she actually admits in her polemic. "She transforms," writes Olson, "but does not reject, the literary realism of the past."[19] Modernist fiction's admittedly experimental preoccupation with the banal, therefore, can be scarcely understood without a consideration of the literary realism of past traditions.

For me, the relationship of the two is embedded in aesthetic modernism's troubled relationship with the philosophical and political modernity of the Enlightenment, a modernity with which traditional realism is inextricably linked. The struggle between longing, fulfillment, and frustration that is at play in the movement between banality and transcendence is structured around the crisis of modernity as it is represented in the embattled aesthetics of literary modernism. Tensions and tremors in the global structure of the British Empire, on the other hand, provide a concrete historical venue for this crisis of modernity, a modernity that makes a disruptive attempt to replicate itself in the colonies. The paradoxical celebration of a negative value such as the banal, in the texts I read in this book, is an affective function of the political condition of their production. The aestheticization of banality in late colonial modernism is therefore underwritten by the core-periphery framework endemic to modernism, a framework shaped largely, though not exclusively, by colonialism. Such a framework, inevitably, has a temporal life as well; the motif of the banal, in that sense, approximates what Heather Love has called "backwardness," following the historian Dipesh Chakrabarty's argument that the definition of modernity is contingent on the identification of the nonmodern.[20] The banal, in these narratives, relates to the trope of backwardness, which Love locates at the critical intersection of modernity as a historical trope and modernism as an aesthetic movement. For Love, aesthetic modernism is marked by a tension between the instinct for novelty on one hand and forces variously structured around the negative and the backward—such as primitivism, decadence, decline, and melancholia—on the other. Temporality is key, as Love points out; for me, banality marks the disenchantment of temporality in the colony, the lacuna created by the perpetually deferred arrival of Western modernity, which promises to capture successfully the excitement of history and progress. Unlike Love, however, who reads "backwardness" in opposition to the instincts of innovation, I approach banality itself as the radical force at the core of the narrative instinct that drives these fictions. Just the way modernism has been understood to make provincialism a metropolitan concern—to bring, in John Marx's words, "provincialism to the metropole"[21]—the most radical modernist fictions reinvent the disenchanted temporal and spatial experience of banality in the colonial periphery as an affirmative narrative force.

Indeed, the vitalization of negative tropes like banality and boredom are usually rooted in the radical politics of disenfranchisement. Patricia Meyer Spacks has convincingly argued that the boredom of middle- and upper-class women in the eighteenth century was the consequence of severe social constrictions that structured their lives. But it was this boredom that helped female authors from the period create narratives of "devious but intelligible social protest."[22] The aesthetic celebration of banality in the fiction of Virginia Woolf, in many ways, inherits the narratives of female boredom and anguish in early English fiction. Woolf, however, is not my subject in this book, except as the most insightful and polemical theorist of the banal in literary modernism; my focus here is on the narrativization of banality and boredom as a function of the political relation between the imperial metropolis and the colonial periphery, a subject on which Woolf's work differs considerably from the fiction produced along the margins of empire. The creative articulation of banality and boredom in women's consciousness, in Woolf's work, however, remains related to the larger politics of disempowerment. My immediate interest in this book is the manner in which such disempowerment appears as a condition of colonial modernity and its affective interplay of desire, longing, and transcendence in fictions shaped by this condition.[23]

Boredom, the close affective relation of the banal, has a complex status in literature and philosophy. It has often been thought of as an affliction that works as an incubator of extraordinary imagination, marking a singular sensibility, as indicated, for instance, in the well-known observations on boredom made by Friedrich Nietzsche, Walter Benjamin, and Søren Kierkegaard.[24] The distinguished history of thought about boredom as a mark of a singular consciousness, combined with the perception of the emotion as an indolent luxury of the materially privileged, however, has obstructed the possibility of understanding boredom as an affective consequence of exclusion and disempowerment. Of considerable significance to my work is recent anthropological research that has chronicled boredom as the pervasive reality of lives on the distant margins of Western modernity, regions excluded by the structures of global capitalism.[25] Boredom, in such locations, is an affective consequence of a perceived nonmodernity and the temporal disenchantment that follows the failed arrival of progress. However, it seems to me that within literary writing, experiences of banality and boredom are yet to be significantly understood as markers of marginality and exclusion. Literature is still significantly attached to the elevating singularity of boredom, as perhaps in some ways it should be. As a literary critic, I too remain committed to the demonstration of the negative or the noncathartic aesthetic of banality *as* an affirmative narrative force. However, I attempt to detach the related affect of boredom from its context of subjective singularity and material privilege, which has been the more dominant model in literary and philosophical criticism. What I hope is noticeable in this approach is how a set of motifs that are not only aesthetically but also politically negative can enable an affirmative narrative instinct. In the fictions I read, the hierarchy between the metropolis and the periphery that creates this disempowering nexus of aesthetics and politics is not only shaped by the late colonial context of modernism but also by the complex legacy of desire and ideology that follows the trajectories of decolonization and the development of postcolonial identity. It remains significant that it is the last phase that is also singled out by recent ethnographers of boredom in the global South as the most visible but theoretically intractable marker of the affective politics of marginality.

As aesthetic and affective indices of the uneven political relations that have marked Western modernity and its global expansion, banality and boredom simultaneously make up both the conscious self of modernist fiction and what Spacks has called its great "hidden Other." The banal insistently negotiates between the aesthetic, the social, and the material. This is a connection that literary criticism has, perhaps not without reason, assumed to be natural. This study seeks to foreground the radical poetics of this historically "naturalized" negotiation along an archival trajectory through twentieth-century world literature in English that reflects the cultural aftermath of the British Empire. Before I turn to this body of fiction, therefore, I would like to examine in some detail the historical development of the aesthetic categories at the heart of this book, as they have evolved within the landscape of European modernity that has globalized itself through the colonial condition.

The Generic Modernity of the Banal

Our current consciousness of banality and boredom and, more crucially, the literary representation of this consciousness comes into being at a significant moment of politicophilosophical modernity in Europe, namely, the Enlightenment in the eighteenth century, although it gathers maximum aesthetic momentum in the late nineteenth and early twentieth centuries, under high modernism.[26] The narrative of the appearance and celebration of the motifs of banality and boredom, I would like to argue, also offers an illustrative version of the larger relationship between the Enlightenment paradigm of modernity and the aesthetic movement of modernism during the late nineteenth and early twentieth centuries. *Modernity* and *modernism*, as such, are two terms that I would distinguish carefully from each other.[27] Within the field of literary modernist studies, the fraught relationship between Enlightenment modernity and literary modernism has been the subject of significant debate, one usually centered on the question of whether that relationship is one of continuity or crisis. In other words, was modernism a continuation of the values of Enlightenment modernity, or did it signal a dramatic break from this modernity? The full range of this debate, which has been explored significantly by scholars of literary modernism, is outside the scope of this book.[28] What I'd like to emphasize here, however, is that literary modernism's singular celebration of the banal encapsulates both the continuities and the discontinuities of modernism's relation with Enlightenment modernity. Through its interest in everyday life, modernist fiction maintains certain continuities with post-Enlightenment notions of the aesthetic, most specifically in the shaping of the fictional world through the mode of narrative realism. But as Woolf's impatience with Edwardian realism reveals most strikingly, the principles around which this quotidian world was organized—those of the rational, socially coherent values traceable to the novelistic realism that rises with Enlightenment modernity—were also to face a profound crisis in the wake of aesthetic modernism. While the constitutive texture of the fictional world sustained itself in the transition, the authorial approach to it changed drastically. The question of whether or not that change in turn radically transformed the fictional world itself remains part of a larger debate over whether the modernist preoccupation with chaos and disorder fully overturned the older narrative of Enlightenment modernity. But reaching a satisfactory conclusion to this larger discussion—which I suspect cannot be resolved definitively—is less important for our purposes than recognizing how the heightening of the banality of the everyday reveals the aesthetic significance of the philosophical relationship between modernity and modernism.

To begin to explore the close mutual relationship of these motifs within the narrative of modernity, it might be useful to step back and look into the etymological and cultural histories of the two words, "banality" and "boredom," that have emerged as extreme evaluative and affective responses to the experience of the everyday. According to the *Oxford English Dictionary*, the earliest recorded use of the word "banal" is in 1753, when it signified obligatory feudal service. *Webster's New Millennium Dictionary* traces the word's roots to the Serbo-Croatian *ban*, meaning "lord" or "ruler"; the *American Heritage College Dictionary* points to its origin in the French (and old French) word *banal*, which it annotates as "shared by tenants in a feudal jurisdiction."[29] As an adjective, *banal* was used to designate things that belonged to feudal serfs (linking it again to *ban*, the Serbo-Croatian word for "lord") or else, again, to compulsory feudal service.[30]

Present-day annotations of the entry include "trite, feeble, commonplace," while noting its original sense of " 'compulsory,' hence common to all." The sense of compulsion or necessity that casts its oblique shadow on the word "banal" and its attendant association with constriction and repetitive regularity, therefore, seem to originate in the communal obligations of the feudal system. Specifically, "banal" looks back to some of the common restrictions that bind the feudal community and define the latter's bond to the feudal lord. This bond finds expression in the essential daily labor of its members, such as the production of food for consumption or obligatory services to the ruler, be they military or civil. Also immediately noticeable here is the double relevance of the word "common"—meaning both "shared by everybody" and "that which is ordinary, ubiquitous, or unoriginal." The slippage of meaning between the two implications of the word "common" seems to hint at the larger transition of patterns in the history of the word "banal." This history, one might say, not only charts a narrative of power and obligation constituting communal lives but also narrates a slow but perceptible transference of meaning over time, from the occupational lives of the politically and economically disenfranchised to a measure of value—or the lack of it. And this is precisely where, I would suggest, the semantic duality contained by the word—that which pertains to everybody and that which is unoriginal—indicates a significant relation between the political and the aesthetic. As it becomes clear from the evolving history of the English novel, the slippage between the two meanings indicates that the nascent genre's preoccupation with ordinary life was linked to the gradually widening social base of its readership, thanks to the acceleration of printing technologies and an emerging middle class.

The earliest recorded use of the word "bore," in the sense I've been using it here, is also in the eighteenth century, though the *OED* is unable to name a precise year. The etymological origins of the word, including the Old English word *borian*, all relate to the other meaning of the word, which pertains to mechanical movement, specifically to making or drilling a hole. The *Random House Webster's* suggests that the word was first used to convey the sense of being "tiresome or dull" in 1768 and that this usage might possibly have come into vogue as a figurative extension of the slow, mechanical movement the verb originally implied. Should this claim have philological legitimacy—and it retains the metaphorical resonance even if it doesn't—slowness, and thus a certain experience of the passage of time, are immediately established as the sociopsychological components of boredom. "The word *bored*," Thomas Dumm argues along similar lines, "has no indisputable etymology that might move one beyond imagining the labor of drilling to explain how the idea of drilling a hole—*to bore*—could also describe the process of being dull and stupefied."[31] That in both cases these terms emerge against the backdrop of the culture of the late Enlightenment, which to a great degree shapes the modern Western conception of aesthetics, is significant as a philological point of departure for this project.

Nor is it accidental that the evolving histories of these two terms are characterized by etymological shifts between the domain of the sociopolitical and that of the affective. Corresponding contexts in literary history show that the rise of the novel as a genre, for instance, marks an intriguing overlap between the celebration of the quotidian and the foregrounding of common humanity in terms of character and narrative. This overlap, I argue, echoes the etymological shifts of the word "banal" between the realm of cultural value and that of the economic stratification of society. The double meaning in the related word "mundane," implying both the ordinary and the secular, indicates these cultural symptoms of modernity as embedded in a secular vision. Locating an emergent earlier moment of modernity, in the late medieval fourteenth century, Michael Hardt and Antonio Negri characterize European modernity as contingent on "the affirmation of the powers of *this* world, the discovery of the plane of immanence" that led to the denial of "divine and transcendent authority over worldly affairs."[32] This modernizing shift away from the plane of transcendence was arguably not only a secularizing move but also a move toward an ontological attachment to the plane of the quotidian. For Henri Lefebvre, too, the era of the emergence of the mundane was "the bourgeois eighteenth century," when "the 'mundane' element burst forth into art and philosophy."[33] Such a shift, reaching full momentum with the Enlightenment, found its natural aesthetic medium in the novel. Distinguishing itself from the older narrative of the romance, the nascent genre revealed a preoccupation with the "mundane" in the sense of "the ordinary" as much as in that of "the secular." Franco Moretti's description of this secular imaginary as constitutive of novelistic realism is illuminating: "It is a new, truly *secular* way of imagining the way of life: dispersed among countless minute events, precarious, mixed to the indifference of the world: but always tenaciously *there*."[34] Though my project focuses primarily on Anglophone literature of the twentieth century, one of its underlying convictions is that the aesthetic of colonial banality remains entangled in a complex and sometimes contradictory relationship with the rise and development of the English novel within the context of the late Enlightenment. It is the eighteenth century that is marked by the rise of the novel and the emergence of narrative realism, the period that also saw the etymological—and perhaps also to a certain extent, conceptual—emergence of the motifs of banality and boredom in the sense we understand them today.[35]

In the system of aesthetic value emergent in the culture of the Enlightenment, an evaluative link increasingly came to be drawn between the concept of "prose" as a certain way of looking at the world and as a certain kind of discourse. As pointed out by Michal Peled Ginsburg and Lorri G. Nandrea, foundational here is Hegel's observation on "the world of prose and everyday" as one of contingency, where the individual is limited by circumstances and context: "As that which prevents individuals from teleologically realizing an implicit internal totality, 'prose' impedes transcendence. In contrast to 'the look of independence and total life and freedom that lies at the root of the essence of beauty,' moreover, 'prose' is a kind of ugliness."[36] This connection between genre and value is embedded in the *OED* annotations on the word "prose," which derives from the Latin *prosus*, meaning "straightforward, straight, direct." Ginsburg and Nandrea refer to obvious links between the dictionary meaning of the word as "the ordinary form of written or spoken language, without metrical structure," and its figurative definition of "plain, simple, matter-of-fact, and (hence) dull or commonplace expression, quality, spirit, etc."[37] The generic and the evaluative meanings of the term "prose" are set up in a relationship of mutuality around semiotic structures of contingency, necessity, and nontranscendence. Such structures, I would suggest, anticipate the constricting networks of historical power that eventually produce banality as a radical narrative instinct in the twentieth century.

However, even though the ordinary begins to find its way into narrative awareness from the late eighteenth century onward, it is not until the development of modernism (first in continental Europe and then in the Anglophone world) that the motifs of banality and boredom come to be foregrounded as modes of a negative or noncathartic aesthetic that could be transformed into a narrative impulse. The notion that a psychic condition such as boredom could constitute a subject of aesthetic representation gained significant literary popularity only since the second half of the nineteenth century. Philosophies of the human condition such as existentialism had a role to play in this celebration of banality and boredom. For Elizabeth Goodstein, the nineteenth century is the crucial period where "the evolution of the discourse on boredom traces the constitution of a new rhetoric of experience—a modern idiom of self-understanding." She points out that no recorded usage of the word "boredom," according to the *OED*, is found before the mid-nineteenth century, when it appears in Charles Dickens's *Bleak House* and subsequently in George Eliot's *Daniel Deronda*.[38]

To my mind, moreover, the echo of Robert Musil's celebrated work in the title of Goodstein's study, *Experience Without Qualities: Boredom and Modernity*, points to the modern nature of the discourse around boredom and specifically to the significance of modernist culture to boredom's aesthetic articulation. Pointing to the concurrence of the concept of boredom with the discourse of modern experience, Goodstein writes: "My overall claim is not that boredom as such is the key to theorizing modernity, but rather the problems of theorizing boredom are the problems of theorizing modern experience more generally."[39] The literary significance of this sociocultural claim about the conjunction of boredom and modernity comes out, probably more richly than elsewhere, in the novel *Madame Bovary*, published, significantly, the same year as Baudelaire's *Flowers of Evil*, a poetic work that pioneered boredom as an index of the modern experience. Traditionally, the innovative force of *Madame Bovary* has been identified in Flaubert's experimental sense of narrative craft. But it is now clear to us that the novel's centralization of the experience of (Emma's) boredom—most notably, its "collapse of 'adventure' into everyday banality," as Franco Moretti has put it, is just as important a component of its radical modernity.[40] More specifically, I argue that if the conceptualization and experience of banality and boredom are crucial components of the subjective experience symptomatic of modernity, they are experiences of lack, or "backwardness," as Heather Love might put it, inseparably connected to the social distribution of power and resources. "The experience of boredom," Thomas Dumm suggests, "may be connected to . . . feeling left out, existing on the margins of events that powerful people represent as central to what matters in the world."[41] Exclusion from agency or even awareness of events, however, rarely implies immunity from the consequences of such events, and the unwilling subjection to such consequences can just as well produce boredom as a mark of one's inability to choose one's own sociohistorical role. Dumm goes on to acknowledge that "boredom may be understood . . . as an expression of discomfort at not wanting to be a part of a larger narrative while being acutely aware that one is."[42] Colonial modernity is acutely caught up in such a narrative of unfreedom, with desire for its imperial counterpart entangled with an acute awareness of one's material and ideological enslavement to it.

Spacks distinguishes carefully between ennui and boredom based on the grandeur and pride of the former's aspirations as opposed to the humbler, more earthbound nature of the latter: "Ennui implies a judgment of the universe; boredom, a response to the immediate."[43] With this distinction in mind, she reads nineteenth-century continental fiction and poetry, notably that by Baudelaire, primarily in terms of ennui rather than boredom. English translations of Baudelaire's poetry have used both terms, as for instance in "Au Lecteur" (usually translated as "To the Reader"), probably the most direct and best-known example of what Baudelaire calls "l'Ennui" in his oeuvre. Such ennui, in Spacks's analysis, magnifies the nobility of the experiencing subject, indicating "the sufferer's awareness of society's intractable corruption and of alienation as its consequence for the sensitive spirit."[44] For Goodstein, on the other hand, the essential modernity of Baudelaire lies in the fact that he democratizes ennui: "In his verses, the ennui that had been the prerogative of the idle rich is represented as having passed to all of those whose lives lack meaning in a world where time has become everyone's burden."[45] The change of understanding of the emotion from one of more active agency to one of almost complete disempowerment is evident in Goodstein's reading of the shift of the meaning as a vice at the beginning of *Flowers of Evil* to an unavoidable fate toward the end of the book, exemplified to perfection in the final "Spleen" poem.[46] Such a set of contradictory approaches reveals how authors like Flaubert and Baudelaire, as chroniclers of the historical transitions between ennui as an elevated, spiritual affliction and boredom as a more earthbound, widespread democratic emotion (though not necessarily designated by those names) become natural sites of debate about the evolution of the mental state as it is represented in literature. Both ennui and boredom share a resistance to affective catharsis, but the cultural history surrounding the two terms contains a clear trajectory of social movement in terms of class, privilege, and imaginative agency. In the end, ennui retains a philosophically and aesthetically elevated status within nineteenth-century European literature, predominantly representing the spiritual resistance enacted within the exceptional and often (though not always) aristocratic sensibility. Boredom, on the other hand, I'd agree with Spacks, is a more materially grounded, demotic affect that is also connected to the collective sensibilities of wider social groups, often those living within conditions of socioeconomic disenfranchisement. Boredom is, I further contend, also an aesthetic of deprivation that closely follows material domination and is not merely the complex, sometimes luxuriant assertion of imaginative agency by a subjective mind whose affliction, in the end, is a mark of its own exceptionality.[47]

The affective focus of my project is also on boredom as a modern experience produced through socioeconomic conditions that are far removed from the glorified individualism and aristocracy of ennui. I focus on banality and boredom as they emerge from global positions of disempowerment, constriction, and the lack of access to resources—the abundance and inequitable distribution of which industrial capitalism makes blatant—rather than the transcendental ennui of a minority of privileged subjects. Boredom, in such a reading, is a symptom of an affective disempowerment where the phenomenon is not merely a function of the drudgery of lowly labor but also of the impoverishment of lives within the ideological and material reality of colonial domination. The acute sense of aesthetic constriction that produces banality and boredom in such lives is the necessary corollary of material, economic, and infrastructural inadequacies felt across the margins of the historical expanse of the British empire. Such inadequacies push their victims not only toward the intense theater of trauma but also toward the pervasiveness of banality and the iterative cycle of boredom.

It is worth noting, however, that throughout much of the twentieth century the most striking conceptions of the family of tropes that form a close descriptive backdrop to the motif of banality—from the empirical category of the "everyday" to the more value-laden concept of the "ordinary"—have been embedded in a network of various power relations. Cultural studies, for instance, has marked both the idea and the practice of the "everyday" as a crucial archive, in spite of the degree of theoretical intractability posed by its idea and the vast, diffuse range of reality embodied in its practice. For cultural theorists, the exhaustive concept of the "everyday" has included the spatial and temporal experience of ordinary life, detailed ethnographic representations of its reality, and the evaluative and affective tropes of banality and boredom. To a degree, therefore, my book explores literary terrains opened by the cultural-anthropological work of Michel De Certeau, Guy Debord, and Henri Lefebvre and, perhaps even more significantly, recent ethnographic analyses of boredom as an affective marker of exclusion from the most thriving narratives of modernity and capitalism in the present world.

Crucially for Lefebvre, the everyday emerges at the site where private sensibility is subordinated to the disciplines of institutional systems and their codes. This subordination produces a passivity on the part of the individual sensibility, and that passivity organizes the quotidian experiences of domestic and familial practices, leisure, and habit. In modern consumer society, the everyday is constituted around a number of autonomous subsystems, such as those of housing, fashion, food, and travel, as they are defined by such structures as the universalizing system of "architectural urbanism, the mechanisms of industrial food production," or "the totalizing system constructed around the automobile."[48] Individual sensibility, personal choices, and decisions are petrified into an "organized passivity" in the face of the bureaucracies of labor and consumption imposed on both public and private lives. The production of the everyday thus necessarily involves the progressive disappearance of private agency, but this erosion of agency is far from uniform across all strata of society. The differential experience of agency and passivity in the embodiment of the everyday is a crucial point where some of my own arguments intersect with those of Lefebvre. "The generalized passivity," he argues, "weighs more heavily on women, who are sentenced to everyday life, on the working class, on employees who are not technocrats, on youth—in short on the majority of people—yet never in the same way, at the same time, never all at once."[49] The boredom generated in women's lives from the constrictions of an oppressive, iterative everyday informs significant components of the texts that I read later on in this book. The culture and structures of officialdom or bureaucracy similarly emerge at crucial points in my project as generators of passivity, monotony, and boredom on both the public and private planes of experience. The "organized passivity" forced upon individuals by bureaucratic structures informs my reading of banality in the lives of Joyce's paralyzed Dubliners as well as in the lives of the agents and consumers of bureaucracy in the global South during and after colonial rule.

What Lefebvre calls the "organized passivity" vis-à-vis the subsystems of consumerism in advanced capitalist societies of the West, however, has also been—ironically, perhaps, but surely not surprisingly—canonized as the principal criterion of happiness in such societies. The most significant political theorist who has continued an examination of this subject is Thomas Dumm, who has identified the United States as the ideal example of the society where the ordinary, in the form of the fulfillment of quotidian consumer desires, emerges as a significant venue of collective values. In *A Politics of the Ordinary*, he locates the American pursuit of happiness at a great distance from "dramas of conquest or war" to "private gratification of desire" on the most banal planes of life. "The ordinary," he writes, "becomes the bland and stultifying ground of American values."[50]

It is tempting to place Lefebvre and Dumm, both theorists of the ordinary or the everyday in advanced metropolitan societies, alongside each other. Dumm sees the everyday production and satisfaction of consumer desires as the canon of happiness in such a society, and a deep sense of irony, even sadness, necessarily accompanies this perception. While Lefebvre directly articulates a sense of the loss of individual agency and private sensibility in the face of such mechanisms of desire satisfaction, Dumm is more ambivalent about the constitution of the ordinary in such a society. In his reading, though the ordinary and the common are significantly marked by the mechanisms of consumption (the "post-Protestant ethic of consumption" is his intriguing name for it), they are by no means exhausted by the latter. The ordinary also stakes a significant claim on the "commonsensical principle of modern liberal democracy" within this very society. "A picture of ordinary people pursuing ordinary goods and leading ordinary lives constitutes an ideal vision of liberal-democratic societies."[51]

It is clear that several of the scholars whose work has come to define the field of cultural studies have predominantly focused their attention on the production of the quotidian in the advanced capitalist societies of the metropolitan West. However, as anthropologists of the global South have shown, the idea and praxis of ordinary life are just as central to the postcolonial state and disciplinary interventions into it. Reflecting on ethnographic explorations of the postcolonial state, Thomas Blom Hansen and Finn Stepputat write: "The constant recurrence of notions of stateness as a guarantee of order and ordinary life is thus not a barrier to critical engagement with the phenomenon of the state, but its most fundamental condition."[52] A global reading of the cultural politics of the quotidian thus also engages in a necessary conversation with anthropology, a discipline that has been closely linked to cultural studies.[53] Indeed, it is more or less agreed today that modern anthropology's predominant archival focus on societies beyond the metropolitan West is partially traceable to the discipline's development within the field of colonial power relations; this agreement has arisen not only because of pioneering works by Foucault and Said but also work by scholars closer to the field, such as James Buzard, Mary Louise Pratt, and James Clifford.[54] If an exploration of the literary representation of banality parallels cultural studies' exploration of the everyday in metropolitan societies, it has a greater, albeit politically more complex relationship with twentieth-century anthropological discourse, which engages in an understanding of societies both within and beyond the metropolitan West through an immersion in the marginal fragments of life. The empirical chronicling of the everyday has always paved the ground for ethnographic knowledge production; however, it is only recently that anthropology has turned its attention to the affective trope of boredom as a constitutive feature of the everyday in spaces excluded or marginalized by the global narratives of modernity, capitalism, and progress, in locations as far flung as urban Ethiopia, aboriginal settlements in Australia, postsocialist Romania, and postcolonial Senegal.

Anthropology's persistent engagement with the textures of everyday life ranges across a wide methodological space, from discursive analysis to sensory immersion. Very much like literary narratives, anthropological studies have often foregrounded the role of the sensuous in the apprehension and absorption of minutiae. Michael Taussig, for instance, working from the overlapping space between anthropology and cultural studies, enacts such a sense-driven absorption of the ordinary everyday, where knowledge "functions like peripheral vision, not studied contemplation, a knowledge that is imageric and sensate rather than ideational . . . knowledge that lies in the objects and spaces of observation as in the body and mind of the observer." Armed with a sensuous, even distracted vision, postmodern cultural forms enact this anthropological exploration of ordinary life: "The ideal-type here would not be God but movies and advertising, and its field of expertise is the modern everyday."[55] Such a vision of anthropological exploration shares with literary fiction not only the everyday as the subject but even the ethos through which to read it.

Beyond sharing an abiding preoccupation with the semantic implications of everyday life, what cultural anthropology has in common with my work is a stake in the historical scope of the fiction that I read. The period of high modernism was indeed a crucial one for anthropology, not least because of the major epistemic changes within it that brought the ordinary within its purview more than ever before. Central to these changes was a clear shift from the evolutionary-comparativist approach of James Frazer to the "functionalist" ethnography led by Bronislaw Malinowski, which foregrounded a fieldwork-driven, empirical study of quotidian life in a given culture, complete with the marginal, minute details that Malinowski called the "imponderabilia" of life.[56]

Just as importantly, the early decades of the twentieth century were also a seminal period for the beginning of a close mutual relationship between literature and anthropology, as becomes clear through the work of both Frazer and Malinowski. James Clifford, who analyzes this relation evocatively, puts the mutual relationship of literary-modernist and anthropological discourse in the troubled light of an emerging global modernity on the eve of the burgeoning disintegration of colonial empires.[57] Indeed, the concerns of anthropology have, throughout the twentieth century, been in constant negotiation with the cultural politics of decolonization and postcolonial identity formation.[58] My concern, as anthropology's has more recently been, is how not only the everyday but also banality and boredom are produced as an index of the differential distribution of global power and resources. To this end, we need to explore how the space of colonial encounters, which Mary Louise Pratt has evocatively called the "contact zone,"[59] is rendered meaningful through a dialectic of the banal and the extraordinary, through which the apparently exotic in alien cultures is transformed into the quotidian component of studied lifeworlds, producing anthropological knowledge in the process.[60]

The Banality of Empire

The four writers whose work makes up the literary archive at the heart of this book—James Joyce, Katherine Mansfield, Zoë Wicomb, and Amit Chaudhuri—come from four different corners of the world that has historically constituted the global British Empire. The fictions of all these writers variously aestheticize the banal as a motif of colonial modernity. In doing so, they mark a global tradition of narrative innovation that draws on crucial affective consequences of the late colonial and postcolonial social reality. Of these writers, Joyce and Mansfield, although they wrote from the political margins of the erstwhile British Empire, have attained canonical status within the tradition of British modernism. Wicomb and Chaudhuri also write from the colonial peripheries of the former British Empire. Wicomb's career has extended from late apartheid-era South Africa to the postliberation present, while Chaudhuri has emerged as a novelist, poet, and critic in postindependence India, in the years leading up to the accelerated globalization of the twenty-first century. The significance of a similar family of themes in their work show these writers' direct or implied links with traditions of British modernism on a global scale beyond the limits of metropolitan Western culture.

Modernist fiction, in moving from the ethnographic account of the everyday to the eclectic investment of symbolic meaning within a radically transformed banal, signals larger epistemic and political shifts associated with the advent of avant-garde modernism on the whole. In my reading, such shifts occur most notably through the uneven relationships between imperial and colonial modernities, relationships within which modernism needs to be located in order to be fully understood. Just as importantly, however, the preoccupation with the banal serves a more sharply polemical function in the works of the two postcolonial writers than it does in the work of their modernist counterparts, who were writing from a context of late colonialism. Wicomb and Chaudhuri are part of a significant tradition of fiction that has been marginalized by the dominant preoccupation with the more grand and spectacular narratives of colonialism, decolonization, and postcolonial development that, for instance, have been the subject of Anglophone national allegories from the global South. Wicomb and Chaudhuri, in other words, celebrate the banal at a time when narrative models are dominated by the spectacle. In doing so, they also delineate significant paradigms of fiction's possible embeddedness in the inaction of the ordinary, in defiance of what Liesl Olson points out is narrative's traditional commitment to extraordinary action that enables the praxis of the plot. Such a celebration extends the radical poetics of high modernism and its departure from traditional aesthetic paradigms that have defined the banal as the polar opposite of literary value and boredom as the affective sign of the failure to convey aesthetic pleasure. The oppositionality endemic to these texts, moreover, hinges on a radical aesthetic response not only to the affective consequences of colonial and postcolonial social reality but also to narratives shaped by such reality.

I read this global body of Anglophone literature not only in its immediate relation to literary modernism but also in relation to the larger, more dispersed legacy of political and philosophical modernity rooted in the European Enlightenment. Some of the most significant theorists of colonialism and postcoloniality have been persistent in their critical engagement with Enlightenment modernity and, on certain occasions, with the aesthetic modernism of the late nineteenth and early twentieth centuries. They range from theorists of the black Atlantic to the subaltern historiographers from South Asia and Latin America.[61] Their insights reveal a highly fraught relationship between European modernity and the colonial world. However, I read this archive of Anglophone fiction as existing in a greater continuity not only with the aesthetics of high modernism but also with some of the major cultural nodes of Enlightenment modernity, such as the rise of narrative realism and its preoccupation with the marginal details of quotidian life. Though this body of literature originates at various points on the periphery of the British Empire, I would make the more conservative claim that their embeddedness in metropolitan aesthetics is central to their very production. These texts variously trace a complex legacy to the narratives of modernism and modernity in the European context, doubtless partly because they are written in English and partly because they make up a body of prose fiction, a genre directly traceable to the tradition of literary modernity that follows the European Enlightenment. It goes without saying that this claim is specifically limited to this archive of literature; it is far from my intention to argue that the diverse range of Anglophone literatures in the world is overwhelmingly traceable to European cultural modernity. Moreover, this relationship varies widely within the body of fiction I read in this book—Joyce and Mansfield, as modernists canonized within the metropolitan canon, demonstrate a closer relationship with traditions of this modernity than that evident in Wicomb and Chaudhuri. More importantly, none of their relations with the literary discourse of European modernity is one of simple, uncritical inheritance. The colonial context of the global British Empire makes this relation one severely ridden with crisis and resistance, as postcolonial interlocutors of the canonized modernist Joyce, such as Andrew Gibson, Emer Nolan, and Enda Duffy, have ably demonstrated.[62] Perhaps the most important thing to note at this point is that I read literary modernism itself as the indication of a serious crisis in the certitudes and principles of Enlightenment modernity. My reading of modernist fiction, therefore, takes as its point of departure a position similar to that of John Marx, who has argued that the radical experimentation of the modernist novel simultaneously hinged on a decline in the imperial confidence of Britain and the increasingly globalized importance of English as a literary language. "The decline of Britain," according to Marx, accompanied "the rise of English." Literary modernism thus not only signaled a crisis in Enlightenment modernity, but it also "joined hands with an interdisciplinary archive of scholarship and commentary to imagine a world of which England was no longer the centre but in which English language and literature were essential components of an abstract or virtual differentiated system that spanned the globe."[63] It is this global system that is the larger context of my literary archive.

Marx's argument about the literary globalization ushered in by modernist literature hinges on an undoing of "the Victorian fantasy of a planet divided into core and periphery, home and colony in favor of a new dream of a decentred network of places and peoples described, analyzed, and managed by a cosmopolitan cast of English-speaking experts."[64] Despite my enthusiasm for the idea of the globalization of Anglophone literature, I remain hesitant about a complete dissolution of the core-periphery binary that Marx sees as endemic in modernism, even though I'm in strong sympathy with the way he reads the norms of metropolitan modernism as framed by "provincial concerns."[65] Literary modernism, for all its radical innovations, in my view remains strongly linked to the cultural logic of the metropolitan and the peripheral, as has been argued by a host of modernist critics, notably Raymond Williams in *The Politics of Modernism*. This is made clear not only by the privileged cultural position of the metropolitan nations but also the heightened significance of select cities and even the artistic cultures of specific neighborhoods within them. The phenomenon of global Anglophone literature, emergent within the historical context of the British Empire, has to a great degree retained similar structures of metropolis and periphery, as Pascale Casanova has argued in the larger context of world literature. Such models of the relation between metropolitan and peripheral spaces help to illustrate banality as symptomatic of a political condition within this global archive of fiction. The embodiment of the banal as a narrative instinct ironizes the binary of the metropolis and the periphery. It is an irony that echoes modernism's export of provincialism to the metropole that has been convincingly argued by Marx and other interlocutors of modernist metropolitanism.

Versions of the relationship between metropolitan and peripheral spaces have driven the biographical and imaginative movements of all four of these writers, leading them to spend most or much of their adult lives away from their places of birth and early years. Joyce carved out his literary vocation in different parts of continental Europe, which promised far greater cultural cosmopolitanism than the late colonial Ireland he left behind. Mansfield felt very much the same way about her native New Zealand, also emigrating to continental Europe and to England, where she was to gain an ambivalent status within the Bloomsbury circle. Zoë Wicomb left behind an apartheid-ridden South Africa to teach in Scotland, where she still lives, and the Indian-born Amit Chaudhuri has similarly carved out his reputation in the metropolitan centers of London and Oxford and has returned to live in India only after eighteen years in England. A culture of ceaseless travel, spatial disembodiment, temporary and permanent border crossings, alienation and homecomings have come to define the literature of the British Commonwealth following empire and decolonization, a field within which the erstwhile stable concept of "British literature" needs increasingly to be situated in order to be fully understood. A field irrevocably marked by a complex range of cosmopolitanisms, the literature of the global British Empire has over the course of the twentieth century come to constitute probably the most significant archive for what Pascale Casanova has called "the world republic of letters."[66] Writers who have emerged as ambassadors for this republic have demonstrated a wide range of relationships to the various physical and cultural spaces with which they have been associated. However, what is especially intriguing about the four writers in my archive is that though they move in person toward metropolitan spaces, their fiction is mostly preoccupied with the locations they leave behind. Dublin occupies almost all of Joyce's oeuvre; Cape Town and Namaqualand and Calcutta and Bombay constitute, for the most part, the respective fictional contexts for Wicomb and Chaudhuri.[67] Cities and suburbs in England and continental Europe occupy a more prominent place in Mansfield's fiction than they do in any of the other three, but most of her memorable later stories are set in the suburban New Zealand that she considered a cultural backwater. The banality of life in places left far behind, in all four of these writers, hinges on a complex interplay of memory, the aesthetics of an eclectic ethnography, and, probably most importantly, the sobering distance from their subjects gained by the fractured sensibility of the exiled writer.

It is almost as if all four had to detach themselves physically from the spatial context of their subjects for an immersion in what Emerson has called "the common," "the familiar, the low" within the culture they left behind.[68] The most important thrust of their cosmopolitanism rests, therefore, not on their depiction of the foreign or the metropolitan spaces toward which they variously gravitated: indeed, the usual equation of the local and the foreign is continually upset in their fiction. Rather, this cosmopolitanism is to be found in the constant negotiation of the alien and the homegrown in the liminal sensibility with which they describe the culture that they inherited by birth. Their ethnographic description of the ordinary as well as their anticathartic celebration of the banal in the colonial periphery emerges as a covert critique of the relation of the metropolitan and the peripheral as it has evolved within the global history of empire. The historical reality of this relation creates realms of possibility and fulfillment beyond the reach of the immediate, which invests the banality of local life with a subtle narrative energy. The intricate web of desire, pleasure, and consumption through which banality and boredom emerge as aesthetic motifs in this literature reveals a relation between the metropolis and the periphery that is both materially structured and ideologically inflected.

The depiction of banality and monotony through the troubled cosmopolitanism of the diasporic literary sensibility, however, is deeply ironic. Severe impediments to mobility generate an oppressive sense of boredom and banality for a vast number of subjects living in the impoverished peripheries of capitalism. In glaring contrast to the privilege of mobility that shapes the worldview of the cosmopolitan artist, these subjects live with no choice to move or travel beyond their immediate space, no freedom to lead a lifestyle of their own choosing. The embodiments of such constriction are widely varied, from Joyce's paralyzed Dubliners, to Mansfield's confined upper-middle-class women in settler society, to the poor creolized inhabitants of rural Namaqualand in Wicomb's fiction. Severe constrictions on mobility and lifestyle practices produce the overarching aesthetic of banality and boredom, something which the biographical and imaginative movement of the cosmopolitan traveler and writer insistently seeks to escape.

An overwhelming sense of the banality of one's life is a damning marker of economic and ideological subordination. Jamaica Kincaid provides a moving example of the afflictions of banality and boredom in peripheral locations in her polemical personal essay, *A Small Place*. At the heart of this affliction is the cultural and material politics of tourism. The question here is who can and who cannot travel. Those who cannot are unable to transcend the banality of their daily existence and can only hate the tourists who turn that very banality into their pleasure. Kincaid's insight into this hatred is poetic:

> For every native of every place is a potential tourist, and every tourist a native of somewhere. Every native everywhere lives a life of overwhelming and crushing banality and boredom and desperation and depression, and every deed, good and bad, is an attempt to forget this. Every native would like to find a way out, every native would like a rest, every native would like a tour. But some natives—most natives in the world—cannot go anywhere. They are too poor. They are too poor to go anywhere. They are too poor to escape the reality of their lives . . . so when the natives see you, they envy your ability to leave your own banality and boredom, they envy your ability to turn their own banality and boredom into a source of pleasure for yourself.[69]

Banality and boredom are here rooted in the oppressive and inescapable materiality of the local—or as Lars Svendsen might call it, its oppressive immanence. And it is again movement that promises transcendence or liberation out of this claustrophobia of banality and boredom; if not the finality of migration, such movement must possess, at least, the recreational temporality of tourism. Being able to move contains the potential to thwart the pervasive banality of the local space that imprisons its dwellers through the misfortune of their birth. Not only does the boredom of these impoverished natives reveal their lack of mobility and economic agency, but in fact their boredom is the very affective force that defines the relation between the natives and the tourist as one of envy and hatred. The disempowerment of banality and boredom revolves around the structure of this relation rather than directly around the spatial polarity of the metropolis and the periphery. Banality and boredom here are not so much definitive characteristics of a particular place or the lives contained there—the privileged tourist, after all, derives pleasure from the very same place—as they are a reminder of the natives' inability ever to escape from them.

The communal experience of the oppressive everyday in such peripheries is determined not only by the lack of resources and privilege but also by an awareness of the tilted allocation of the same across the globe, an awareness made acute by the cultural hegemonies that usually follow economic imperialism. Not only the empirical experience of the everyday but, more crucially, the feelings of excitement, lack, and monotony that structure such experience are shaped in the image of this center-periphery model by the ideological impact of cultural hierarchies that necessarily follow the economic pecking order. Antiguan beaches might be the objects of desire and excitement for the European or American traveler, but they are, for those travelers, still realistic, attainable objects. In contrast, the technological or cultural wonders, say, of Western metropolitan centers are infinitely more desirable to the native confined to a location in the global South, as she can rarely aspire to consume such pleasures as a tourist of leisure. The sociocultural superstructures of metropolitan power, ranging from the canons of "high" literature to today's globally consumed popular subcultures, have in various ways worked to affirm this hierarchy of value within which the banal and the exciting have been produced as categories.

How does this aesthetic marker of exclusion and disempowerment energize narrative fiction in the twentieth century? This is the key question for this book, one that I feel is best asked within the global body of fiction that can be situated within the category formerly called British Commonwealth literature, a domain of culture that ranges from the canon to the periphery, not unlike the shared history of the former British Empire, which it acknowledges on a plane of cultural symbolism. All four writers discussed in this book, through their complex negotiations of biographical and imaginative movements between metropolitan and peripheral spaces, reveal levels of awareness of this global inequity of material and cultural power that range from the direct to the implicit. At the same time, distance from the spaces of their biographical origin—spaces that also come to define their principal subjects—enable in them a detachment from the most dominant political narratives through which the periphery often asserts itself against the metropolis. Anticolonial nationalism, in all these instances, is variously complicated by an investment in the banality of the everyday, which is located at a remove from the spectacular venues of mainstream struggle.

Beyond the common points of awareness shared by the diasporic literary sensibility, however, there remains an important difference between the divided sensibility of the early-twentieth-century modernist writer and the writer from the late-twentieth-century global South. The representation of the banality and monotony of life predominantly becomes, in the hands of the late colonial modernist, an index of the colonial power relation between the metropolis and the periphery. For the two late-twentieth-century writers discussed here—one from a culture poised on the cusp of liberation and the other from a developing postcolonial nation-state—the representation of the banal also resonates with a clearly articulated theoretical polemic that has begun to call for a departure from the ceaseless valorization of the mainstream narrative of spectacular struggle and development.[70] If in the work of Joyce and Mansfield the constitution of the oppressive everyday is an effect of empire, in the work of Wicomb and Chaudhuri, the banal, while similarly linked to the sociopsychological consequences of imperialism, also significantly emerges as a locus of cultural resistance to the spectacular narratives of colonialism and its nationalist heirs. Their clear departure from the sensational struggles staged in the grand theater of the national public sphere and canonized in the headlines of mainstream historiography, such as wars, riots, genocide, and political upheavals, are a covert critique of the narrative preoccupation with the aesthetics and the politics of the spectacle. The relation of the description of the quotidian and the affective invocation of banality with the cultural politics of colonialism and postcoloniality, therefore, undergoes significant historical transformation over the course of the twentieth century. This book seeks to capture some of the most significant points of the fictional deployment of the contrarian aesthetics of banality within the cultural context of colonialism and postcoloniality, along a transnational body of texts where the literary enactment of such motifs meets with theoretical polemics over the politics of their representation.

Some additional explanation of my archival scope might be relevant, particularly the chronological leap that follows my discussion of the canonical modernist authors to a focus on the last decades of the twentieth century. Though considerably past the turbulent midcentury decades of decolonization in most parts of the world, the late twentieth century is an especially pertinent time to examine the epistemological and political implications of the banal in Anglophone postcolonial literature. Just as a sense of the power of the banal object or situation is found in Joyce's theory of the epiphany or Woolf's articulation of the stream-of-consciousness method, the last decades of the twentieth century set the stage for a curiously similar debate about the revelatory power of the quotidian and the marginal within the cultural politics of postcolonial fiction. It is in the context of these debates about the experiences of quotidian life as an important constitutive space for antiapartheid struggle that Kelwyn Sole foregrounds his argument that banality is an index of power and oppression.[71] An exclusive focus on what Sole calls "the brutal displays of power and victimhood" tend to marginalize awareness of structured inadequacies within all aspects of the quotidian life of oppressed groups, including "basic needs such as clean water, sanitation, electricity, transport and housing" that mark out the disparity between the center and the periphery.[72] It is within such quotidian inadequacies, as opposed to the spectacular dialectic of violent oppression and struggle in the colonial period, that Kincaid's immobile natives are also stuck, trapped in envy for the visiting tourists who derive aesthetic pleasure from aspects of local lives that appear banal and iterative to the impoverished natives. Some distance, it seems, had to be achieved from the grand and spectacular moment of liberation, and the traumatic memory preceding that moment, to pave the way for a renewed fictional attention to the everyday.

The intense conflicts of decolonization had suspended, as it were, the possible fictionalization of an ordinary everyday, erecting instead the grand and dramatic narrative of power, domination, and struggle as the very condition of postcolonial writing during the decades immediately following independence. This narrative continued to dominate postcolonial writing, in most cases, to the last quarter of the twentieth century.[73] It is not in fact until the later years of the century that a handful of writers from locations in the global South begin to *consciously* question the postcolonial novelist's aesthetic and ethical stake in the historically valorized narratives of colonialism and decolonization. In two of these contexts in particular, late apartheid-era South Africa and postindependence India, the consequence of this growing detachment has been a gradual discovery—or "rediscovery," as the South African writer Njabulo Ndebele has called it—of the semantic potential of the mundane everyday at several removes from the dramatic conflicts in the public sphere.[74] The mundane and marginal fragments of indigenous life, consequently, have come to find champions not only in aesthetic practice but also in principle, against what is still the deafening noise of the national narrative of decolonization, independence, and development in the imaginative conceptions of the nascent nation. Forms of weariness with the narrative of the spectacle have led these writers not only to produce fiction that is remarkable in its removal from the obvious spheres of struggle and suffering, be they wars, riots, genocide, or other headline-grabbing political upheavals, but also to articulate vocally a theoretical polemic against the enslavement of the novelistic imagination to such spectacles. Taken together, this body of fiction charts a trajectory from the aesthetics of the banal to that of the ordinary that might be read as an affirmative movement from the condition of lack and unfulfilled desire structured by colonialism to a polemic about the representation of postcolonial reality that is of pointed relevance to the present.

• CHAPTER 1 •
James Joyce and the Banality of Refusal

> *Epic savagery is rendered impossible by vigilant policing, chivalry has been killed by the fashion oracles of the boulevards. There is no clank of mail, no halo about gallantry, no hat-sweeping, no roistering! The traditions of romance are upheld only in Bohemia. Still I think out of the dreary sameness of existence, a measure of dramatic life may be drawn. Even the most commonplace, the deadest among the living, may play a part in a great drama.*
>
> —James Joyce, "Drama and Life"

If the radical aesthetic of the banal thrives at the urgent confluence of modernist innovation and colonial anxiety, it has no greater exponent than James Joyce, who transforms the banality of provincial life into an unprecedented narrative force. If the successful artist, in Joyce's fiction, charts a troubled arc of migration from the provincial margin to the metropolitan center, his path is littered with bodies that fail to do so. Bodies of Dubliners, almost always male, whose desire for the energetic aesthetic culture of the metropolis is stifled by the paralysis that pervades the colonial periphery like dreary smog. Such is the defining reality of the life of Little Chandler in the story "A Little Cloud": "A dull resentment against his life awoke within him. Could he not escape from his little house? Was it too late for him to try to live bravely like Gallaher? Could he go to London? There was the furniture still to be paid for. If he could only write a book and get it published, that might open the way for him."[1] The story is driven by Little Chandler's realization of the glaring contrast of his own life with that of his old friend, Ignatius Gallaher, who is back in Dublin on a short visit. Gallaher has apparently cut a "brilliant figure on the London Press" and has matched his success with a promiscuous, bohemian, and richly exciting life in London and Paris (57). Little Chandler has stayed back in Dublin, married, had a child, and let his literary ambitions be swallowed up by the dreariness of a clerical job at the King's Inn. After a few drinks with the flamboyant Gallaher at the elegant and expensive Corless's bar, he returns home, his rekindled poetic ambitions locked in a losing struggle against the realities of his domestic life: the small child, the furniture yet to be paid for, and the parcel of coffee that he has forgotten to bring home for his wife. Poetry rises in a last gasp against the prose of this world, to lose itself in the wails of the child, the anger of his wife, and his own shame and remorse at having shouted at his child. "Little Chandler felt his cheeks suffused with shame and he stood back out of the lamplight. He listened while the paroxysm of the child's sobbing grew less and less: and tears of remorse started to his eyes" (70).

"To labor," writes Hannah Arendt, "meant to be enslaved by necessity, and this enslavement was inherent in the conditions of human life."[2] Little Chandler's life seems caught up between the conflicting demands of the human condition famously described by Arendt. He is constrained by what Arendt calls "labor," the activities essential to the biological sustenance of the body (or the bodies of those one procreates), those that were traditionally hidden from public view. From within such constraints, surrounded by his wailing child and unpaid-for furniture, he longs to etch his literary signature on the world, to articulate a string of words that, for Arendt, shapes "action": "With words and deeds we insert ourselves into the human world, and this insertion is like a second birth, in which we confirm and take upon ourselves the naked fact of our original physical appearance."[3] But at the end of Joyce's story, Little Chandler is left not only within the constraints of labor, but also crushed under its moral burden. He "felt his cheeks suffused by shame . . . tears of remorse started to his eyes" (70). Action, in the Arendtian sense of the term, remains an unborn dream, with the words of poetry we know he will never write; he will go back to his job as a clerk the next day, to provide for himself and his family, to keep his child from wailing.

In Joyce's fiction, the banality of daily life and the desire for aesthetic transcendence are not so much polarized as held in a mutually enabling dialectic. Nowhere is it brought out more famously than in *Ulysses*, where the aesthetic is indeed embodied *through* the banal. In many of the stories in *Dubliners*, however, the banality of immediate life and the transcending impulse of the aesthetic appear in a relationship of bitter mutual hostility. In Little Chandler's story, this bitterness takes an especially painful shape—that of the Arendtian duality of labor and action; of the claims of private, biological life and those of the literary artist, lived in the light of public glory. These entwined hostilities are subsumed within what is perhaps the most pervasive artistic duality in Joyce—that of the periphery and the metropolis. It is a duality that is no less true for the artist manqué than for the fulfilled artist. No less for Little Chandler than for Stephen Dedalus. In Little Chandler's story, the banality of daily, labor-burdened life in the colonial periphery of Dublin is brought into a pointed contrast not only with the glamorous cosmopolitanism of London but with something more than that, by the manner in which the city appears as a realm of infinite, undefined possibilities, of a life of public action and glory. And Gallaher was one who had realized the possibilities. He was not only "a brilliant figure on the London press" but also a man who looked the part. "You could tell that at once by his travelled air, his well-cut tweed suit and fearless accent" (57). A figure like him only deepens the depressing contrast between the infinite potential of the metropolis and the paralytic nothingness of the periphery: "There was no doubt about it: if you wanted to succeed you had to go away. You could do nothing in Dublin" (59). For Chandler, the excitement of meeting Gallaher morphs unnoticed into the excitement of encountering the metropolis, farther and farther away from the prosaic reality around him: "Every step brought him nearer to London, farther from his own sober inartistic life" (60).

The ironies of history pave his path. To the English critics, Chandler hopes to be accepted as a melancholic Celt caught in the wistful nostalgia of a mythical past. "The English critics perhaps would recognise him as one of the Celtic school by reason of the melancholy tone of his poems" (60). Joyce's skepticism of the Celtic revival in late-nineteenth-century Irish literature reveals itself in this spark of satire on the way the Irish poet manqué dreams of being accepted by the imperial literary establishment. Not one to offer "the cracked looking-glass of a servant"[4] to his colonial masters like Stephen Dedalus, Chandler can only focus on enhancing the marketability of his name to them: "Thomas Malone Chandler, or better still: T. Malone Chandler" (60). Gallaher, too, turns out to be a bit of a fake as the story proceeds, or at the very least a poseur. His condescending friendliness demeans Ireland as much as it demeans Little Chandler: "Gallaher was only patronizing him by his friendliness just as he was patronising Ireland by his visit" (60).

That's our cue not to take too seriously the polarity of the metropolis and the periphery. The aesthetic tension between the banality of an uneventful dailiness and the promise or lure of artistic glory in Joyce's work parallels the historical tension between colonial periphery and the imperial center. But the mutual hostility, in both situations, is deeply overlaid with irony and hence rarely to be taken at face value. Stephen Dedalus, the true artist, would realize this later in his migration back and forth between provincial Dublin and metropolitan Europe. But it takes Stephen Dedalus a long time to arrive, and to arrive specifically at this deceptive dialectic of the banality of the periphery and the artistic possibilities of the metropolis. Into his making goes all the Dubliners unable to see the deceptive nature of this dialectic, all those disheartened, paralyzed, trapped, disenchanted by what to them is the deadening banality, the utter marginality, and the historical vacuum of life in the far periphery of modernity and progress. And since long before they are old enough to understand the true implication of their marginality: the boy in "Araby," Eveline from the story named after her, Little Chandler, Farrington from "Counterparts," and, finally, Gabriel Conroy from "The Dead."

The banality of colonial life is damningly articulated in the striking Joycean motif of paralysis crippling late-nineteenth- and early-twentieth-century Ireland. The musty, long-enclosed air in the houses in the blind street in "Araby," "the odor of dusty cretonne" in Eveline's nostrils, the sentences copied ad infinitum by the clerk Farrington, and the provincial Irish culture so feared by Gabriel Conroy all breathe the tired air held prisoner by the claustrophobic and iterative life of colonial Ireland, banished to the margins of modernity under the rule of Stephen's "two masters"—"the imperial British state . . . and the holy Roman catholic and apostolic church" (*Ulysses*, 6). What is truly radical about Joyce's fiction is that this aesthetic expression of the historical marginality of the colony becomes one of its most powerful narrative forces. Everybody is driven away by the banality of this life—though more fail to flee it than those who succeed—yet it is this aesthetic of banality that in turn drives Joyce's narrative of Dublin.

Of all of Joyce's work, *Dubliners* is perhaps most immediately driven by this aesthetic of banality. *A Portrait of the Artist as a Young Man* concludes with the artist's decision to leave the periphery, not, however, for England, but for metropolitan locations in continental Europe; it is a move that parallels his decision to transform banality into the material of a new aesthetic. Together, they offer a promise to turn the banalized, unheroic, and subordinated reality of colonial life into the stuff of art. *Ulysses* is, of course, the delivery of this promise.

Thus, in Joyce's fiction, neither the radical aesthetic import of the banal nor Ireland's peripheral relation to imperial modernity is fully realizable without the other; symbiotically, they make up a subaltern narrative force that, in time, will unsettle the aesthetic relation between the metropolis and the periphery. To make sense of this apparent paradox, we need to turn to the claims of the banal, the trivial, and the marginal that repeatedly stir unease through Joyce's fictional and critical work.

Transience, Banality, and the Critique of Historicism

Twenty days into the new century, on January 20, 1900, an eighteen-year-old Joyce presented, at the session of the University College Literary and Historical Society, a paper titled "Drama and Life." I've quoted one of the most striking passages from the paper in the epigraph to this chapter. "Still I think," the passage concludes, "out of the dreary sameness of existence, a measure of dramatic life may be drawn. Even the most commonplace, the deadest among the living, may play a part in a great drama."[5] It is striking because, at the outset, it proposes "the most commonplace" as a proper subject for drama, the literary genre most dependent on conflict and spectacle, as evident in the adjective derived from it: *dramatic*. Beyond that, it contains a larger literary elegy for a spectacular form of aesthetics that has died along with the fading of the epic and romance. This shift of emphasis from grandeur to banality is an apt description of a crucial transformation of aesthetic value from its classical tradition to that of post-Enlightenment modernity. As hinted in the last sentence of the passage above, Joyce's own fiction would stake some of its most striking claims for the excitement of "the most commonplace," where the epic and the romance would come alive in a curiously inverted form, through the ironic outbursts of mock-heroism. "The most commonplace," as such, is not only part of Stephen's authorial credo but of his creator's as well. "It is my idea of the significance of trivial things," Joyce wrote in a letter to his brother Stanislaus, "that I want to give the two or three unfortunate wretches who may eventually read me."[6]

As fictionalized in the extant manuscript pages of the autobiographical *Stephen Hero* (more autobiographical than the final, completed novel *A Portrait of the Artist as a Young Man*), Stephen's paper triggers off a maelstrom of outrage and scandal. Behind this outrage, which climaxes with his championing "scandalous" modern authors like Ibsen, is a sustained onslaught on certain established principles of the aesthetic that has been incubating in Stephen's mind for a long time. Key among these is "the antique principle that the end of art is to instruct, to elevate and to amuse."[7] A disciple of Thomas Aquinas, Stephen is "unable to find even a trace of this Puritanic conception of the esthetic purpose in the definition which Aquinas has given of beauty" (79). What brings about this obsolescence of the "antique principle" of aesthetics is a widening of the aesthetic criteria, far beyond the moral, spiritual, and pedagogic mandate of Horace, into a process that is indifferent to moral and spiritual uplift, leading up, in the end, to the realm of the ordinary and the common. "The qualifications he expects for beauty are in fact," Stephen writes, "abstract and common" (79).

Beauty, for Stephen, hinges on patterns of perception and cognition rather than on elements of spiritual uplift or moral sanctification. The utterly ordinary becomes beautiful only when the aesthetic is severed from the sublime. This causes alarm among the authorities in the Jesuit college, who view it as a counterintuitive invocation of Aquinas, one of the most influential Jesuit theologians. The conflict culminates in Stephen's conversation with the rather amicable college president, whom Stephen bewilders with the claim that the Thomist aesthetic is so far detached from spiritual sanctification that it would apply to "a Dutch painter's representation of a plate of onions" (95).

This is probably the argument the college president finds most baffling during his exchange with Stephen before the Saturday Stephen is to read out his paper, which is to trigger further uproar:

—Pulcra sunt quae visa placent. He seems to regard the beautiful as that which satisfies the esthetic appetite and nothing more—that the mere apprehension of which pleases . . .

—But he means the sublime—that which leads man upwards.

—His remark would apply to a Dutch painter's representation of a plate of onions.

—No, no; that which pleases the soul in a state of sanctification, the soul seeking its spiritual good.

—Aquinas' definition of the good is an unsafe basis of operations: it is very wide. He seems to me almost ironical in his treatment of the 'appetites.'

(95)

This is a crucial moment in Stephen's personal rebellion against Jesuit theology's moral and pedagogic control of Ireland. Confident of this control over the Irish people, the president expresses his cynicism about the effect Stephen's theories might have: "I do not predict much success for your advocacy in this country, he said generally. Our people have their faith and they are happy. They are faithful to their Church and the Church is sufficient for them. Even for the profane world these modern pessimistic writers are a little too . . . too much" (97). The shocking pervasiveness of Stephen's aesthetic theory, by foregrounding the banalized elements of the everyday as fit subjects of artistic representation, disrupts this religious didacticism. For him, there is no place for "instruction" or "elevation" in his own allegiance to the Thomist trinity of "Integritas, consonantia, claritas" (96). In her reading of *The Portrait of the Artist as a Young Man*, Rebecca Walkowitz identifies "triviality as a tactic of heresy and insubordination."[8] What she calls triviality I call a meditated and consciously theorized aesthetic of the banal that becomes the crucial point of difference between Stephen's and the president's positions and that culminates in their respective interpretations of Thomism.

The Thomist criteria for beauty, however, might be "abstract and common" (79) but there is in fact a clear structure to it, one that, according to Stephen, travels across cultural and historical differences. The structure derives neither from the powers of romance or spectacle nor from the promise of spiritual uplift. "You know what Aquinas says," Stephen tells Cranly, near the end of the available manuscript pages of the draft: "The three things requisite for beauty are, integrity, a wholeness, symmetry and radiance" (212). The object is perceived in its distinction from the rest of the world and in its integrity as a singular thing. This also establishes its symmetry in the eyes of the observer. As a consequence, what emerges as clear and striking is the quidditas of the object, its essential whatness, a point that we find Stephen also making in *Portrait*.[9] It is at this point of recognition, when "its soul, its whatness, leaps to us from the vestment of its appearance," that the third and the most ambiguous quality, radiance, emerges, and the cumulative effect of all three qualities leads even the most ordinary object to its epiphany: "The soul of the commonest object, the structure of which is so adjusted, seems to us radiant. The object achieves its epiphany" (*Stephen Hero*, 213).

The "commonest object," therefore, comes to occupy centrality in Stephen's theory of the epiphany. In fact, the more insignificant the object, the better suited it is to the unreliable narration of modernism. Garry Leonard points out the significant but overlooked fact that the subject—that is, the character experiencing the epiphany—is passive during the epiphanic moment. "The object, as a 'special point,' announces itself, and 'the soul of the commonest object' becomes 'radiant.'"[10] The very qualities of the banal object that frustrate paradigms of good, functional details characteristic of normative modes of knowledge production are also the ones that respond to the destabilized ontology of modernism. In her exploration of the banal object in modernist fiction, Naomi Segal argues that its dullness and solidity provide a concrete ontological mooring in fiction of unreliable narration. Choosing the example of the "epiphanising" clock of the Ballast Office that comes up in Stephen and Cranly's conversation, she points out that the degree of the insignificance of the object itself is directly proportionate to the degree of intensity and power of the "sudden spiritual manifestation" that Stephen theorizes.

The reasons behind the significance of the banal object are related to the literary self-consciousness of the narration:

> The banal object is singularly well-fitted for this type of problematic text. Its ontological status is no less paradoxical. For while the whole point of its appearance is that it should be dull, commonplace, resistant, solid, concrete, it is of course no more so than any other existent in a literary text. The more the narrator insists on the difficulty of rendering it in language the more cynical the alert reader is likely to become. The use of the "excessively solid object" in a text is a sign of what one might call the literary selfconsciousness with its back to the wall. And this feeling is of course exactly what the texts aim to reproduce.[11]

The unique "solidity" of the banal object, in other words, actually helps to produce its quidditas for the observer and, consequently, its "radiance" in the moment of the epiphany. Elevating the banal object disrupts aesthetic paradigms that seek to keep them merely functional or atmospheric. This disruption is theorized by Stephen in his exchange with the college president.

In the most disruptive of these moments, the banal object approaches a kind of radical alterity. Segal describes Marcel's reactions to the scattering of banal objects in the hotel at Balbec in *A la recherche du temps perdu*. Such objects, during his first visit there at the age of eighteen, seem to threaten him in their utter alienness, but they return many years later in joyous epiphanies through the rush of involuntary memory, triggered by the feel of uneven paving stones or the sound of a spoon tapping against a plate. As before, the revelatory power of the perception is contingent on the banality of their sites. Their ordinariness guarantees that that they have not been actively sought out: that they are *not* the work of voluntary memory, as objects canonically invested with symbolic significance and meaning tend to be, but have been given anonymously, like sanctifying grace. The erosion of the subject's agency, to a degree, destabilizes the subject-object binary. Following this attrition of agency, the consequent recognition is utterly and completely unexpected. The banality of the object shapes its representation as "radically alien" to the perceiver, "separate from any mental categories of ownership or symbolism by which he might possess it."[12] The preservation of the radical alterity of the banal object makes the experience of encountering it a process akin to what Emmanuel Levinas has described as the encounter between the Self and the Other, in which the Self communicates with the Other without the latter losing its radical alienness.

The correspondences between the Joycean epiphany and the Levinasian encounter, however, become fully meaningful only when the banal object resists the epiphany in spite of having invited it. In the typical Joycean epiphany, when the epiphany is successful, the subject demonstrates more agency over the object than the Self does over the Other in the Levinasian encounter. As Stephen argues, the mind has to be in a certain state of readiness to receive the epiphany, which in turn illuminates the object before the mind. Though, as Leonard points out, the experiencing subject remains in a certain state of passivity at the moment of the epiphany, the epiphany is still contingent on a clarity and distinction that is, in the end, resisted by the Levinasian Other. Stephen's arguments here are in fact allied to the Western tradition of aesthetic-epistemological perception that Levinas critiques. For Levinas, the Other remains obscure in spite of the encounter, preserving its radical alterity before the Self and thereby resisting epistemological domination of the former by the latter. While Segal focuses on the successful epiphanization of banal objects, I would argue that it is when the epistemological opacity of the banal object frustrates the epiphanic possibility that the encounter approximates Levinasian ethics. In this, Joyce—especially in his later fiction, as we shall see below—explored wider possibilities than what the young Stephen allows in his aesthetic theories in *Stephen Hero* and *Portrait*.[13]

This is where the ethical import of this encounter with alterity becomes synonymous with a significant aesthetic instinct of modernism that the Joycean epiphany helps to define. Contrary to what the college president might believe, the aesthetically adventurous is thus also the ethically responsible. The need to seek out the unnamable or ideologically unavailable significance of the banal object brought forth by involuntary memory coincides with the need to exceed traditional conceptions of the subject-object relation. Just as Levinas felt it necessary to go beyond the ontological traditions of Western philosophy, the aesthetic chronicler of the banal has to leave the domain of his or her own mind to follow the quirky, phantom lives of the watering cans and paving stones, which, in the end, always lie just a little beyond the reaches of human subjectivity.

The epistemological opacity of the banal object cuts off the easier route of symbolism. In such instances, the opacity implies that the epiphany is often a more complex and fragmented process than the metaphoric elevation of the ordinary or the sordid. When in "Clay," Maria, during the Hallow Eve games, fails to realize what the "soft wet substance" that she has touched is or what its prophetic significance could be, such a failure of realization—a failure of symbolism, as it were—becomes a moment when the epiphany is invited but resisted. Such a frustration not only erodes the mechanism of signification but is also linked to the marginalization of the desolate Maria, who, till the end, is unable to partake fully in the knowledge, much less the significance, of the situation. The failure of the invited epiphany, scattered through Joyce's fiction, is a complex process that has been infrequently theorized. Liesl Olson, who has recently argued that the epiphany is predominantly a tactic of failed aesthetic illumination, points out the gulf between Stephen's theorization of the epiphany and its actual practice in Joycean fiction. "Joyce is drawn to the romantic nature of epiphanic moments if only to deflate them."[14] The highly irregular conferral of significance on the most banal of objects or situations, leading to a suppression of the epiphany as frequently as to its fruition, troubles the theoretical apparatus of signification itself.

In *Solid Objects: Modernism and the Test of Production*, probably the most important scholarly attempt to read the solidity of the physical object in modernist literature as a gesture of resistance, Douglas Mao locates the celebration of this resistance in modernist writing:

This feeling of regard for the physical object as object—as *not-self, as not-subject*, as most helpless and will-less of entities, but also as a fragment of Being, as solidity, as *otherness* in its most resilient opacity—seems a peculiarly twentieth-century malady or revelation, in any case; or rather, we might say, the open acknowledgement of such a feeling seems one of the minor trademarks of the writing of this period.[15]

The legacy of "object-love," according to Mao, is carried along parallel planes by Theodor Adorno and John Crowe Ransom. Ransom contrasts the relationships shared respectively by science and aesthetics with the object—the former aiming to "devour," the latter merely seeking to "cherish." Adorno's *Negative Dialectics* pursues a more radical argument, wherein the object "materializes in an ongoing campaign against the reasoning subject's inevitable, and inevitably violent, move to reduce every thing in the world to a concept."[16] Both Ransom and Adorno are united in their strong critique of Hegel, whose philosophy not only establishes the hegemony of the subject but also the supremacy of the abstract concept over the concrete materiality and the earthy particularity of the object.

The traditional relation between the subject and the object is subverted by the failure of symbolism that occurs often in Joyce's fiction. Even the successful epiphany involves a radical temporality that stages a critique of an ideological vision behind forms of political authority. Garry Leonard has argued that the epiphany's emphasis on the ephemeral, the perpetually vanishing present of historical time, performs a striking critique of the grandeur of the historicist narratives of imperialism. Joyce's fiction, Leonard argues, "consistently presents what is beneath notice as that which is most noticeable."[17] Drawing on various examples of the insignificant and the ephemeral in *Ulysses* as well as from *Dubliners*, such as "the odour of dusty cretonne" in one's nostrils in "Eveline" and Maria's purse in "Clay," Leonard shows how "throwaway" objects are heightened in their short-lived intensity, leading to a privileging of the nonhistoricized "now" as opposed to the imperial historicism valorized by authority figures who betray their investment in the grand narratives of teleological history framing the pedagogic vision within which the boy in the early stories of *Dubliners* finds himself. The boy's world in *Dubliners* is one where the lowbrow exotica of the Apache Chief in boys' magazines such as *The Halfpenny Marvel* is held in ironic contrast to Julius Caesar's Gallic Wars. "What is this rubbish?"

Father Butler asks with a frown upon catching Leo Dillon in class with the boys' magazine. "Is this what you read instead of studying your Roman history?" (13). In colonial Ireland, considerable pedagogic authority rests with figures like Father Butler, who has little doubt about the proper methods and canons of historiography, and with those like the headmaster Deasy in *Ulysses*, who, notwithstanding his faulty knowledge of Irish history, declares absolute confidence in a historiographic vision that is unrelentingly teleological.

In the stories of *Dubliners*, the popular exotica of the Wild West fans a desire for excitement in the boy for "real adventures" (14), a desire that is deeply ironized in the stories themselves. Real adventures of the dimension he longs for never happen to him; revelation of a different kind arrives through highly ephemeral epiphanies that are shaped exactly by the kind of banality that he seeks to escape. This is a world where the exoticizing impulses of popular histories about distant cultures are always doomed to frustration through the epiphanic revelations of the banal—the grand Oriental Bazaar for which the boy in "Araby" waits all week with bated breath climaxes in the banal jangle of unused coins in his pocket and his hearing "a voice call from one end of the gallery that the light was out" (26). The transient banality of the epiphany, therefore, mocks the exotic spectacle of popular imagination as much as it ironizes the grandeur of imperial history that frames Jesuit pedagogy.

The moment of the epiphany is one of the most significant sites where modernist experimentation comes together with a radical critique of dominant modes of knowledge. It is striking how such ephemera celebrated in Joyce's fiction resonate with the projects of contemporary postcolonial, especially subaltern, historiography. Temporality as a site of anticolonial epistemological resistance is also one of the main concerns of many of these projects, such as Dipesh Chakrabarty's *Provincializing Europe*. Chakrabarty speaks of "subaltern pasts," those irrational moments of history that cannot be integrated within the dominant, rational, teleological, and historicist narratives, those which "are marginalized not because of any conscious intentions but because they represent moments or points at which the archive that the historian mines develops a degree of intractability with respect to the aims of professional history."[18] Temporality in Joyce's fiction often illustrates this intractability, significantly though not exclusively around the problem of the transient and amorphous experience of the epiphany. In this sense, the conversation between Stephen and Mr. Deasy in the "Nestor" chapter of *Ulysses* is not just about history but also about historiography. The nightmare from which Stephen is trying to awake is not simply history itself but certain methods of conceiving, institutionalizing, and enforcing it, such as the model of religious teleology embodied in Deasy's platitude: "All human history moves towards one great goal, the manifestation of God" (28). Stephen's famous response to this vision approximates Joyce's valorization of the intractable fragment in the historian's archive, the banal experience of a momentary street noise. If for Deasy all human history moves toward the manifestation of God, for Stephen, God is "a shout in the street" (28).

Shouts on the street, transient moments, shapeless, evanescent experience. It is with such historic marginalia in mind that Patrick Williams draws attention to Walter Benjamin's sense of the "fragment" as a marker of fractured modernist temporalities, as opposed to "the seamless narratives of dominant historiography." The Benjaminian "fragment," for Williams, challenges dominant historiography by foregrounding the banal and the ephemeral aspects of the everyday. The fragment resides in "disregarded or 'insignificant' objects and forms" that are held in opposition to "great cultural monuments and aesthetic canons."[19] Benjamin's awareness of the signifying potential of ordinary objects and practices—be it old books in his collection, walking in the city, or the possibilities promised by the experience of boredom—thus not only resonates with Joyce's belief in the power of the banal and the marginal but also with the unspeakable or the unrepresentable in institutional modes of history writing, as the subaltern historians have repeatedly pointed out. The irrational aspects of history, Chakrabarty argues, end up in a subaltern relation to the dominant ideologies of history as an institutionalized discipline. If figures like Deasy, Father Butler, and Stephen's college president can be seen as representing dominant positions of historiography and aesthetics that frame institutional authority in the world of Joycean fiction, the banal objects and situations foregrounded by epiphanies and Stephen's theories occupy methodologically disruptive locations. Inasmuch as they inscribe temporalities—mostly transient ones—they are the "subaltern pasts" of such dominant models for the production and consumption of history.

Frequently, it is the very *realization* of the sense of ordinariness and ephemerality of situations that is the reward of the epiphany. At the end of "Araby," therefore, the distressing banality of the deserted fair around which he had woven high expectations drives the boy to see himself, in that brief, concluding moment, as "a creature driven and derided by vanity" (19). The realization is accompanied by the fragments of an exchange that can only appear to him as banal and to which he can only listen "vaguely":

>   —O, I never said such a thing!
>   —O, but you did!
>   —O, but I didn't!
>   —Didn't she say that?
>   —Yes. I heard her.
>   —O, there's a . . . fib!
> (19)

This meandering, semicoherent exchange of flirtation predicts a very similar situation in *Stephen Hero*, where Stephen, far more mature and intellectually articulate than the boy in "Araby," comes across an exchange between a young man and a woman. Stephen, who by this point is in the process of shaping his literary vocation, thinks "of collecting many such moments together in a book of epiphanies" (211). If Stephen the artist-protagonist finds in "this triviality" (211) the material for epiphanies, the boy in "Araby" is *in* the epiphany himself, without realizing it, in the banality of frustrated desire and the transience of the experience that can only remind him of lost time and opportunity.

A Homeric Shield for Fourpence: The Banal Object in Symbolist Naturalism

The epiphany hinges on the spectral life of the minute and marginal detail, which grows and prospers with the literature of modernity. For Naomi Schor, the exemplary historian of the detail in modern European literature, the aesthetics of the minutiae is linked to feminized labor, as against classical and neoclassical valorization of the ideal with no particulars, which shapes the masculine structure of Western literary and philosophical imagination. The specific historical forces behind the rise of the detail in late-nineteenth- and twentieth-century literature also "include secularization, the disciplining of society, consumerism, the invention of the quotidian, the development of the means of mechanical reproduction, and democratization."[20] In Joyce's oeuvre, the most celebrated instances of industrial capitalism, democratization, consumerism, and the jagged cityscape of commercial urban modernity—all in a critically transitional phase—are contained in *Ulysses*, the epic of the advertisement canvasser and his sordid-heroic modern odyssey. It focuses on the life of a provincial capital situated on the margins of the empire, in its semifeudal smallness and immediacy, caught in the troubled waters of subaltern nationalism and imperial exploitation. Moreover, it is chronicled through an encyclopedic abundance of ethnographic details, less in the ordered descriptions of naturalism than in the disruptive matrix of what Edmund Wilson had termed "symbolic naturalism." *Ulysses* is, therefore, expectedly a chaotic celebration of the banal fragment, which is scattered in various incarnations throughout the novel. One of its most conscientious readers, John Bishop, has argued that *Ulysses* is a novel where the evaluative meaning of the word "banal" comes to engage the sense of economic and political marginality that shapes the etymology of the word.[21] The banal is produced in the interwoven lives of the provincial petit-bourgeoisie who would have embodied the sociopolitical periphery of the feudal economy subjected to the constrictions of banality in the original sense of the term. In a novel like *Ulysses*, such a connection is in fact not a mere metaphor but a real convergence of the aesthetic and the political. Banality gives aesthetic form to the fractured and incomplete model of urban modernity that shapes the novel's landscape, emerging, in the process, as a radical narrative instinct in its own right.

One of the most celebrated banal objects (a necessary oxymoron) that makes its odyssey through Bloomsday is the "sweet lemony" fourpence worth of soap that Bloom buys for credit at the chemist's toward the end of "The Lotus Eaters." Shuffled around different parts of Bloom's person, the forgotten yet unforgotten soap keeps making its appearance at rather regular intervals, charting, as it were, the progress of the day. As he settles down in the cab that will take him, Martin Cunningham, Mr. Power, and Simon Dedalus to the cemetery where Paddy Dignam's funeral is to take place, the soap, a hard edge pricking his bottom, reminds him that he is sitting on it. The need to transfer it to a more comfortable part of his person deepens in Bloom's consciousness—sensuous and disconcerting, occasionally but not entirely forgettable—a need that is not satisfied till they can all step out of the carriage. But his pocket is hardly a pit of oblivion for the soap. It returns in the Aeolus episode, and not "ONLY ONCE MORE," as the section title promises (101). The act of dabbing his nose with his handkerchief here rewards Bloom with the "Citronlemon" fragrance of the soap, which returns to his mind on the occasion. Upon this remembrance, he takes it out of his handkerchief and puts it back where it originally had been, in the hip pocket of his trousers. Again, right at the end of the "Lestrygonians" episode, while he is flustered and disturbed at the sight of Blazes Boylan, his hand, out of some inexplicable desire of security and self-effacement, goes into a frenzy in his pockets, only to come up with the soap again. In the "Sirens" episode, as he stands up in the pub, ready to leave, the soap feels sticky behind, indicating the possible sweatiness of his body. Instead of deflecting his thoughts onto other things, as it did previously, this time the soap draws them inward, as it were, into an intense awareness of his own body, which of course is never very far from Bloom's thoughts. In "Nausicaa," a similar strain of contemplation of his own physicality, this time of possible male odors that might be attractive to women, brings him to insert his nose into the opening of his waistcoat, to be greeted by the same lemony smell of the soap. An involuntary action reminds him of the soap again in the "Circe" episode, when the thought of pickpockets makes him automatically insert his hand inside his pockets, where he identifies, along with the soap, his purse, the purchased book *Sweets of Sin*, and the potato. But even a banal object cannot be kept from attaining surrealist proportions in "Circe." The soap soon rises in the east as the sun, containing the freckled face of Sweny the druggist in its disc. The "soapsun" sings too, claiming a magical cleansing partnership with Bloom: "We're a capital couple are Bloom and I. / He brightens the earth. I polish the sky" (360). At last, it is in the "Ithaca" chapter that the soap finds the use for which it was intended, as Bloom uses it to wash his hands: "To wash his soiled hands with a partially consumed tablet of Barrington's lemonflavoured soap, to which paper still adhered (bought thirteen hours previously for fourpence and still unpaid for), in fresh cold neverchanging everchanging water . . ." (550).

None of these recurrences of the soap in *Ulysses* is anything more than ephemeral and would therefore seem invested with what Garry Leonard calls "nonhistoricized significance." The literally infinitesimal nature of the motif is reflected, moreover, on both the spatial and the temporal plane. Beyond the small and "partially consumed" dimension of the object itself, its figuration in space is forever limited and forever diminishing, except for its solar incarnation in Nighttown. It either remains wrapped in Bloom's handkerchief or snuggled in his hip pocket; it never wanders beyond the range of Bloom's sensory organs or, for that matter, his physical person. Even so, repeated, scattered fragments of its self-effacing but disruptive appearance succeed in becoming something of a fractured objective correlative of Bloom's day, often signifying his mental (curiosity, agitation) and physical (discomfort, sweat) state as well as the mood and texture of the particular imaginative universe it happens to be located in at the moment—attaining, correspondingly, surrealist proportions in "Circe." On the whole, however, the manner in which the soap appears throughout the novel ensures that it accumulates a certain epistemological opacity that frustrates the easy attachment of aesthetic and cultural significance. It is, I would argue, the perfect example of a banal object that resists epiphanization. The significance of this resistance becomes clear in the location of the soap—or the lack of it—in the larger aesthetic framework.

The soap's intermittent eruption throughout the text not only negates its possible integration into larger conceptual or thematic wholes but also ruptures any possibility of subordination to human subjectivity. Bloom's very purchase of the soap is the result of an afterthought, since he is unable to get the face lotion in Molly's recipe, which he has misplaced. And subsequently, every time the soap makes its appearance in the text, it is either the accidental result of some other intended action (sniffing down his waistcoat for odors, dabbing his nose with the handkerchief, feeling his pockets at the thought of pickpockets) or because of some discomfort caused to his person by an irregularity in its position (pricking his bottom from his hip pocket, sticking to his behind with his sweat). It is only in its final reference in "Ithaca" that we return to the soap as the real object of action, when Bloom uses it to wash his hands. At all other times, even though the soap takes us to (or is reached through) various motifs representative of Bloom's eclectic mind, its specific appearance is contingent on some banality or some marginal, meaningless accident.

One explanation of the disruptive appearances of the object can be found in the description of Joyce's aesthetic by a contemporary critic, Edmund Wilson. In *Axel's Castle*, Wilson argues that Joyce's narrative method involves a convergence of naturalism and symbolism. The careful chronicling of the continuous but marginal and disruptive appearance of the partially consumed cake of soap throughout the novel illustrates the chaotic merging of the naturalistic penchant for detail and the symbolic elevation of such detail. More importantly, the novel reveals the place of the banal detail at the convergence of the two aesthetic modes. As Naomi Segal points out, ordinary details abound in naturalistic fiction, but they are generally functional, infinitesimal as the functions may be. They help to affirm the nineteenth-century man's "fetishism of facts," his belief in science and progress, and, consequently, his "delight and trust in the visible world."[22] In their more important incarnations, they aid plot and prefigure as omens, as they do in Stendhal and Tolstoy. Moreover, they help in characterization, as idiosyncratic personal possessions or components of human attire. In all, they are "human-centered, imbued with the significance of a perceiving consciousness," they are organized in strict subservience to the exploration of human subjectivity, and their relationship is usually in keeping with the functions and values such objects are assigned in the material world. But while naturalism locates man in a vast material world with the plenitude of objective details, the symbolist selects a few objects and seeks to transmute them with transcendental significance. Therefore, as Segal argues: "The existence of the banal object begins only when the two extremes are brought up against one another and come into conflict. The encounter with the banal is the challenge that the Naturalist assumption makes to the Symbolist assumption, when objects which have no place in the poet's world intrude and make their claim."[23]

Bloom's soap is a perfect example of an object that has managed to escape the orderly world of naturalism to flirt with the symbolist assumption, but it is one that also refuses to surrender fully to the transcendental impulse of symbolism. In the kind of fiction of details Virginia Woolf had accused Arnold Bennett of writing, the soap would have perhaps been bought, put to proper use, and kept in its usual place, the narrative consequence being either the creation of setting, for example, the establishment of the lifestyle or the character of the protagonist. On the other hand, in either a symbolist or a romantic world, the soap would be one of the handful of objects highlighted by the narrative and would be invested with a unique metaphoric power, thus elevated above and beyond its usual functional role. Emergent at the chaotic intersection of symbolist aesthetic and an encyclopedic naturalism, the Joycean banal deconstructs the binary between the two. It is in fact this indeterminacy that shapes its life as a banal object.

In Bloom's pocket, this life thrives next to that of its more famous neighbor, the potato that Bloom consciously carries like a talisman. He steps out of the house for the very first time in the morning, to get kidneys from the butcher for breakfast, with the assurance: "Potato I have" (46). But the potato is the more famous object not merely because it is talismanic for Bloom; it is so because, as Catherine Gallagher and Stephen Greenblatt point out, it is at once a "historically overdetermined" signifier and the ultimate antipoetic object of gross materialism.[24] If anything, we might guess, it is talismanic for Bloom precisely because of its overdetermined materialism in the historical context of colonial Ireland, rightfully ensconced in the physical body of the eclectic materialist Bloom. But Bloom's pocket is a space of murky materialism where the opaque ends up replacing the talismanic; shook up at the sight of Blazes Boylan near the museum gate right at the end of "The Lestrygonians," he looks for the potato in his pocket: "Try all pockets. . . . Trousers. Potato. Purse. Where?" (150). Instead of the potato, it is the soap that his hand encounters, which, oddly, becomes his symbol of safety. "His hand looking for the where did I put found in his hip pocket soap lotion have to call tepid paper stuck. Ah soap there I yes. . . . Safe!" (150).

If the potato can hardly be considered a banal object in the sense the soap can be, its value as a symbol is just as complicated. It is but a symbol of antisymbolism, something of an antisymbol itself. The perfect object for the "materialist imagination," Gallagher and Greenblatt point out, the potato embodies the materialism associated with the colonized poor of Ireland who eat it, as opposed to bread, which is not only more expensive and therefore the proper staple for the wealthier classes but which is also capable of being wholly spiritualized through the Communion. The potato becomes therefore not so much a symbol but a metonymy for the "idea of the autochthonous people, people who are part and parcel of the land, as medieval serfs were imagined to be."[25] The potato eaters, in other words, are banal people in the feudal sense of the term.

The materialism of the potato finds its perfect embodiment in the idiosyncratic sensuality of Leopold Bloom, which never veers far from the erotic. If Bloom's hand seeks the potato frantically at the upsetting sight of his wife's lover, its next significant appearance does not happen until we enter the sexually carnivalesque atmosphere of Nighttown. Now we see it rubbing shoulders not only with the soap but with *Sweets of Sin*, the soft-porn novel that he has bought for Molly: "*Bloom pats with parceled hands watchfob, pocketbookpocket, pursepoke, sweets of sin, potatosoap*" (357). Soon, the young prostitute Zoe, reaching into Bloom's pocket seductively to feel his testicles, finds the potato, which she brings out: "*Her hand slides into his left trouser pocket and brings out a hard black shrivelled potato. She regards it and Bloom with dumb moist lips*" (388). Bloom tells her that it is "A talisman. Heirloom" (388). It is indeed an object linked to the memory of his mother—just a little while ago, feeling the potato in his trouser pocket, Bloom identified it as "Poor mamma's panacea" (356), which has contributed to its talismanic property. Symptomatic of the fluid sexuality and ambivalent kinships of the world of *Ulysses*, the talisman from his mother now passes on to the prostitute Zoe, and that is the last we see of the potato in the novel: "*She puts the potato greedily into a pocket then links his arm, cuddling him with supple warmth*" (389).

The chaotic mix of symbolism and naturalism that foregrounds the banal object, as such, does so through a range that spans from the opaque to the oddly symbolic. The third object (not) in Bloom's pocket, next to the soap and the potato, is only conspicuous in its absence throughout the day. This is the key to the house, for which he feels his trouser pocket right as he leaves in the morning, finding the potato instead. "On the doorstep he felt in his hip pocket for the latchkey. Not there. In the trousers I left off. Must get it" (46). The soap, the potato, and the (absent) key are foregrounded in the novel in an ascending order of symbolic richness, with the key possessing not only the richest symbolic meaning but also the most crucial plot function. The various symbolic meanings of the key and how they relate to Bloom's odyssey throughout the day are famously embodied in the "Aeolus" section of the novel, around the Keyes advertisement, which relates to the motif of the key both as pun and symbol. The functional role played by the forgotten key is fulfilled in the equally famous passage in "Ithaca" where Bloom, returning home with Stephen late at night, is forced to climb the railings of his house and enter it through the scullery door, as he has left the key at home, in the pocket of another pair of trousers.

It turns out that Bloom's pocket is a pretty revealing slice of the world of *Ulysses*, and the objects that are there, no more or less than those that should have been there but are absent, embody the tension between the naturalist and the symbolist that shapes a narrative universe teeming with banal objects. The plenitude of ethnographic detail chronicling the real historical and geographic compass of turn-of-the-century Dublin exhibits naturalism's penchant for creating a true-to-life atmospheric canvas replete with referential details. Yet without the disruptive entry of symbolist aesthetics into this universe, objects such as the bar of soap, the potato, or the set of keys could never have chalked out marginal, disruptive lives of their own. The duality of the naturalist and symbolist use of objects has long been noticed in Joyce criticism, perhaps most famously by Robert Martin Adams, who distinguished between the surface—that which provides historical or atmospheric context—and symbol, which represents themes and patterns of abstract importance.[26] An object such as the soap is, in some ways, better explained by the undefined tension between surface and symbol rather than as a categorical binarization of the naturalist and the symbolist. The life of the banal object teases but never quite satisfies symbolism's urge to elevate such objects into transcendental significance. It continues to be variously symbolic of Bloom's day and his character, his fears and his fetishes. Yet it does so in such a fragmented, transitory manner that it falls far short of the symbolic depth or grandeur of Mallarme's flowers or Yeats's swan. It refuses to be organized in the ordered universe of naturalistic fiction, in keeping with its conventional material utility, or in subjugation to the dominant consciousness of the subject. But neither does it quite attain the transmuting power of the object *chosen* by symbolism. This transformative power can only be attained by a privileged few, unlike the chaotic plethora of banal objects and practices strewn throughout *Ulysses*. Sometimes, if a banal object assumes a symbolic importance beyond the scope of its immediate materiality, it does so through a uniquely Joycean turn of language, often through a comic pun. Such is the empty biscuit tin that the one-eyed citizen throws at Bloom in a frenzy of anger in "The Cyclops" episode, an act that seems to mirror Lenehen's comment earlier in the episode where he says that "*Throwaway*. . . . Takes the biscuit" (267), inasmuch as Bloom is, like Throwaway, the dark horse of the day.

A particularly apt Joycean device through which this unresolved tension of the symbolist and the naturalist is mediated is the list, which in *Ulysses* is a pseudostructured but actually capricious assortment of mundane details. Lists are also singled out by Liesl Olson in her attempt to demonstrate the resilience of the ordinary in the face of aesthetic transformation, where the desire to narrate the everyday is as palpable as the frustration of such desire. Herein lies the unique indeterminacy of the Joycean position with respect to the everyday detail, which perceptive critics from Wilson to Olson have identified over the more aesthetically recognizable transcendence offered by symbolism alone. This indeterminacy reveals an essential truth about the narrative representation of the ordinary in Joyce's novel, that "the everyday is a foil to the very act of interpretation itself."[27] Lists abound most famously in "Ithaca," a chapter whose parody of the catechistic method and also perhaps of the Socratic dialogue, is well known. The pseudostructure of the numerous lists in the chapter also foreground a unique relationship to the marginal and quotidian object, where Bloom's amateur and absurd scientific vision shows a curious affinity with Stephen's perception of quidditas. Modeled on an exchange between the two characters, the chapter brings to a comic climax the relationship of the Bloomian and the Dedalusian visions, most significantly in their commitment to the materiality of the banal object. Bloom, however, is the host in this chapter, and it is his worldview that provides the crucial framing apparatus to this exchange, shaped by a mind that fascinates itself endlessly over "inventions now common but once revolutionary," especially when facilitated by a certain physical state, that of "reclining in a state of supine repletion to aid digestion" (559). Lists are the most striking component of this apparatus, and they range far and wide in nature, from the detailing of the homely contents of the "lower, middle and upper shelves of the kitchen dresser, opened by Bloom" to the more absurd lists of the "various inventoried implements" in the hypothetical "Bloom Cottage"—"Eeltraps, lobsterpots, fishingrods, hatchet, steelyard, grindstone, clodcrusher, swatheturner, carriagesack, telescope ladder, 10 tooth rake, washing clogs, haytedder, tumbling rake, billhook, paintpot, brush, hoe and so on" (551, 586). The movement between the listing of familiar objects in domestic settings and the more exotic and absurd collections, often in imaginary situations, reflects the tension between an ethnographic naturalism and a disruptive symbolism that shapes the narrative mode of the novel on the whole.

On the other extreme, the ordinary detail can be made to serve in a far more rigidly organized regime, in more traditional models of realism that would suppress the radical ascendancy of the banal. Joyce's trivia plays equal havoc with this regime. And it is no coincidence that the polarization of these two modalities of ordinary detail and the subsequent categorization of the "good" and the "bad" is theorized by one of Joyce's fiercest critics, Georg Lukács. As Naomi Schor points out, Lukács takes Hegel's organicist ideal of all parts' complete, ordered subservience to the whole and refracts it through nineteenth-century historicism to come up with his Marxist version of the "good" detail, which contributes to the social, material function of art: "details meticulously observed and depicted with consummate skill and substituted for the portrayal of essential features of social reality and the description of the changes effected in the human personality by social influences."[28] As opposed to the "good" details of Tolstoy and Balzac, Lukács gives the examples of the "bad" details of Flaubert and Zola. Suspicious of what he considers the subjective distortion of merely apparent reality in Joyce's method, Lukács argues that "the crux of the matter is to understand the correct dialectical unity of appearance and essence."[29] Unlike Segal's (or, for that matter, Wilson's) binarization of symbolism and naturalism,

Schor sets Lukács's applause of realism (which he sees as socially responsible) in contrast to his antipathy for naturalism, which for him is decadent, bourgeois, a version of petty Western realism, abounding in details variously categorized as "inessential," "isolated," "superficial and unconnected." Schor argues that for Lukács, "the target aimed at through the critique of naturalism is actually modernism."[30] Lukács's sense of the complicity between naturalism and modernism is again best justified by the abundance of naturalistic detail in the archmodernist Joyce, who came under the fiercest fire from Lukács on grounds quite similar to the objections expressed by the Marxist critic against the "bad" details of naturalism.[31] Unable to reflect a grasp over "the total complex of reality," fiction such as Joyce's, Lukács concludes, "never rises above the level of immediacy, either intellectually or artistically. . . . Hence the art they create remains abstract and one-dimensional."[32]

A Commodity Misplaced

Disrupting the Lukácsian dictum of the "good" detail, Leopold Bloom's "citronlemon" soap appears throughout the novel, erupting through the empirical realism of the "everyday," threatening aesthetic or epistemological totality. It is subservient neither to plot nor to character; it radically disrupts both, at the oddest and the most transient of moments. In fact, it exhibits many of the attributes of the "bad" detail, namely, superfluity, isolation, marginality, and idiosyncrasy. The soap's dislocation from its original context of material use, moreover, indicates a relation with dominant economic modes as diffuse as that of the relation it shares with established aesthetic parameters. The very production of banality in Bloom's bar of soap is partially a function of its relation with consumer capitalism within the culture portrayed by the novel.

Constructions of the binary of aesthetic ideology and consumer capitalism, through the respective figures of Stephen Dedalus and Leopold Bloom in *Ulysses*, have figured in many readings of the novel, yet this binary has been deconstructed in Joycean scholarship at least since the mid-1990s. Garry Leonard points out how the supposedly solid distinction between timeless art and the ephemeral marketplace dissipates both in Stephen's theorization of the epiphany as well as in his "marketing" of the concept to Lynch. Lynch, with his short attention span and his need for material incentives like cigarettes as Stephen "sells" him his aesthetic theories, plays, in jest, the role of the consumer in a free market. But in Joyce's imaginative universe, the location of the commodity itself troubles consumer culture. This troubling is an important precondition of the production of banality. This is, after all, a world whose modernity is not only secular but antitranscendental, framed in a mock-heroic vision that imagines heaven as a place "equipped with every modern home comfort, " including telephones, elevators, water closets, hot and cold water (248)—an infrastructure set to satiate the needs of modern consumerism. Heaven, in this worldview, is not only incorporated into a landscape of secular modernity but also brought down from the plane of the transcendental to that of banal creature comforts. We realize that alternative chronicles of history, such as advertising, fashion, and the commercial news media, in *Ulysses* are not incompatible with the aesthetic process of the epiphany; they are all marked by a disruptive transience. The soap, as with several other banal objects and practices in the novel, similarly deconstructs the binary of the artistic and the consumerist.

Bought for fourpence at the chemist's, the soap, a mass-manufactured product, would seem to exemplify the consumer capitalism that pervades so much of Bloom's life and, indeed, the entirety of the novel. That would have perhaps been its entire configuration in a work of traditional realist fiction, where the object of everyday detail is relegated to its usual position and function of material contingency, which in this case would be within the cycle of consumerism and the subsequent material pleasure and utility such consumerism is supposed to produce in the lives of individuals. But even though it is produced in Bloom's life through an act of commercial transaction—albeit as an afterthought—throughout the novel, the soap is divorced from its conventional function until the very end, in "Ithaca." Instead of being consumed by washing, it is "partially consumed" by Bloom's sweat, sticking to his body at the oddest of points and times. As Bloom's window shopping in "Lestrygonians" shows, in Bloom's life and mind, motifs of buying and selling rarely function smoothly along the dominant logic of consumer capitalism—they are rather released in the eclectic narrative of symbolist naturalism, in the associative stream of consciousness where the banal and the "exotic" are pushed together cheek by jowl—pin cushions and silk underclothes, the spices of the East, advertisements of Agendath Netaim. Bloom's ambivalence toward the ideologies behind consumer capitalism is made clear in his response to the idiom of advertising, which often implicitly links capitalism to the colonialist project. Professionally, Bloom is dedicated to shaping and foregrounding the discourse of consumerism, but he is no less of a critic of this discourse. "He is," writes Marjorie Howes, "both an architect and critic of the processes that commodify the memory of nationalist heroes like Robert Emmet, the 'gallant pictured hero in Lionel Marks' window,' or enable a cake of soap to generate consumer demand by appropriating the ideology of colonialism."[33] Not that it is unlikely that he also occasionally "buys"—pun intended—the principles behind such discourses or their implication in the colonialist project; the soap, after all, does come to claim the cleansing and illuminating powers that also form the ideological backbone of empire: "He brightens the earth. I polish the sky" (360). Through Leopold Bloom, the banalized commodity's location within and subsequent dislocation from its ideologically interpellative function refracts colonial Ireland's ambiguous relation with the more advanced models of capitalism of the time.

The totality that Lukács accuses Joyce of failing to probe is the entire complex of society held in a relation of determinism to the capitalist mode of production.[34] In this argument, the Joycean banal object merely remains on the plane of immediacy, unable to probe beneath it to understand the structure of totality framed by capitalism. I think, however, that an object as the soap proves otherwise, reflecting, through its fractured lives through the novel, a different model of capitalism, one at once emergent and fragmented, that shapes the urban landscape of *Ulysses*. A careful reading of the life of the soap reveals patterns of its dislocation from the circuits of mainstream capitalism and of late colonial Ireland's fractured relation with its institutions. Daniel Moshenberg, who also refers to the soap in his reading of the novel, sees in its journey the three stages of the Marxian circuit by which the commodity is transformed into commodity capital. After its purchase, however, the soap disappears from public circulation, and its continual appearances throughout the day are always private, invisible to others: "As the visible sign of the invisible, the soap can also be seen as signifying the unseen but felt antisocial fragments within the city, and thus interrupts the fiction of Dublin as unified, homogeneous capital."[35] Dislocation from the public circuits of capitalism, therefore, becomes a metonymy of the state of capitalism in late colonial Ireland. For Leonard, the subaltern relation that the "semi-colonial" Irish shared with British/European consumer capitalism shaped their inevitable disappointment with it: "But as the object is approached, it fades, then disappears. The semi-colonial subject is 'caught out'—flush with the feeling of expectation and promise, yet suddenly crushed and disoriented by the unbearably keen awareness of the relatively hopeless life she has been trying to ignore."[36]

This disappearance of the commodity from its promised function of material satisfaction is literalized not only by the phantom life of the soap throughout Bloomsday but by its actual physical diminution during it, in Bloom's pocket, by his sweat and under the pressure of his body. Throughout the novel, it is subsequently misappropriated and fetishized—often both at the same time—and this "reobjectification" outside its original circuit of existence, as Bill Brown might put it, leads to its production as a "thing" rather than the "object" it initially was.[37] Curiously, this emergent "thingness" turns the soap into a singular detail as much as it causes it to disappear into the very everydayness that defines the ethos and the atmosphere of the novel, not unlike the simultaneously mundane and extraordinary figure of Bloom himself.

The Ethnography of Everyday Life in the Colony

The emergence of banality as a radical aesthetic value in Joyce's fiction cannot be fully appreciated without attending to the way the more descriptive category in its backdrop, everyday life, was being subtly reinvented as a significant vehicle of knowledge in the early decades of the twentieth century. The major venue of this reinvention was the discipline of anthropology, where the everyday was beginning to emerge as a key epistemological category. Moreover, this emergence itself was a significant departure from the older cast of the discipline, which was far more deeply pervaded by the value system of an imperialist world order. This was the story of anthropology's transition from James Frazer to Bronislaw Malinowski, a transition that foregrounded the epistemological potential of the everyday as a space where imperial structures of knowledge could be dislodged from the center. This new anthropology—and the ethnographic fieldwork as its methodological framework—provides a larger epistemic backdrop to Joyce's narrative radicalization of the aesthetic of banality.

Many recent anthropological readings of Joyce identify in *Ulysses* a critique of imperialist models of anthropology. Marc Manganaro's *Culture, 1922: The Emergence of a Concept* draws attention to the "dailiness" and the "ordinariness" of the matter documented in *Ulysses*. "*Ulysses* as ethnography," writes Manganaro, "as the literary record of a people, a culture, one among many which, like *Argonauts*, records the events of a day in terms of their typicality, and does so for ethnographically-relevant reasons."[38] Such ethnographic recording is a departure from comparative-evolutionary models like Frazer's *The Golden Bough*, which categorizes the culture of various peoples as "ancient," "modern," "primitive," and "civilized," thereby constructing clear hierarchies (in which contemporary British are at the top and African tribesmen at the bottom). To an extent, Joyce's own physical absence from Dublin while he wrote about it—with his brother Stanislaus answering his queries on factual details of its civic life—bears the mark of the Frazerian armchair anthropologist. However, in the plenitude of its ethnographic detail rooted in the average quality of everyday life, *Ulysses* resembles the empirical ethnography emerging at the time rather than Frazer's hierarchical taxonomies of cultural values.

Joyce, moreover, as James Buzard has argued, approximates the position of the autoethnographer, portraying not an alien culture but one's own, and in a mode in which the ethnographic self is constituted in a unique detachment from his culture.[39] The image of the artist as "God paring his fingernails" is, in that sense, also of the archetypal autoethnographer who portrays his own culture from a detached vantage point. In an earlier essay, Buzard had traced the emergence of autoethnography to the 1930s, which was also when it gained the support of Malinowski, who, more than anybody else, represented the new ethnographic turn to the discipline of anthropology.[40] The representation of one's own culture, whether in ethnographic discourse or in fiction that borrowed from the former's methods—of which Joyce's novel remains the most important early example—has to remain committed to the apprehension of the everyday. Joyce's exhaustive exploration of a single day in the life of a given culture, moreover, not only had a special relevance to the Malinowskian functionalist anthropology but also to an intriguing counterpart in the anthropological discourse of the late 1930s. This was the focus of the amateur research organization Mass-Observation's project to undertake a book-length study of British life on a single day, May 12, 1937, initially formulated by the poet and journalist Charles Madge, the anthropologist Tom Harrison, and the filmmaker and painter Humphrey Jennings. The autoethnographic intent of this project was of great political significance, as it proceeded with the assumption that a "civilized" culture like Britain could be studied through methods till then reserved for approaching cultures and communities peripheral to the metropolitan Western world.

Even though Mass-Observation gained the approval of Malinowski himself, as James Buzard has pointed out, May 12, 1937, was not exactly an ordinary day in British life, being the coronation day for George VI.[41] June 16, 1904, on the other hand, was as close as it could get to a perfectly ordinary day in the life of the contemporary Dubliner. Barring the personal importance the day had for Joyce as the day of his first walk with Nora Barnacle (later to be his wife) in the evening at Ringsend, the event closest to being special for the communal lives of Dubliners on that day was the race for the Ascot Gold Cup, eventually won by the dark horse Throwaway. It was, by all measures, a perfectly average day, its ordinariness noted by several contemporary readers, among them Arnold Bennett ("the dailiest day possible"), Stuart Gilbert ("a perfectly ordinary day, in fact"), and Ezra Pound ("never goes beyond the average").[42] From an anthropological point of view, Manganaro points out, the smallness, the provinciality, the ordinariness of life in Dublin makes it a more desirable object of study: "that a smaller civic unit—a provincial city on the margins of Europe—is much more appropriately considered as 'culture' because it is more readily discernible, mappable, recognizable, than its more complex and heterogeneous neighbors (Paris, London)."[43]

While modernism's debt to James Frazer is well documented through T. S. Eliot's acknowledgments in *The Waste Land*, it is only more recently that critics have begun to note that the crucial year of 1922 also saw the publication of Malinowski's ethnographic account of the western Pacific islands, *Argonauts*, along with Joyce's novel and Eliot's poem. As Manganaro has argued, *Argonauts* ushered in the more empirical ethnography of Malinowski, with its focus on the most banal of details in studied cultures—the "imponderabalia" of everyday life, as Malinowski called them.[44] In the Malinowskian model, the ethnographer reconfigures elements that would otherwise appear exotic into ordinary components of everyday life within the context of that given culture. Just as a shared anthropological interest in myth bridged Jessie Weston and T. S. Eliot, both *Argonauts* and *Ulysses* share an ethnographic interest in the plenitude of marginal details of quotidian life.[45]

For Malinowski, the ordinary is paradoxically a means of apprehending alterity, since his functional method works through an awareness of cultural relativism to focus on the most trivial of details in the given culture from the perspective of the locals. To work through such perspectives is to bring out the "dailiness," even the banality, of alien lifestyles and to situate them within the comfort zone of one's own understanding. Such "dailiness" is an integral component of autoethnographic writing, where the ethnographer's detachment produces his own culture as an appropriate subject of study. The ordinary and the everyday are as essential to the depiction of the given culture in autoethnographic discourse as they are to the aesthetic imagination in Joyce's novel. Any perception of *Ulysses* as the masterwork of ethnography—as Manganaro has argued it to be—must acknowledge the place, indeed, the ethnographic primacy of the daily and the ordinary, the minutiae of "trivial" details like the "coolwrapped soap," "stillflowing taps," "halffilled" kettles, to say nothing of the bulk of factual information about the culture of Dublin at the turn of the century. The fact that much of this information has been revealed to be inaccurate—and quite a bit of it because of Joyce's deliberate transcription of mistakes in the ethnographic sources to which he himself turned—at the same time tempers his relation with the discipline of anthropology with an element of parody. Such inaccuracies underlie fiction's necessary relation with ethnographic knowledge production; specifically, it highlights Joyce's flirtation with anthropological verisimilitude in fiction.

Manganaro points out the kinship between Joyce's Dedalus and Malinowski's ethnographer in their attention to the texture of everyday life, from which they carve out aesthetic and anthropological insights respectively. Moreover, this anthropological paradigm has a striking affinity with the worldview of symbolist naturalism that readers have identified in *Ulysses*. Within this narrative paradigm, the ordinary, indeed, "the most sordid of objects," for both the artist and the ethnographer, is filled with higher possibilities than objects and situations that are significant according to traditional aesthetic or social norms. "In both texts," writes Manganaro, "the protagonist sculpts out of sundry quotidian experience (living out of native Dubliners and Trobrianders) triumphant distantiation in the form of exquisitely wrought moments of vocational omnipotence, in which any ordinary event, person, or object can become filled with revelatory possibility."[46] The foregrounding of such sordid objects, "the low, drab, and ordinary of Malinowski's insistence" often becomes, in Joyce's fiction, the occasion for epiphanic revelations,[47] while in ethnographic studies, it contributes toward the emergence of definable cultures. Such a deployment of the banal also turns out to be, in literature as in cultural anthropology, not only a deconstruction of binaries of "superior" and "inferior" cultures and civilizations but also a disruption of similar hierarchies between what is and what is not an appropriate subject of representation. The conventional orientation of the center and the periphery is unsettled in the aesthetic as much as in the cultural-anthropological order.

In *Ulysses*, one such everyday practice rich in aesthetic and ethnographic significance that plays out against the backdrop of the cityscape is that of walking in the city. Walking, in fact, through the motif of urban flânerie, has come to occupy a significant place in the modernist city text, from Baudelaire to T. S. Eliot. In *The Practice of Everyday Life*, Michel de Certeau, writing of a very different city, New York in the 1970s, as seen from the top of the World Trade Center, singles out the practice of walking in the city as a component of the urban language system. "The act of walking," he writes, "is to the urban system what the speech act is to language or to the statements uttered."[48] Walking is an example of an everyday practice that becomes a privileged signifier in the cultural anthropology expounded by de Certeau as in the aesthetic order of *Ulysses*, as well as in several stories of Dubliners, like "Two Gallants," "Counterparts," and "A Little Cloud," not to mention Stephen's walks with Lynch and others during the discussion of his aesthetic theories. Leopold Bloom's wandering through the city is perhaps the most significant speech act of the language system of *Ulysses*. Another crucial enunciation of this speech act would also be the "Wandering Rocks" episode, which epitomizes the movements of almost all the characters in the novel during the day. Made up of nineteen short sections, this is something of the central episode of the book, where almost all the characters make at least one appearance; almost all of them are shown to be walking through various parts of Dublin between three and four in the afternoon. Consequently, this is also the chapter where the perceiving subjectivity of the narrative is more pluralized and fragmented than anywhere else, where the viewer of one episode is the viewed of a following section. Little distinction is made here between the subjectivities of Bloom, Stephen, Father Conmee, the one-legged sailor, Blazes Boylan, Tom Kernan, Simon Dedalus, Almidano Artifoni, or any of the various others who appear and are given their pride of place in terms of the dominant subjectivity of the moment. As such, the duality of the perceiver and the perceived is shifted around in rapid succession, reiterating the symbolic deconstruction of the self and the other that remains such a tantalizing part of the novel's narrative consciousness.

But it is in fact through the figure of Bloom as the urban flâneur that the full signification of colonized subjectivity is articulated. In *The Subaltern* Ulysses, Enda Duffy locates in Bloom's flânerie a vision of urban subjectivity that is an integral part of the shared experience of modernity.[49] Even so, both the private subjectivity and the larger milieu that together enable this flânerie bear the mark of the uneven relation between the imperial center and periphery. The immediate context of this flânerie is the subjective consciousness of a Jewish man, half an outsider in this society, and its larger horizon is that of a late colonial city in the margins of the empire. As such, Duffy distinguishes between the "more purposeful" tours of Clarissa Dalloway in the imperial capital of London and the "aimless wandering" of Leopold Bloom in the colonial city of Dublin.[50] Unlike the flânerie of Baudelaire and Woolf, flânerie in the colonial city is a consumption that is always overshadowed by exploitation, and it records an interpellation into the colonial regime of control and surveillance. Duffy's reading of flânerie also recalls Rachel Bowlby's suggestion of gendered power relations embodied in Woolf's depiction of flânerie. Bowlby demonstrates the ineluctable maleness of the figure of the flâneur, because of the woman's societal exclusion from the practice of flânerie, and the radically liberating potential of Woolf's fiction in its depiction of the emergence of the female passante, a projection of male desire, into the empowered figure of the female flâneur, as in *Mrs Dalloway*.[51] It remains important, however, not to see Duffy's postcolonial inscription of the flâneur in Woolf within a master discourse as a contradiction of Bowlby's feminist reading. Rather, one can locate at crucial points the ways two different discourses of subalternity relate to each other. To return to Joyce, the dialectic of the two flâneurs—the imperialist and the colonized—holds for Duffy the analogy of the Hegelian lord and bondsman. As a paradigmatic text of postcolonial modernism, *Ulysses* successfully establishes the invigilated subjectivity of the colonized "other" through the language system of an everyday practice that, till the advent of literary modernism, occupied, at best, the fringes of aesthetic imagination.

It is by scouring such fringes of imagination that Walter Benjamin arrives at a definition of boredom as "the dream bird that hatches the egg of experience," the bird who is driven away by "a rustling in the leaves."[52] For the young Stephen Dedalus, the potential in the boring, the stagnant, and the paralyzed have proved rich in their promise long before their value could find a mellower, more mature articulation in Leopold Bloom's more ambivalent flâneur sensibility.

Long before *Ulysses*, in *Stephen Hero*, the utter banality of the subject of epiphanies is seen as deriving from the "paralysis" of Irish provincial life:

> A young lady was standing on the steps of one of the brown brick houses which seem the very incarnation of Irish paralysis. A young gentleman was leaning on the rusty railings of the area. Stephen as he passed on his quest heard the following fragment of colloquy out of which he received an impression keen enough to afflict his sensitiveness very severely.
> The Young Lady—(drawling discreetly) . . . O, yes . . . I was . . . at the . . . cha . . . pel . . .
> The Young Gentleman—(inaudibly) . . . I . . . (again inaudibly) . . . I . . .
> The Young Lady—(softly) . . . O . . . but you're . . . ve . . . ry . . . wick . . . ed
> This triviality made him think of collecting many such moments together in a book of epiphanies. (211)

The scene recalls a similar exchange between a man and a woman at the end of "Araby," described above, also similarly vacuous but for a faint patina of flirtation. In the short story, the banality of the exchange helps to shape the deflation of experience that is at the core of the boy's epiphany at the deserted bazaar. But it is an experience that the young boy is unable to place within a conscious aesthetic. The more mature Stephen, however, is able to perceive the aesthetics of triviality as the staple of the epiphany, but he does so by placing the experience within its historic context, which accounts for the poignant political resonance of such triviality and stagnation. If the epiphany embodies a radical aesthetic, its radicalism is rooted most crucially in the banality of its subject; that this banality is itself the aesthetic marker of Ireland's political and cultural marginality is now beginning to dawn upon the young Stephen, who will soon leave this marginal location in order to fulfill the mission of the autoethnographic artist. The heightened banality and the provincialism of Dublin that makes it a privileged field of anthropological enquiry also become, in Joyce's fiction, a powerful if indirect index of the political and economic marginalization of colonial Ireland. The narrative of Dublin can only be radically new because *nothing* happens here; *nothing* happens here because it is too far from the imperial center where the excitement of progress, history, and modernity is concentrated.

Suddenly, Joyce's Dublin looks very much like Benjamin's dream locale for storytelling, even though it might only be situated at an unwieldy intersection of that past and the present into which it is being rapidly precipitated. In *Ulysses*, the boring, the banal, the trivial—everything that is truly peripheral, indeed, antithetical, to traditional literary imagination—is the very stuff of Joyce's art, and in this he embodies a strand of modernist aesthetics that celebrates the alien and the marginal in a way rarely witnessed before. By foregrounding the affective texture of life far from the metropolis, Joyce reinvents the fractured modernity of the colony as a groundbreaking narrative mode.

• CHAPTER 2 •

Katherine Mansfield and the Fragility of Pākehā Boredom

Miss Mansfield, we in New Zealand have laid proud claim to you because you were born and brought up a New Zealander. Although you spent most of your adult years in England and the Continent, you always looked back to these southern antipodean islands as the main source for your stories. On our part, we have long since acknowledged that New Zealand could not fulfill your expectation of Life, Art, Literature and Experience. The world was waiting in England, Germany, Switzerland, Italy and France.

—Witi Ihimaera, *Dear Miss Mansfield: A Tribute to Kathleen Mansfield Beauchamp*

Desire and Domesticity in the Backwaters of Empire

In Katherine Mansfield's best-known story, "Prelude," Stanley Burnell, who has just moved to a new house, is delighted by his new life in the wide-open space of New Zealand countryside: "Ah, it was splendid to live in the country—to get right out of that hole of a town once the office was closed; and this drive in the fresh warm air, knowing all the while that his own house was at the other end, with its garden and paddocks, its three tip-top cows and enough fowls and ducks to keep them in poultry, was splendid too."[1] It is the very same space that drives his sister-in-law, the young, single, and attractive Beryl, into a well of despair:

> We have got neighbors, but they are only farmers. . . . But my sister who lives a mile away doesn't know a soul here, so I am sure we never shall. It's pretty certain nobody will ever come out from town to see us. . . . Such is life. It's a sad ending for poor little B. I'll get to be a most awful frump in a year or two and come and see you in a mackintosh and a sailor hat tied on with a white china silk motor veil. So pretty.

(117)

To Stanley, on the other hand, country life not only offers immediate pleasures, but more crucially, it is an investor's paradise. "I've got the place dirt cheap," he says, "You see land about here is bound to become more and more valuable . . . in about ten years' time" (89).

In Katherine Mansfield's fiction, the New Zealand countryside of her childhood becomes many things. Probably captured most memorably in the stories centering on the Burnell family—"Prelude," "At the Bay," "The Doll's House," "The Little Girl"—they often make up a dreamy, mist-covered natural idyll where the mythical aloe blooms once in a hundred years; to the children, it is a magical and unreal landscape. Nothing stands out more, however, than the vast, bare expanse of this landscape, evoking the Karori countryside to which Mansfield's own family had moved, away from the city of Wellington, when she was six years old. To Stanley Burnell in "Prelude," this bare, unclaimed space represents the settler colonial's dream—"dirt-cheap" land that is bound to rise in value in the coming years. It is a dream, however, that is of no interest to the women in his family. Even as he shares the excitement of his clever real estate investments with his wife Linda, he has to check to see if she is still awake and is in fact listening to his financial success story. Murmuring from a half-dreamy state, Linda calls him "Mr. Business Man," a name of endearing sarcasm. And Beryl, Linda's younger sister, writes a letter to her friend Nan Pym, venting her depression and tedium at being trapped in what to her is a vacuous space of utter social barrenness and, eventually, a sexual death. Unlike her entrepreneurial brother-in-law, the blank space of the settler colony represents to her one long stretch of fatal boredom.

When does empire become a space of boredom? When does its infinitely expansive space fail on its promise of romance and drama and become an agoraphobic venue of unrelenting, deadening tedium for the European colonial or settler? Historical and anthropological research, in recent years, have uncovered boredom as the affective consequence of life in the far provinces of the historical British Empire, where the deadening tedium of the everyday contrasts with the social and historical excitement of the imperial metropolis. It is a tedium that betrays the exotic romance of empire as promised by popular fiction and "exhibitions, juvenile literature, music hall entertainment, radio, advertising, film and organizations such as the Boy Scouts."[2] In his essay "Imperial Boredom," the historian Jeffrey Auerbach chronicles the daily lives of a number of imperial administrators and their wives, including Garnet Wolseley as the governor of

Natal; William Denison as governor-general of New South Wales; the marquess of Hastings and Lord Auckland, both as governors of Bengal; and H. G. Keene, as the assistant subcollector in Mathura, to reveal the oppressive banalization of their daily lives. Auerbach provides a perceptive diagnosis of this imperial boredom: "The boredom that nineteenth-century colonial officials experienced was largely the product of unmet expectations about the landscape, combined with the increasingly bureaucratic and ceremonial nature of imperial service."[3] While reality was ill served by the imagination of popular culture, the burden of boredom was also accentuated by the sense of social and cultural marginality embodied in these provincial spaces. In other words, while haunted by the unrealized specter of imperial adventure, the colonial administrators and their families also suffered from the kind of vacuousness experienced by Beryl in the wide-open New Zealand country, the boredom bred in the backwaters of empire. And how very ironically so—just when they should in fact be defined by the excitement represented by Stanley Burnell and his lust for wide-open colonial land!

As a member of the settler colonial population and, significantly, as a woman, Beryl, however, suffers alienation and disempowerment far more intense and pervasive than the bored colonial administrators of the British Empire. Her boredom with life in what appears to be the provincial backwaters of Karori is an affective index of her social and sexual isolation, from where the socioeconomic affluence of the metropolitan heart of empire, England, and even its colonial incarnation in regional government seems to contain the objects of impossible desire: "A young man, immensely rich, has just arrived from England. He meets her quite by chance. . . . The new governor is unmarried. . . . There is a ball at Government house. . . . Who is that exquisite creature in *eau de nil satin*? Beryl Fairfield" ("Prelude," 89).

The white settler colonial community, Robert Young points out, occupies an ambiguous historical space. Named the "in-between class" by Young,[4] their racial and cultural moorings derive from the imperial society that governs the colony from Europe. They claim ideological affiliations with the metropolitan center of empire, avowing careful distance from the indigenous peoples of the colony with whom they often have—as in colonial New Zealand—a history of violent conflict. At the same time, they are a colonial population, often ridden with the anxiety of living on the margins of modernity, of the perpetual fear of being left behind, of being excluded from the excitement of metropolitan power and affluence. Dreaming of this empire, its economic and political might as romanticized in the figure of the wealthy young man just arrived from England, Beryl Fairfield is dejected at the thought of vegetating in the provincial tedium around her.[5]

Beryl, no doubt, remains a partly parodied figure, a receptacle of a fractured authorial sympathy. But she serves a crucial purpose in Mansfield's New Zealand bildungsroman, made up by stories about the Burnell family. Shaped by her despair, restlessness, and boredom in the social wilderness of the country, Beryl embodies a gendered critique of the masculinized ambitions of settler colonialism and its fantasy of open, unclaimed space as territory prime for economic investment. To the settler colonial woman, especially if she is young, with unrealized social, cultural, and romantic ambitions, the masculine dream of expanding into undiscovered country opens up a world not of imperial adventure and romance but of unrelieved, agoraphobic boredom. If the masculine imagination of the settler colonial fantasy is centrifugal, the feminine imaginary reveals itself to be centripetal. Driven to tedium by the blank open spaces of the colonial territory, the feminine imagination seeks instead the promise of social and cultural modernity embodied in the metropolitan center of empire. As a larger phenomenon, the centripetal desire of colonial modernity is scarcely gendered—the fractured relation this modernity has to its imperial ideal is a historical reality that encompasses both men and women. Mansfield's stories, however, reveal a gendered fissure in the settler colonial imaginary, one made obvious and immediate in Stanley and Beryl's respective responses to the family's move to the country. Beryl, in fact, is a less than sympathetic characterization of the anxieties that preoccupy many of Mansfield's female protagonists and characters and, indeed, of the author herself, whose life was marked by a ceaseless movement between the margin and the center, between the colonial backwaters of suburban Wellington to the heart of the metropolitan avant-garde in Bloomsbury.

The landscape of the New Zealand countryside of her childhood comes back as a natural idyll of magical possibilities in Mansfield's best stories, those published in the last few years of her life. The magic of this natural landscape, however, is far more alive to the children than to the adults. Grown women suffer more ambiguous fates in Mansfield's world. Often they seem locked in a failing quest for a life that is socially, conjugally, or aesthetically fulfilling. One of the most pervasive affective markers of this failure is a realization of the iterative, restrictive banality of their lives and the boredom that comes with it—to which one must eventually surrender. This boredom marks a gendered response to the perceived fracture of colonial modernity as it exists, hesitant and incomplete, on the antipodean margins of the British Empire. The possibility of a fuller, richer, and aesthetically meaningful life, which haunts many of Mansfield's characters—and, curiously, provides the narrative entropy to much of her fiction—is enabled by the shadow of a fuller life that is visible in fragments from the margins but that will always remain outside the sensual reach of the colonial subject. Even the calm texture of quotidian domesticity that makes up a significant part of her fictional world is molded by the replication of metropolitan social values and norms in the colony. The colonial writer who had so eagerly desired and gained entry into Bloomsbury but was simultaneously derided for her colonial origins offers telling stories of futility, restlessness, and emptiness, of a world where such desires are teased but never satisfactorily fulfilled. Beryl Fairfield only represents the most obvious—and scarcely the most sympathetic—of the fractured quests of a fuller life outside one's reach. Mansfield's fiction is pervaded by this aesthetic unfulfillment, which casts a shadow even on the stories that do not have a recognizably colonial setting. This unfulfillment, and the tedium that is its bitter fruit, provides the larger affective context to Mansfield's oeuvre.

Many of these desires, and the story of their frustration, can be traced to Mansfield's personal biography. If, with the Irish modernists, the fervent cultural nationalism of anticolonial struggle led to an erosion of colonial desire, for the upper-middle-class white settler community in New Zealand, this desire for the imperial metropolis was far more intense and pervasive, as this community fervently traced its ideological underpinnings to England and to the British Empire. New Zealand in the nineteenth century, as Claire Tomalin points out in her biography of Mansfield, was on the margin of empire in the most extreme sense. It was for many a colony of Australia in the way that Australia was a colony of England, "the very last place, the furthest you could go, the end of the line."[6] If Ireland's physical proximity to England and continental Europe ironized its cultural marginalization, for the white settlers in New Zealand, the twelve thousand miles that separated them from their "home" pushed them to do their best to offset the "alien" local landscape by investing it with all they could associate with England, a place that many had never seen. "The wooden bungalows, the municipal buildings," writes Tomalin, "the schools and shops were built to match English mid-Victorian buildings."[7] The ideological power of this yearning for the imperial metropole was powerful enough to shape the consciousness of natives assimilated into the colonial mainstream, as it is evoked by Witi Ihimaera in *Dear Miss Mansfield*, the Māori writer's tribute to his Pākehā predecessor:

> The London that was waiting for Mahaki and Susan had been the capital of a colonial empire and was now the mother to the Commonwealth. It was Britannia and, under an earlier Queen, had sent out English settlers to a land far to the south—New Zealand. There, in uneasy alliance with the natives, and perhaps because of the natives, the colonists had established a *new* England. But life, legislation, traditions and culture were still determined from the place of satanic mills. It was to be expected that at least once in their lives most New Zealanders should visit the Home Country and, if possible, attend the new Elizabeth at the Court of St. James.[8]

Katherine's grandfather, Arthur Beauchamp, migrated from England to New Zealand, eventually attaining prosperity there as a merchant after a failed attempt as a prospector in the goldfields of Australia. His son, Harold, rose to success rapidly when his time came, ultimately becoming the chairman of the Bank of New Zealand and a prominent member of the settler community in Wellington. Knighted later in life, Harold Beauchamp epitomized the successful colonial merchant not only in his professional career but also in spirit—in his complete identification with England and all things English. When Anthony Trollope visited New Zealand in the 1870s, when Harold was a boy, he noted Harold's conviction "that England is the best place in the world and he is more English than any Englishman."[9] Harold traveled to England as soon as he was able to, and, as Tomalin points out, the very first trip was made in 1889, "a year after the birth of his third daughter, Katherine."[10] It was this tradition of Anglophilia in which Katherine was born and raised and that shaped her own yearning to be part of a metropolitan European modernism. But even though she would subsequently come to be incorporated as part of the English modernist canon, during her lifetime, her colonial origins would never cease to shadow her sense of personal identity:

> I am the little colonial walking in a London garden patch—allowed to look perhaps, but not to linger. If I lie on the grass, they positively shout at me:

"Look at her, lying on our grass, pretending she lives here, pretending this is her garden, and that tall back of a house, with windows open and the coloured curtains lifting, in her house. She is a stranger—an alien. She is nothing but a little girl sitting on the Tinakori hills and dreaming: 'I went to London and married an Englishman and we lived in a tall grave house, with red geraniums and white daisies in the garden at the back.' "[11]

Biographical sources have convincingly established Katherine Mansfield's troubled status within the Bloomsbury circle as much as it has revealed her sense of discontent and inadequacy in what seemed to her the colonial backwaters of New Zealand. Such feelings were exacerbated after her return home after her first few years in England, an experience that doubtless shaped her decision to live in England and continental Europe for almost the entirety of her adult life. Critical, biographical, and editorial interventions have also tended to emphasize Mansfield's relationship with and place within metropolitan European culture and have diminished the sense of personal importance that her colonial home had for her.

Even so, most of her best work, especially the late stories, have colonial settings. Much of her fiction set in Europe also strongly echoes the ambience and landscape of colonial New Zealand, as in the early collection *In a German Pension*. It is especially in light of these facts that a significant lacuna in Mansfield studies becomes glaring, one that has recently begun to be addressed by scholars such as Mark Williams, Bridget Orr, Ian Gordon, Lydia Wevers, and Elleke Boehmer. This is the issue of her relationship with the colonial history and landscape of her native country, doubly complicated by her own attachments to metropolitan Europe and her ambiguous distance from her country of origin. Traditional Anglo-American criticism has tended, often rather simplistically, to construct a "European" Mansfield with little or no relationship to her colonial roots. Such critical trends were partly set in motion by her husband John Middleton Murry not only in his commentary on her work but through his highly selective editing of her writings, especially her diaries and notebooks, which are only now beginning to undergo restoration. The colonial implications of her writings have also generally been ignored by criticism that has otherwise provided valuable insights into the radical dimensions of Mansfield's work with respect to gender and sexuality, such as seminal studies by Kate Fullbrook, Claire Hanson, and Sydney Janet Kaplan, and the biography by Claire Tomalin.[12]

Ironically, as Bridget Orr points out, even when Mansfield's work has been read in the context of its New Zealand setting, as in fact was done in an earlier approach by C. K. Stead, it has relied upon a simple binary. In this construction, the raw colonial elements of her work are seen as occupying a negligible and marginal portion of her oeuvre, while her true aesthetic complexity is understood to emerge in contexts that are either European or colonial settings domesticated and diluted to the point where they become weak versions of middle- and upper-middle-class English society.[13] Stead thus minimizes the importance of New Zealand, even in the few Mansfield stories where he acknowledges a distinctively colonial setting, reading them as minor distractions from Mansfield's genuine—and resolutely European—aesthetic vocation. The more subtle interplays of race and colonial class relations that are at work in some of Mansfield's most significant stories, Orr argues, are ignored by Stead, for whom the picture of New Zealand reality can only be captured by regional realism in the manner of the short-story writer Frank Sargeson. "Such an assumption," Orr writes, "installs Sargeson as the true father of New Zealand letters, and Mansfield's production of regional texts is seen as proleptic only, a false start—she 'anticipated' or 'foreshadowed' a whole genre of New Zealand fiction but the true origin, oddly enough, comes later."[14]

My reading of boredom as a colonial condition in Mansfield's stories builds upon the approaches opened up by Orr, Wevers, Gordon, and Williams. Mansfield's understated relationship with the landscape of New Zealand is as important to my approach as is her insistent disavowal of her colonial roots and subsequent identification with English culture. This relation with colonial history and landscape, often expressed through allegory or metonymy, extends not only to the complexities of the English settler society but occasionally even to the influence of Māori culture, people, and history, with which settler colonialism had been locked in a deeply troubled relationship. Overlooked points of Mansfield's relationship to the culture of her birthplace include accounts of her travels through New Zealand countryside in her notebooks as well as her abandoned novel *Maata*, centering on Martha Grace Mahapuku, a theme that the Māori writer Witi Ihimaera takes up in his collection addressed to Mansfield.

Mansfield's stories, often thought of as psychological sketches, have a tonal and textural ambivalence that draws from a play of desire, distaste, longing, and disillusionment that shaped her back-and-forth movement between New Zealand and Europe. Colonial subordination to metropolitan modernity, in this worldview, is further aggravated by a feminine discontent with the centrifugal instincts of a masculinist settler colonial imagination that seeks to expand to the furthest spatial limits of the colony. The very tangible fabric of banality in her stories reveals more about the perturbed colonial history from which they consciously distance themselves than one might identify superficially. From underneath this sanitized, quiet, and uneventful surface, the feminized upper-middle-class domesticity in Mansfield's stories forms a quiet dialectic with the promise of trauma and violence lurking within colonial and indigenous landscapes. Such violence is literalized only occasionally, but even when it is not brought to surface, it forms a silent undertow in the ambience of her fiction.

Between "Māoritanga" and White Modernism: Colonial Ethnology and *The Urewera Notebook*

The narratives of modernity and colonialism in nineteenth- and early-twentieth-century New Zealand were replete with violence and conflict between Māori and Pākehā—the indigenous tribes and the European settlers, as they are known in the Māori language (and in New Zealand English), respectively.[15] The confusion perpetrated by the Pākehā over the deceptively worded Treaty of Waitangi of 1840 stands as both the epistemological culmination of this conflict and as its textualized metaphor. Such conflicts have left lasting marks on turn-of-the-century colonial and settler writing as much as on Māori literature later into the twentieth century, as evident in the tension between European and indigenous forms of modernism that mark both traditions of literature.

Bridget Orr convincingly accounts for the way modern New Zealand literature has evolved from the colonial stereotypes of the nineteenth century to the celebration of regional identities and cultures in the twentieth century.[16] According to her, turn-of-the-century women writers like Katherine Mansfield and Jane Mander were among the first to help this literature move beyond simplified colonial romance and comedy by introducing a "distinctly female perspective." Nationalism, however, does not stir the Pākehā literary imagination until the 1930s, when writers like Frank Sargeson and Robin Hyde begin to adopt authentic modes of regional realism. Pākehā writers continued to dominate the literary scene through the 1950s and 1960s, mostly through large-scale family dramas of provincial life and historical novels. But it wasn't until the 1970s that real change came about in the relative cultural homogeneity of New Zealand literature, with the emergence of the Māori Renaissance in New Zealand literature.

Katherine Mansfield occupies a critical position in this literature not only because of her pioneering role in the development of New Zealand's literary identity but also with regard to questions of legacy and canonization. European high modernism eventually overcame perceptions of "the little colonial" to integrate Mansfield's place within its metropolitan canons. Specifically, she is now acknowledged as a member of the Bloomsbury group and, in the light of her literary aesthetic and authorial worldview, is often mentioned in the same breath as other major female modernists such as Virginia Woolf, Dorothy Richardson, and Elizabeth Bowen. On the other hand, Māori writers of the latter decades of the twentieth century have traced significant parts of their legacies from Mansfield, consequently casting her in the light of "Māoritanga," or Māori-ness. The most prominent of these claims on Mansfield's legacy has been Witi Ihimaera's *Dear Miss Mansfield*, a collection of short fiction that responds to Mansfield's writing, offering new perspectives on her relation with Māori culture. The Māori protagonist of Ihimaera's novella "Maata," Mahaki, somewhat ironically shares much of the author's fascination with Mansfield, significant aspects of which are summarized in his "Letter" to *Dear Miss Mansfield*:

> Miss Mansfield, we in New Zealand have laid proud claim to you because you were born and brought up a New Zealander. Although you spent most of your adult years in England and the Continent, you always looked back to these southern antipodean islands as the main source for your stories. On our part, we have long since acknowledged that New Zealand could not fulfill your expectation of Life, Art, Literature and Experience. The world was waiting in England, Germany, Switzerland, Italy and France.[17]

Even though Mansfield has occasionally suffered from the perception of her being a minor writer in the context of British and European modernism, she has been long considered a major writer in New Zealand by Pākehā and Māori writers alike. Reading her stories with this awareness, we can identify two significant places where we can reassess her relation with colonial, especially indigenous, cultures: her reception by later Māori writers and her own documentation of her relationship with indigenous cultures and landscapes.

Specifically, I argue for a reading of Mansfield's fiction and nonfiction based on the complex and often-contradictory realities of white settler colonial society and the more distant but looming landscape of Māori culture and history. It is an intriguing relationship between two very different forms of colonialism existing in an explosive contact zone. In Mansfield's stories, this contact is often dictated by the pivotal performance of gender. Gender enacts the distinction of private and public spaces and accordingly marks a rift over the expansionist ambitions of settler colonialism. While Mansfield's location within the domestic world of settler society has been obvious, her relationship with the world of indigenous culture has only just begun to be addressed.

The most concrete evidence of Mansfield's interaction with Māori culture is contained in her notebooks chronicling her travels through the New Zealand countryside. Many of the significant aspects of her New Zealand stories, including the depiction of specific settings, mood, and characterization, are derived from entries in her travel notebooks. The route through which she processed her relationship with Māori culture becomes clear, therefore, if we read her notebooks and her stories together. This relationship is marked by a tension between the idyllic and romantic picture of Māori culture painted by turn-of-the-century ethnology and the colonial violence to which such cultures were subjected. The genocide and trauma that were a part of Māori history under British domination was, in fact, not too remote from Mansfield's own time. Mansfield's journal entries record her closest contacts with Māori cultural and historical landscapes, most significantly those in *The Urewera Notebook*, which is her account of her camping trip through Urewera country at the age of nineteen.

As Mark Williams has pointed out, Mansfield passed through Te Whaiti in 1907, where a few years earlier there had been a government store run by the ethnographer Elsdon Best, who went on to write several monographs promulgating a romanticized account of Māori culture. A reading of some of Best's surviving works helps us, in the first place, to locate him in the Frazerian tradition of turn-of-the-century anthropology, in which human cultures and civilizations are placed in global hierarchies of value and progress. Such subjective evaluations seep through Best's descriptions and analyses in works like *The Māori as He Was* and *Spiritual and Mental Concepts of the Māori*, as, for instance, when Best writes about Māori religious ideals: "a barbaric folk such as the Māori is usually much more religious than are peoples of a higher culture stage—than ourselves, for example."[18] But while such hierarchies are validated within the parameters of rationality, they are also complicated within a system of abstracted spiritual values: "It is for us to read the lesson contained in these beliefs and conclusions of man the barbarian. It is for us to retrace our steps down the path of intolerance, and regain the broad highways of altruism—to tread the four-way path of Tane over which, from all quarters of the fair earth, the souls of dead fare on to Hawaiki-nui, the domain of purification."[19] Best's ethnographic account of the Māori as a significant cultural "Other" in colonial New Zealand forms part of the contemporary European anthropological projects that crucially shaped the intellectual climate of modernism, as is also evident in the writings of Franz Boas, Ruth Benedict, and Bronislaw Malinowski. In spite of its location within this larger intellectual tradition, there is little doubt that the ideological underpinning of an anthropological project such as Best's had more in common with James Frazer's evolutionary comparativism than any other model of anthropological knowledge production contemporaneous with literary modernism. Specifically, Best's approach to culture clearly belonged to the late-nineteenth-century episteme where, as James Clifford points out, "culture was still generally thought of in the singular" and that assumed that "people had higher or lower degrees of culture."[20] That later in the twentieth century Pākehā critics would often read Māori writing primarily as a form of ethnographic discourse becomes something of a literary-critical counterpart to this phenomenon.

What is also striking is that Best's idyllic portrayals contain no hint of colonial violence, especially the bloody conflicts over road surveys between the European and the Tuhoe people in 1895, which left their lasting mark on the Ureweras, where Best had his store and through which Mansfield passed in 1907. This was, as Ian Gordon describes it, "the great pumice plain between Rangitaiki and the Waipunga River."[21] In *The Urewera Notebook*, Mansfield's entries often reflect a perception of the romance and beauty of Māori life and people: "There is one great fellow I see—who speaks English—black curls clustering round his broad brow—rest almost languor in his black eyes—a slouching walk and yet slumbers in his face passion might and strength." A historical awareness of Māori anger and the marks of trauma and violence, on the other hand, intrudes far less often, only in the occasional passage, as for instance in her description of Opipi: "at last we come on Opipi—the scene of a most horrible massacre—only 2 men were saved." Again, she writes about another camping site where, in 1866, a conflict between British forces led by Major Fraser and the Māori had left most of the Māori combatants dead: "Round us in the darkness the horses were moving softly with a most eerie sound—visions of long dead Māoris—of forgotten battles and vanished feuds—stirred in me."[22]

Mansfield's awareness of the indigenous historical, cultural, and demographic landscape was largely a reflection of the calm, idyllic, and picturesque version propagated by turn-of-the-century colonial ethnology, such as that exemplified by the work of Elsdon Best. Only at the rarest of moments is this version intruded upon by the darker knowledge of colonial violence, as for instance in this passage early on in the notebook, which evokes a surrealist aesthetic: "Everywhere on the hills great masses of charred logs—looking for all the world like strange fantastic beasts, a yawning crocodile, a headless horse, a gigantic gosling, a watchdog—to be smiled at and scorned in the daylight, but a veritable nightmare in the darkness. And now and again the silver tree trunks, like a skeleton army, invade the hills."[23]

The surreal nightmare promised by this landscape cannot be too distant from the submerged historical reality behind this world. This is the reality of violent conflict that has shaped the structure and trajectory of white colonial society. Like surrealism, this reality is caught in a muted tension with the calm and idyllic picture of indigenous society painted by colonial anthropology. Literary modernism shared with turn-of-the-century anthropology a crucial climate of disciplinary development, where the latter was undergoing significant methodological and ideological changes that would eventually shape the discipline that we recognize today. Katherine Mansfield, while predominantly deriving her worldview from the older model of anthropological epistemology, also seems to be positioned at this moment of disciplinary transition.

This subdued tension is an important key to reading her short fiction. In the following pages, I explore the way in which Mansfield's stories metaphorically and metonymically refract her broader imagination of the colonial landscape. This incorporates the colonial English middle- and upper-middle-class worldview, including not only its intricate social fabric, its repetitive, predictable, and restrictive routine, but also the historical shadows of disorder and violence lurking close by. As a characterological presence, the Māori remain marginal in her fiction, appearing on the rarest of occasions as shadowy, romanticized figures. The lingering threat of violence that haunts many of her stories and erupts directly in a few derives almost exclusively from the dark underclass of the white settler population let loose in the colonial wilderness. Runaways, convicts, prisoners, and murderers inhabit this space, worlds apart from the still and tepid domesticity of the world of garden parties. It is an atmosphere of anarchic disorder that makes for a stark contrast to the economic pragmatism of Stanley Burnell, to whom the open space represents an investment opportunity, or to the restless Beryl, for whom it evokes nothing but boredom and social isolation. The haunting nature of this colonial violence reveals itself, however, only as a shadow of the oppressive, iterative everyday that appears to make up the central fabric of Mansfield's fiction.

"Why Must You Suffer So?": Colonial Desire and Female Tedium

The dominant atmosphere of Katherine Mansfield's short stories, based on middle- and upper-middle-class lives, is usually constituted by a quiet, quotidian domesticity, which is a common precondition of the lives of her female characters. This atmosphere of domesticity ranges from the dreamily idyllic to the drearily monotonous. This is the defining quality of the lives of the confined housewife Millie in the story "Millie"; the children Kezia, Lottie, and Isabel and their young aunt Beryl in "Prelude";[24] the quiet, routine-encased everyday experiences of Miss Brill in the story "Miss Brill"; and the middle-aged unmarried daughters of the dead colonel in "Daughters of the Late Colonel." This gendered tedium pervades Mansfield's colonial and British/European stories alike.

A gendered relationship between domesticity and boredom has been identified as a significant component of the worldview of English prose fiction from its very beginnings. Patricia Meyer Spacks argues that the boredom that pervaded the lives of middle- and upper-middle-class women in eighteenth-century England and often found creative manifestation in women's literature was a consequence of the web of limitations imposed by patriarchal society on female lives. The dialectic of boredom and anguish that shaped such lives provided narrative impetus to works of "intelligible social protest."[25] Carefully distinguishing such boredom from the grander trope canonized in literature and philosophy—"ennui"—Spacks points to the very concrete, historically located material politics behind the force and pressure of such "gendered" boredom:

The boredom to which women are destined, according to conduct books by men and women alike as well as women's novels, is not a condition of the soul. . . . The boredom of women, as it emerges in these texts, constitutes an imposition of intricate social pressure: pressure to conform to the rules that forbid free choice or action, and pressure to deny their conceivable understanding of their relatively inactive lives as tedious. Narratives of female misery, however fantastic, reveal resentment of such imposition.[26]

The lives of Katherine Mansfield's female protagonists can be located within similar traditions of patriarchal control. Many of Mansfield's female characters, for instance, appear trapped within the cycle of what Hannah Arendt calls labor. Labor, for Arendt, is the activity of the *vita activa* that is essential to the daily, biological sustenance of the body but which leaves no trace or impact beyond its immediate context, as opposed to action, through which individuals express their personalities and form sustainable relationships with the public realm. Labor, on the other hand, was originally confined to the household sphere.[27] The oppressive tedium and gritty materiality of this quotidian labor absorb many of Mansfield's female characters. The nature of their absorption in this labor varies according to class. "Life of Ma Parker," for instance, reveals the very bottom rung of this labor in Mansfield's world; it foregrounds the Sisyphean life of an old woman who works as a cleaning lady, performing part of the labor of others' lives to make her own living. And it is labor that is presented to the reader as dreary, depressing, and ugly, though it seems unlikely that Ma Parker thinks of it as such. The particular home where she works in this story belongs to a character identified only as "the literary gentleman"; it is an identification that foregrounds the Arendtian duality of labor and action. Identified only in terms of the action through which he seeks to articulate his individuality in the public realm, the literary gentleman outsources the dirty business of labor—cleaning and housekeeping—to "a hag," maintaining what to him is a simple system: "You simply dirty everything you've got, get a hag in once a week to clean up, and the thing's done" (251).

In Mansfield's world, characters like the literary gentleman offer ripe material for satire. In fact, reading her stories, it is impossible not to wonder at the biting negativity around almost all the characters identified as writers, artists, and musicians. This might come across as surprising in the work of a writer who lived most of her life and crafted her work in the celebrated artistic milieus of European modernism. Some of it, however, might be explained by Mansfield's marginal status within that milieu and the coldness and hostility she occasionally experienced there as a writer from a distant, antipodean colony. But I believe that this insistent satire is, most significantly, directed against the pretentious position that art is always in danger of assuming, a position of detachment from and transcendence beyond the tedious and gritty business of life's daily sustenance. Art that seeks to elevate itself above the banality of this sustenance, that wishes to keep itself clean of the "toast crusts, envelopes, cigarette ends" (251) will not escape Mansfield's satire. If class bears the burden of this gritty labor in "Life of Ma Parker," in "Mr Reginald Peacock's Day," the weight of daily drudgery is borne by marriage. Reginald Peacock is the vain and selfish music teacher who spends his day in an eroticized fantasy of his imagined artistic excellence (as it is with most of these satirized figures, there is little actual evidence of any kind of real talent). His day is filled with the daily music lessons he offers to admiring young women and is punctuated by outbursts of disgust and hostility for his wife, who has to interrupt his lessons to ask for money to buy milk for their son.

The literary gentleman is further damned by the affectionate sympathy of Ma Parker, whose perspective frames her story. "But Ma Parker bore him no grudge. She pitied the poor young gentleman for having no young to look after him" (251). Reginald Peacock needs no help from others; his own point of view, dripping with a sexualized artistic vanity, gives him away. He is a poster boy for the distaste that bohemian artistry professes for what it sees as the unregenerate banality of domestic life, its restrictive chores and obligations. His distaste, moreover, glares with misogyny: "The truth was that once you married a woman she became insatiable, and the truth was that nothing was more fatal for an artist than marriage" (121). A ludicrous vanity shapes his own perception of himself as defined by a poetic naïveté about the burdensome prose of the world: "Looking back, he saw a pathetic, youthful creature, half child, half wild untamed bird, totally incompetent to cope with bills and creditors and all the sordid details of existence" (121).

Women caught in the banality of this daily labor, in Mansfield's fiction, often live far apart from the world of aesthetic glory and its iconic paradigms. Ma Parker was born in Stratford-on-Avon, yet she had never heard the name of Shakespeare till she came to London. "Yes, she was born in Stratford-on-Avon. Shakespeare, sir? No, people were always arsking her about him. But she'd never heard his name until she saw it on the theatres" (252). Stratford, to her, meant nothing but a comforting memory of the quotidian, shaped by the labor of her own mother: "Nothing remained of Stratford except that 'sitting in the fireplace of a evening you could see the stars through the chimley,' and 'Mother always 'ad 'er side of bacon, 'anging from the ceiling'" (252). The most ironic encounter between literary romance and the prosaic reality of work happens over the literary gentleman's remarks upon hearing that Ma Parker's late husband had been a baker. To the gentleman, who knows the working-class professions merely through mediocre literary clichés, baking is "such a clean trade" (252). "And didn't you," he asks, "like handing the new loaves to the customers?" (252). Ma Parker had neither the mindset nor the luxury to aestheticize her husband's work, preoccupied as she was with her own daily labor, often literally that of birth: "I wasn't in the shop a great deal. We had thirteen little ones and buried seven of them. If it wasn't the 'ospital it was the infirmary, you might say!" (252). Hearing this, the literary gentleman can only shudder in horror, "taking up his pen again," returning to the sanitized aesthetic of his privileged pursuit. Ma Parker is left with the memory of her husband dying of consumption, with "flour on the lungs," as "the doctor told her at the time," the result of the daily pollution of his body by what literary cliché imagines to be "a clean trade" (252).

Mansfield, in these stories, is a fierce parodist of the pretensions of transcendence that art is capable of making over the banality of labor. Tentative whisperings of imagination, such as those often associated with children in her work, obtain a far richer sympathy in Mansfield's vision than the conscious rituals of artistic life. She seems keenly aware, moreover, that this ritualized life of the arts is likely to be embedded within a masculine subjectivity, that the banal labor needed to clean the debris of everyday life is far more likely to be left to women. Her aesthetic vision remains firmly rooted in this labor, and it is the banality of this labor that provides narrative energy to her fiction. Often this entropy is generated through the scathing edge of satire.

Ma Parker and Reginald Peacock's wife, however, are not the kind of women who script a conscious quest for aesthetic fulfillment that lies beyond the weight of their quotidian labor. Reginald Peacock's wife comes across as silent and embittered; her husband's deeply narcissistic perspective, which frames the story, refuses her voice or agency beyond fragments of such quiet bitterness. Ma Parker, on the other hand, has so deeply internalized the endless Sisyphean tragedy of her life through her patient and absorbent humanity that she cannot imagine looking for a real change to this life, only a quiet place where she can hide herself and "where she could have her cry out—at last?" (256)—a place, she realizes, that does not exist for her. But there are other women in Mansfield's fiction who are weighed down not so much by the Arendtian burden of daily labor but by the oppressive tedium of an everyday that limits freedom to choose their lifestyle or the ability to form meaningful relationships with other people. While none of them are trapped in a life as punishing as Ma Parker's, a range of Mansfield's female characters are still imprisoned in a vacuous tedium from which they all seek various forms of aesthetic, social, and sexual meaning. Giorgio Agamben reads the bored subject as a captive who is suspended from all possibilities of free choice, without control of circumstances; all of these women lead lives that are imprisoned by time and space, both of which, particularly in settler colonial contexts, appear prolonged and expanded beyond measure.[28] In stories like "Miss Brill," "Millie," and "Prelude," women are only too conscious, often painfully so, of their entrapment within lives defined by severe aesthetic and affective poverty. As such, these stories, wholly or in part, are driven by the quest for affective and aesthetic meaning. *What makes for a meaningful life?* is the urgent question that lies behind most of her stories, a question that she frames most powerfully in terms of women's experience. Like the significant ellipses that often mark human exchange and interaction in Mansfield's stories, this question looms large and heavy; no possible answer to it seems reachable. In the end, it is the question and the lacuna around it that shapes her stories.

Few lives in these stories are more telling that of Miss Brill, in the story named after her. Miss Brill's weekly highlight is her little Sunday outing, where she watches the afternoon crowd and the band playing in the park. She is timid, in need of continuous self-assurance that she is partaking in a reality that is interesting, even enthralling, while sustaining herself on other people's conversation, on which she eavesdrops greedily: "Miss Brill always looked forward to the conversation. She had become really quite expert, she thought, at listening as though she didn't listen, at sitting at other people's lives just for a minute while they talked round her." It was disappointing when people did not speak, but "there was always the crowd to watch" (226). Watching becomes enthralling enough for the scene to take on the dimensions of the theater, though one suspects that what makes the experience enthralling is not so much what she sees but a desperate internal need to convince herself that she's indeed having an enthralling experience: "Oh, how fascinating it was! How she enjoyed it! How she loved sitting here, watching it all! It was like a play. It was exactly like a play. Who could believe the sky at the back wasn't painted? . . . They were all on the stage. They weren't only the audience, not only looking on; they were acting" (227).

In a moment, she goes from being an observer of this wonderful theater to one of its participants, an actress herself. The transformation merely ironizes the obvious but unmentionable backdrop of the story—the sterile dullness of Miss Brill's life, of which this Sunday spectacle was the weekly highlight. "Even she had a part and came every Sunday . . . she was part of the performance after all. . . . Yes, I have been an actress for a long time" (227–228). She is driven by an intense need to participate in the imagined excitement of other people's lives, but she can imagine doing so only through the framework of a theatrical spectacle. Such an imagination accentuates not only the banality of her own life but also a sense of her own utter marginality to the (supposedly) exciting lives of others, in which she can only participate through this imaginary framework. Her fear of her own marginality is well founded; this particular Sunday afternoon comes to a crushing end as she listens eagerly to an attractive young couple, in her imagination "the hero and the heroine," only to realize their disgust for her: "Why does she come here at all—who wants her? Why doesn't she keep her silly old mug at home?" (228). The theater that she anxiously seeks to enter is repelled by her; its protagonists think she belongs to the tedium of her home, which is exactly what she is anxious to escape.

But in Mansfield's world of female boredom, youth breeds its own frustrations, as we see in Beryl's sense of frustration and futility about her own life. If the lack of the beauty of youth deprives Miss Brill a place in the theater of life's excitement, for Beryl, youth and beauty ironize, deepen, and in some ways precipitate the intensity of her plight. Since the settler society primarily shapes the arcs of women's lives in terms of marriage and defines its success according to the social yardsticks of marital success, in spite of being young, spirited, and beautiful, and perhaps more so *because* of it, Beryl has a more deeply oppressing sense of the banality of her own life. Beryl's social and romantic desires, of course, center not only on the social excitement of the city that is an "awful" bus ride away but gravitate toward the ultimate object of white settler fantasy—England: the metropolitan center of empire. Beryl, as such, emerges as situated despairingly in a material and ideological network that is structured around male leadership of the immediate family, the social and commercial ambitions of the settler colonial enterprise, and, in the final instance, the economic and political might of the imperial center.

Spacks delineates a close relationship between boredom and psychosis in female life. Middle- and upper-middle-class women in late-nineteenth- and early-twentieth-century England and America were often subjected to mind-numbing regimes of medical surveillance and control, and these have been acutely analyzed by Foucauldian and post-Foucauldian studies of discipline, authority, and domination.[29] While there is no specific medical surveillance that proscribes the movements and actions of Mansfield's numerous female protagonists, the structures, ideologies, and the economies of society push them into deeply constricted spaces. The striking affinity between the worldview of Mansfield's stories and early English fiction on the subject of female constriction and disempowerment in turn can be traced to the peculiar sociopsychological constitution of the English settler colony. Specifically, such an affinity speaks to the cultivation of norms that are perceived as defining the social fabric of the imperial metropolis. The predicament of these female characters, along with several other behavior patterns, social institutions, customs, and habits, indicates a replication of English social and ideological structures in the colonial peripheries. The colonial replication of metropolitan values, therefore, not only introduces the sense of lack and frustration characteristic of the lives of middle- and upper-middle-class English women into the lives of their New Zealand counterparts but also reveals the fixation of a collective gaze on the social structures of the metropolitan heart of empire.

Rupturing the Quotidian

In "Millie," an ironic tribute to this object of settler colonial desire is crystallized in the colored print on Millie's bedroom wall, titled "Garden Party at the Windsor Castle": "In the foreground emerald lawns planted with immense oak trees, and in their grateful shade, a muddle of ladies and gentlemen and parasols and little tables. The background was filled with towers of Windsor

Castle, flying three Union Jacks, and in the middle of the picture the old Queen, like a tea cosy with a head on top of it" (25). The tribute is ironized by Millie's irreverence: "Millie stared at the flowery ladies, who simpered back at her. 'I wouldn't care for that sort of thing. Too much side. What with the Queen an' one thing an' another'" (25). To her, the Queen appears as "a tea cosy with a head on top of it." But her personal mockery of the ideal object of settler desire hardly renders her free of a larger social structure that is shaped by this very desire, even though she inhabits a space far apart from the middle-class world of the Burnells and the Sheridans. She finds the picture a little absurd, a little distasteful, but still it is the overarching presence in her own bedroom. She is confined within a social fabric that models itself on imperial social norms—specifically, within the feminized space of its interior, with the literal unveiling of which the story begins: "Millie stood leaning against the veranda until the men were out of sight" (24). The defining characteristic of this space that Millie inhabits is the overarching sense of confinement, repetitiveness, and boredom against which the protagonist is left to struggle. There is a certain vacuum in the quality of Millie's life; time here appears to be repetitive: "And then she sat, quiet, thinking of nothing at all, her red swollen hands rolled in her apron, her feet stuck out in front of her, her little head with the thick screw of dark hair, drooped on her chest. 'Tick-tick' went the kitchen clock, the ashes clinked in the grate, and the venetian blind knocked against the kitchen window" (25).

But this is only the first half of "Millie." We soon realize the fragility of the domestic interior enabled by the social structures of settler colonialism. The feminized tedium of this interior is intruded upon by violence in a masculinized external landscape that, as Ian Gordon notes, is significantly derived from *The Urewera Notebook*. Drawn by a noise, Millie steps into her backyard and stumbles upon the injured young Englishman Harrison, who has murdered Mr. Williamson, a member of the local settler community. It is a strange moment of almost maternal affection that drives her to feed and care for the boyish murderer shaken by the trauma of his own action. "She broke the bread and butter into little pieces, and she thought, 'They won't ketch him. Not if I can 'elp it. Men is all beasts. I don't care wot 'e's done, or wot 'e 'asn't done. See 'im through, Millie Evans. 'E's nothink but a sick kid'" (27).

Admitting the murderer into the folds of her protective care, Millie reveals the fragility of the veneer separating the sheltered tedium of domesticity from the violence of the external landscape; it is a veneer that, in Mansfield's stories, is always more fragile than it seems on the surface. This revelation culminates in a strange and disruptive emotional reversal for Millie. Later in the day, after she has fed and cared for Harrison and sent him on his way, the men of the house return home and begin a frantic hunt for the murderer. The story ends with the men hunting down Harrison like an animal and Millie breaking into a hysteria of excitement at what promises to be the revenge killing of the same boy she had nourished and tended to a few hours back:

> And at the sight of Harrison in the distance, and the three men hot after, a strange mad joy smothered everything else. She rushed into the road—she laughed and shrieked and danced in the dust, jiggling the lantern. "A-ah! Arter 'im, Sid!
> A-a-a-h! Ketch him, Willie. Go it! Go it! A-ah, Sid! Shoot 'im down. Shoot 'im!" (28)

"Millie" literalizes a tension that characterizes much of Mansfield's fiction, though usually in a more subtle, covert, or metaphorical form: a tension between a routine-encased domestic space on one hand and the powerful undercurrent of violence and trauma on the other, both of them uneasy and unavoidable legacies of colonial history. The ambience of colonial life outside the domestic sphere probably owes much to the tradition of colonial writing that Lydia Wevers identifies as "a discourse of exteriority," contingent on visible markers of difference, such as clothing, landscape, and even certain behavioral stereotypes including violence, adventure, and conflict.[30] But while the public space of colonial history in New Zealand is inevitably ridden with conflict, violence, and trauma, the white settler society tries its utmost to ensure the construction of a feminized domestic space seemingly sheltered from such conflicts. It is indicative of Mansfield's cultural and historical sensitivity as a writer that she is able to see through this fragile shelter imposed by settler colonial society.

The occasional eruption of the violent colonial reality in Mansfield's stories is almost exclusively experienced by the white settler underclass. Only a fragmented awareness of violence against the Māori appears in the rare entry of *The Urewera Notebook*, which sometimes shapes elements of her fictional setting. As Ian Gordon, the editor of *The Urewera Notebook*, observes, the description of the store at Rangitaiki is one of the sources of Mansfield's story "The Woman at the Store." Located far outside the urban and suburban English settler lifestyle, with its tea parties and country houses and everyday routine regulated by caretakers and governesses, this is one of the rare stories in Mansfield's oeuvre that captures the wilderness of the backcountry landscape and refracts it through a worldview that is bitter, savage, and unforgiving. "There is no twilight in our New Zealand days, but a curious half-hour when everything appears grotesque—it frightens—as though the savage spirit of the country walked abroad and sneered at what it saw" (13). It is one of those stories where the fragile barriers separating the private and public spheres have been shattered and their gender politics turned inside out with vengeance. The unkempt interior of the house appears in an ironic contrast with the colonial flavor of the décor, which makes up a destructive counterpart to the well-trimmed colonial domesticity of "Millie." In the present story, this is what the room looks like: "It was a large room, the walls plastered with old pages of English periodicals. Queen Victoria's Jubilee appeared to be the most recent number. . . . Flies buzzed in circles round the ceiling, and treacle papers and bundles of dried clover were pinned to the window curtains" (13). The life led by the lone woman and the half-crazed child whom the travelers come across is a combination of desolation, monotony, and bareness: "'Good Lord, what a life!' I thought. 'Imagine being here day in, day out, with that rat of a child and a mangy dog'" (13). The child provides concrete form to the kind of violence that only lurks in the dark crevices of the souls of Kezia, Laura, Lottie, and the other children of families such as the Burnells and the Sheridans. Her drawings are the most frightening of all: "And those drawings of hers were extraordinarily and repulsively vulgar. The creations of a lunatic with a lunatic's cleverness. There was no doubt about it, the kid's mind was diseased. While she showed them to us, she worked herself into a mad excitement, laughing and trembling, and shooting out her arms" (17).

In one of the pictures she draws for the visitors we get a direct hint of the distorted mind of the child and the violence that has shaped her life. The drawing also reveals what is perhaps her darkest secret—that her mother had shot and killed her own husband, the child's father. Just in the way the frail surface of a restful domestic atmosphere is shattered by Millie's violent excitement in the conclusion of her story, the erotic atmosphere of intoxication in "The Woman at the Store" is punctured by the violation implicit in the child's picture:

"I done the one she told me I never ought to. I done the one she told me she'd shoot me if I did. Don't care! Don't care!"

The kid had drawn the picture of the woman shooting at a man with a rook rifle and then digging a hole to bury him in.   (19)

Both "Millie" and "The Woman at the Store" were written soon after Mansfield left her country of birth, never to return again. As Andrew Bennett points out, along with the story "Ole Underwood" they make up a triad of early New Zealand stories that "centre around violence and lawlessness—indeed, all three centre on an act of murder."[31] Within Mansfield's oeuvre, these darker stories offer a contrast to the more ostensibly pleasant, ordinary, domestic everyday that seems to form the staple of her work. "The Woman at the Store," for instance, frames a nightmare world that quickly vanishes with the end of the story, as if it had never existed: "A bend in the road, and the whole place disappeared" (19). More often than not, however, the suggestions—or reality—of violence very subtly disrupt the texture of ordinary domesticity within the framework of a single story. It is intriguing to note that Mansfield's recollection of the "most horrible massacre" of Opipi is made in the same notebook entry that describes the store that forms the setting of the story "The Woman at the Store," just a few lines apart from each other. Her awareness of a traumatic colonial history rooted in the same landscape that served as the setting of the story clearly influenced her depiction of what is one of the bleakest, bitterest, and darkest ambiences in her work. Indeed, the colonial massacre casts a shadow on her description of the store in Opipi, where conflict and bitterness seem to hang heavy, coloring the attitudes of the two Māori men at the store: "Then lunch at Rangitaiki," she writes, "the store is so ugly—they do not seem glad or surprised to see us—give us fresh bread—all surly and familiar—and they seem troubled."[32] This is a crucial example of the way in which ravaged indigenous landscapes and histories get metonymically transformed in Mansfield's imagination, where violence, bitterness, and trauma are often divested of their mooring in indigenous history but continue to linger ominously.

Shadows of the indigenous presence in colonial New Zealand appear in Mansfield's stories in a way that is very different from the violence and lawlessness that often mark the lives of the white settler underclass. If the Māori represent a dramatic departure from the dominant societal norm of the domestic everyday, they do so through images of romance and beauty foreign to the worldview of white settler life. In "How Pearl Button Was Kidnapped," Mansfield creates a dreamy, allegorical tale that explores the duality of restriction and freedom, the banality of routine and the excitement of spontaneous behavior through a romanticized opposition of Western and non-Western cultures. This opposition clearly reflects Mansfield's understanding of the relation between the European and the Māori, which often surfaces in *The Urewera Notebook* and is evidently influenced by essentialized constructions of Māori culture dominant at that time. In the story, the dark women, their physical descriptions and dress, the children they nurture, and the community of people they live with all strongly resonate with the way Mansfield perceived and wrote about them in *The Urewera Notebook*, perhaps, as Gordon argues, as a result of the warm welcome her camping party had received from the Māori guide and his family. Mansfield's prose, in this passage, is animated by a happy romance:

> The child saying "Nicely thank you," the shy children, the Mother & the brown baby—thin & naked, the other bright children, her splendid face and regal bearing. Then at the gate of the P.O. a great bright coloured crowd, almost threatening looking—a follower of Rua with long Fijian hair & side combs, a most beautiful girl of 15, she is married to a patriarch, her laughing face, her hands playing with the children's hair, her smiles.[33]

Her delight in the company of the Māori is mirrored by her love for what she considers authentic Englishness. Her pleasure in the company of the English comes up in an entry on the next page of the notebook: "Here, too, I meet Prodgers—it is splendid to see once again real English people. I am so tired & sick of the third rate article. Give me the Māori and the tourist but nothing between."[34] For Mansfield, the self-image of settler colonial society is shaped by a kind of self-loathing framed, on one hand, by admiration of "real English people" and, on the other, by the romance of the Māori. In her fiction, while the former embodies a significant social impulse underlying settler society, the latter casts a rarer, more fragmented shadow, shaping landscape and atmosphere more often than characters. "Pearl Button" is one of those rare stories populated by figures who evoke the Māori. Reading the allegorized duality of the story, Kate Fullbrook writes: "The salient features of this story belong to the romantic tradition that glorifies the 'naturalness' and 'freedom' of the savage over the inhibitions and pleasure-denying aspects of mechanical civilization."[35] Pearl

Button is from "the House of Boxes," where people's lives are boxed in by routine, none more than those of the women, confined to the labor of sustaining the everyday. Even the little girl knows it all too well. When the dark women ask her where her mother is, she's quick to answer: "'In the kitching, ironing-because-its-Tuesday'" (20). For the child, to whom the world only makes sense through patterns, the causal connection between labor and routine is central and obvious. But far on the other end of the settler everyday lie the stirrings of a radically alien culture that offers a promise of unscripted freedom.

Grown women, in Mansfield's world, are often trapped in the colonial world of suffocating rules and prohibitions; tedium is such an overarching reality of their lives that that they often fail to notice it. The children, most of whom are female, seem to enjoy a relative degree of possibility and open space, though even in their lives the strictures of a patriarchal colonial system loom close by. Pearl Button, who in the House of Boxes is already trapped in such a life, enters a world of beauty, drama, and excitement, where she does her best to act according to the social decorum in which her society has already trained her: "She carefully pulled up her pinafore and dress and sat on her petticoat as she had been taught to sit in dusty places" (21). She is terrified when she spills fruit juice on her dress, but this is a world where such things do not count as social infractions: "'That doesn't matter at all,' said the woman, patting her cheek" (21). In her reading of the story, Fullbrook argues that Pearl Button escapes into this world rather than being kidnapped in it: "Pearl, who is not kidnapped at all, rather *escapes* from the world of masks into the world of freedom, only to be forced by the police, as if she was a criminal, to abandon her loosely structured utopia to be schooled into the rigid categories of women 'ironing-because-it's-Tuesday' and men who inevitably 'go to offices.'"[36] Indeed, at the end of the story, when Pearl is taken back to the world from which she came, it feels that she is carried away not back to home but to a prison: "Little men in blue coats—little blue men came running, running towards her with shouts and whistlings—a crowd of little blue men to carry her back to the House of Boxes" (23).

Mansfield's fiction moves between the comforts of the quotidian to the oppressiveness of boredom. But it is also haunted by the specter of transgression. But the specter takes bodily form only in rare fragments, sometimes through spells of intricately wrought fantasy that seek to disrupt the rules of social conduct. If Beryl is subjected to limitations imposed by the patriarchal structures of middle-class settler society in "Prelude" and is pushed to indulge in the fantasy of excitement over imaginary suitors from England, she herself embodies forbidding authority to Alice, the servant girl, who seeks respite in even richer fantasies. Alice's fantasies derive partly from her interest in the reading of dreams and partly from the imagination of clever retorts she knows she will never actually make to her employers. At Beryl's appearance, Alice slips the *Dream Book* "under the butter dish . . . Alice was a mild creature in reality, but she had the most marvellous retorts ready for questions that she knew would never be put to her. The composing of them and the turning of them over and over in her mind comforted her just as much as if they'd been expressed" (111). If authority limits her life, she has carved out an imaginary life where she disrupts this authority and lights things up with the sparks of disruption.

Transgression takes various shapes in Mansfield's stories. It disrupts not only the texture and landscape of domestic tedium but also the material and ideological structures of colonial life that upholds this class and gender-bound social landscape. Such transgression might be enacted through Alice's imaginary retorts, the liberating kidnapping of Pearl Button, or even the murderous violence of the woman in "The Woman in the Store" or Millie's aggressive frenzy. If Pearl Button's story inscribes the short-lived liberty of a child in allegorical terms, the duck-slaughtering scene in "Prelude" exhibits violence, excitement, and pain in a momentary burst, narrated with excruciating realism:

> Pat grabbed the duck by the legs, laid it flat across the stump, and almost at the same time down came the little tomahawk and the duck's head flew off the stump. Up the blood spurted over the white feathers and over his hand.
>
> When the children saw the blood they were frightened no longer. They crowded round him and began to scream. Even Isabel leapt about crying: "The blood! The blood!" Pip forgot all about his duck. He simply threw it away from him and shouted, "I saw it. I saw it," and jumped round the wooden block. (108)

The sight of blood seems to provide the children a release for the tension and fear of the preceding moments and gives them a sense of closure to the whole drama. It is at such moments when the distance between them and the "diseased" child in "The Woman at the Store" becomes thin, drawing out, as it were, a dormant dimension of cruelty and bloodthirstiness in their natures.

In Freudian terms, the triumph of the id over the superego is revealed in the spontaneous violence of these children. But the triumph, in this scene of "Prelude," is neither decisive nor complete. The headless body of the duck is caught in a series of muscular paroxysms, imitating its live steps on its way back to the stream, as if it wants to escape its death and mutilation in one phantasmagoric effort. While little Isabel finds it hilarious, squealing, "it's like a little engine. It's like a funny little railway engine," for Kezia—the girl whose characterization is marked with autobiographical echoes to Mansfield—it suddenly becomes a nightmare that desperately needs to be restored to normalcy:

> But Kezia suddenly rushed at Pat and flung her arms round his legs and butted her head as hard as she could against his knees.
> "Put head back! Put head back!" she screamed. (109)

The children, especially the girls Kezia, Lottie, and Isabel, are located in the limited open space this society offers its female children but withholds from its adult women. As they move around in that space, the three girls seek out the new and the exciting and the dramatic, a quest that indicates the presence of a potential adult discontent in themselves, if only in an embryonic form. If the constriction of the private, domestic life of women and female children creates unfulfilled, banalized spaces carefully screened off from a more disturbed external landscape, the frail veneer of separation suffers periodic ruptures, often caused by a transgressive female sensibility where violence and liberation are mutually indistinguishable. Whether it is literalized in Millie's outburst or symbolized in the children's excitement over the slaughter of the duck, such ruptures shape a continuous narrative of covert tension in Mansfield's work.

In *The Predicament of Culture*, James Clifford reads the fragmentation of experience, the disruption of power structures, and the diffusion of cultural relativism reflected in early-twentieth-century French art, literature, and ethnography through close, interconnected generic networks. All these genres were driven by the need to make sense of a complex reality shaped by the conflict of the familiar and the "exotic," the self and the other, the local and the global. In their efforts to interpret reality, Clifford argues, both the ethnographer and the surrealist engage in a drastic reshuffling of it, as the stability of an available reality is contested more than ever.

To state the contrast schematically, anthropological humanism begins with the different and renders it—through naming, classifying, describing, interpreting—comprehensible. It familiarizes. An ethnographic surrealist practice, by contrast, attacks the familiar, provoking the eruption of otherness—the unexpected. The two attitudes presuppose each other; both are elements within a complex process that generates cultural meanings, definitions of self and other.[37] Such an ethnographic practice situates different cultures in a relationship of eruptive mutual contact that also begins to define the traumatized global modernity shaping the backdrop of literary modernism. Ethnographic surrealism, similarly, depicts the coming together of competing values—no longer mutually hierarchical—as the means of apprehending a reality that is strikingly disruptive and perilously unstable.

If the early-twentieth-century destabilization of colonial empires contributes to what Clifford calls ethnographic surrealism's eclectic juxtaposition of the alien and the familiar, the colonial setting of Katherine Mansfield's fiction—complicated by the triad of the absent metropolis, the in-between settler class, and the indigenous communities— projects this juxtaposition with a deceptive subtlety. Mansfield represents that intriguingly transitional sensibility within the chapter of New Zealand literary history that precedes the cultural nationalism of the 1930s—which is captured, for instance, in Frank Sargeson's distinctive regionalism—but that has already begun to depart from the stereotypes of colonial life in the nineteenth century. Even so, it is very much a Pākehā perception of the colonial landscape. It is a landscape that is, moreover, pushed to the margins of the worldview of white settler society as embodied within an upper-middle-class female sensibility. But the unnamed traumas of this marginalized landscape both shape and threaten the daily security of domestic settler life. The seamlessly ordinary and humdrum surface of this life is riven by an undercurrent of violent ruptures in the social fabric of colonial society. The most striking way in which Mansfield's work recalls Clifford's model of contested global modernity is the deceptiveness with which it does it, through the unlikely and understated network of boredom, idyll, and violence that straddles both her fiction and her nonfiction.

• CHAPTER 3 •

The Dailiness of Trauma and Liberation in Zoë Wicomb

Help me remove my baby from my back
because it is time to make love:
the only chore I do without
my baby on my back

—Boitumelo Mofokeng, "With My Baby on My Back"

Reality and Weirdness

Published in 1988, James Clifford's *The Predicament of Culture* is an insightful exploration of metropolitan modernist aesthetics against the backdrop of a troubled global modernity in the late nineteenth and early twentieth centuries. It is, moreover, representative of a critical momentum in the developing relationship between literary and anthropological discourse in the late twentieth century. The book has been considered a critical work in the so-called literary turn in anthropology, which was already exemplified by the influential collection co-edited by Clifford, *Writing Culture*, published in 1986.[1] In his introduction to the collection, Clifford points to the rising popularity of literary approaches in a range of disciplines he calls "the human sciences," noting several anthropologists who have shown an interest in literary theory and practice, including Clifford Geertz, Victor Turner, Mary Douglas, and Claude Levi-Strauss. Their interest, he claims, has precedents in an earlier generation of anthropologists, such as Margaret Mead, Edward Sapir, and Ruth Benedict. Examining the rhetorical constitution of ethnographic discourse as opposed to its supposedly scientific or objective "core," Clifford argues that any understanding of the "literariness" of the discipline must hinge not merely on "good writing or distinctive style" but on the larger way "literary processes—metaphor, figuration, narrative—affect the way cultural phenomena are registered."[2]

In *The Predicament of Culture*, Clifford identifies a spectral affinity between ethnography and surrealism. "Surrealism is ethnography's secret sharer," he writes, "for better or for worse—in the description, analysis, and extension of the grounds of twentieth-century expression and meaning."[3] At the heart of this affinity is a dialectic that is essential to both literary and anthropological discourse—between the familiar and the alien, the ordinary and the strange. In literary criticism, a preoccupation with this dialectic has had a long and distinguished critical history, ranging from Russian formalism to recent critical interest in the ethical implications of literature following the work of Emmanuel Levinas.[4] And significantly, in an essay in *Writing Culture*, Vincent Crapanzano identifies a Levinasian understanding of Otherness that must lie at the heart of the ethnographer's work: "He must render the foreign familiar and preserve its very foreignness at one and the same time."[5] In *The Predicament of Culture*, Clifford substantiates this dialectic by drawing attention to Bronislaw Malinowski's prescription of balance between the "coefficient of weirdness" and the "coefficient of reality," which must constitute the ethnographer's reading of alien cultures and their lifestyle practices. The ideal study should be able to contextualize the initial appearance of alienness in other cultures in terms of the normal, regular, or ordinary, even as a sense of their strangeness and difference is preserved for the reader. This relationship between the ordinary and the strange is dialectical (in a Hegelian or Marxist sense) rather than simply oppositional—they complement and, indeed, make each other possible by their mutual antithetical coexistence. For surrealism, an integral component of the absurd is the quotidian, with which the absurd enters into a disruptive relationship. Anthropological humanism takes the strange and alien in foreign cultures and tries to render it comprehensible, to establish it as part of the ordinary and the everyday as they are produced within the studied cultures.

A similar dialectic of the familiar and the strange also forms the foundation of our pleasure in literature. Empathy—an affect that is crucial to our appreciation of fictional characters—hinges on our recognition of the familiar and the identifiable. But familiarity alone does not make art. A successful literary work also depends on a rendition of the utter strangeness of the familiar, whether achieved through language, formal structure, narrative, or other means of aesthetic innovation. The unresolved tension between the familiar and the strange that forms the core of aesthetic pleasure can also relate to a similar negotiation of the banal and the transcendental or, to use a more immediate set of terms, the boring and the interesting. "The act of writing," Patricia Meyer Spacks reminds us, "implicitly claims interest (boredom's antithesis) for the assertions of questions or exclamations it generates." Banality and boredom, by defining the condition of aesthetic failure, form the "displaced, unmentioned, and unmentionable possibility" of literature.[6] Beyond that, however, there is a specific cultural-historic implication to this narrative that culminates in the haunting kinship of ethnography and surrealism delineated by Clifford. While the classic charge of literature is to transcend the banal, the more empirical category of the everyday has, since the Enlightenment, given the emergent world of prose fiction its unique shape, and high modernism has radically engaged the banal as a subject of aesthetic representation in its own right. That anthropology's functionalist turn—led by Malinowski—was preoccupied with the mundane "imponderabilia" of everyday life around the time when modernism's interest in the banal culminates in its radical poetics is surely significant in the light of Clifford's identification of the modernist affinity of ethnography and surrealism.[7]

The ethnographic definition of alienness also has a concrete material implication. Historically, this definition has evolved through anthropology's exploration of cultures that are alien to the European ethnographic gaze, rooted outside the metropolitan West. Accordingly, the interaction of the ordinary and the dramatic shaping the mutual affinity of ethnography and surrealism derives much of its significance from the encounter between the metropolitan literary-modernist subject and cultures alien to this subject. Black Africa provided the most significant of these cultures, but the indigenous cultures of the Pacific islands and parts of Asia also figured extensively in such anthropological encounters. Such cultural "otherness"—whether or not it was always conceived as such—constituted significant components of the contemporary aesthetic instinct, famously exemplified in the exhibition of African masks that influenced Picasso and the conception of Cubism. Anthropology, even in its most traditional versions, had made such "otherness" its principal object of enquiry. Studies of the development of modernism and of nineteenth- and early-twentieth-century anthropology have established that some of the main historical influences behind the importance of the non-Western "Other" included the growth, consolidation, and ultimately the disintegration of colonial empires around the world. It was the growing immediacy of the indigenous cultures of the colonies that catalyzed intense aesthetic and anthropological interest in such cultures. This interest was most visible within the metropolitan centers of Europe that were colonial powers—most significantly France but also Britain and other nations.

The coming together of such competing values brought about by the colonial encounter, in this landscape of ethnographic surrealism, produced a reality that is no longer unified, homogenous, or epistemologically uncontested. Even the anthropological imagination of the colonial encounter embeds itself within this epistemological conflict. Peter Pels has identified three ways in which anthropologists think of colonialism: "as the universal, evolutionary progress of modernization; as a particular strategy or experiment in domination and exploration; and as the unfinished business of struggle and negotiation."[8] Each of these processes entails acts of epistemic and material violence, leading to a violation of discrete and demarcated spatial boundaries, thus placing mutually inconsistent modes of imagining history in a potentially explosive contact. Mary Louise Pratt uses the term "contact zone" to describe the space of this interaction, which she defines as "the space of colonial encounters, the space in which peoples geographically and historically separated come into contact with each other and establish ongoing relations, usually involving conditions of coercion, radical inequality, and intractable conflict."[9] The epistemological consequence of this contact is the production of a reality whose shape, contours, and texture are more contested than ever before. The Malinowskian "coefficient of weirdness" is set into conflict with the "coefficient of reality" in a rapidly changing order where such values often become interchangeable over time. While this conflict is central to the actual experience of such cultural realities, it is perhaps even more crucial in the representation of such realities, as surrealism and ethnography illustrate in their respective contexts. This epistemic conflict in many ways lies at the heart of the historical process of colonialism, with the colonial power seeking to normalize—or, to use Roland Barthes' terms, turn into the ahistoric structure of myth—the European paradigm of history, the success of which completes the ideological work of colonialism.

The instincts of high modernism, whether in literature or the visual arts, manifestly trouble this ideological project of colonialism, as Clifford's demonstration of ethnographic surrealism illustrates. However, if experimental modernism's negotiation of the ordinary and the fantastic is incomplete without its historic encounter with cultural otherness from its colonial empires, it is just as important to examine this negotiation within discourses within which the colonies have produced themselves. The anthropological equivalent of this discourse is autoethnography, which defines texts "in which colonized subjects undertake to represent themselves in ways that *engage with* the colonizer's own terms."[10] If it is possible to understand the epistemological and aesthetic conflict in the colonial contact zone as an unresolved dialectic of the familiar and the strange, the banal and the dramatic, it is worth exploring how autoethnographic discourse has produced this tension.

My archive here is the literary equivalent of autoethnographic discourse, the cultural act through which fringes of the empire outside the range of Western civilization have written back to the metropolitan center—Anglophone postcolonial literature from the global South. Anglophone literature, especially the genre of prose fiction that traces part of its legacy to the European Enlightenment, is one of the most significant cultural products of the global British Empire, especially in locations in the global South where literature in English has come to constitute a new archive inextricably linked to colonialism and the development of postcolonial identity. Within this global body of Anglophone literature, however, I wish to turn to a historically specific moment. If colonial contact and contestation over the representation of reality is marked by a continuing tension between the spectacle of colonial intrusion and the ordinariness of local spaces, this particular moment of cultural history marks, for the first time, a clearly articulated polemic regarding the respective importance of the ordinary and the spectacular in the representation of postcolonial reality. It is an inevitable debate for any discourse that takes narrative form, as historians and narratologists of the twentieth century have come to understand alike. The fundamental question, in history and philosophy as in fiction, has been whether narrative, a temporal category, can possibly unfold outside its obligation to unique events. Or are the endlessly repeated conditions of human life, which make up the domain of the ordinary everyday, also an appropriate venue for narrative? Is the ordinary everyday, as Stanley Cavell believes, a viable ground from which to appreciate better the eruption of events, or does an exclusive or predominant focus on events define an epistemological self-sufficiency? To rephrase this in terms of the dialectic identified by Clifford, do the ordinary and the dramatic throw each other into relief? Or do the full implications of the dramatic tremors along the arc of global history become clearer through an exclusive attention to the turbulent events themselves?

Late-twentieth-century Anglophone cultural politics in certain locations of the global South intervenes in this conversation through a range of forms. These forms include debates over the respective significance of turbulent upheavals of colonial and postcolonial history and the constitution of an ordinary everyday outside the major signposts of conventional historiography; between the aesthetic and political import of representing the dramatic happenings in the public sphere on one hand, and, on the other, the fragments of quotidian life as experienced in the intimate folds of the private sphere; between bold lines of fictionalized history visible on a national plane, on one hand, and the culturally idiosyncratic minutiae produced in regional spaces that trouble and disperse the notion of modern nationhood, on the other. Not that these categories are all held in distinct and demarcated spaces all the time, but it so happens that in the course of this debate—carried out implicitly in fiction and explicitly in theoretical writing—many of these categories have come to be perceived as polarities. This, therefore, is the most opportune moment to examine not only the aesthetic exploration of the everyday but also the presentation of such an everyday within the radical affective frameworks of banality and boredom in English-language literature from the peripheries of empire beyond the cultural limits of the West. To do that, we need to begin with an examination of the evolving tension between the representation of the historical spectacle and that of the everyday within the cultural politics of Anglophone postcolonial fiction.

Genre and Narration in the Colony

A quick survey of fiction and criticism from postcolonial cultures written in European languages through much of the twentieth century confirms an argument that has only recently begun to be articulated by a handful of voices—an argument that, if essentialist, is doubtless strategically so. This argument points to male postcolonial fiction writers' predominant focus on abstracted versions of the colonial struggle in larger, national spaces, in public lives of nations constructed more by a pan-national bourgeois sensibility than by those embedded in local realities. Moreover, the incidents valorized by dominant models of historiography—such as riots, genocides, wars, nationally organized anticolonial movements, and electoral upheavals—have been more often the subjects of male writers. The most celebrated and prominent site of these subjects has been the much-theorized "national allegory," a genre that has established itself as a predominantly masculine construct. The novelistic national allegory, invested in the very concept of "nationhood" and its evolution in larger public spaces, focuses on some of the most spectacular stories of the nation. This focus on the dramatic is usually embodied through narrative techniques rooted in the fantastic, the magical realist, and the mythical. Many of these features are to be found in the canonical postcolonial national allegories, such as Ben Okrie's *The Famished Road*, Gabriel Garcia Marquez's *One Hundred Years of Solitude*, and Salman Rushdie's *Midnight's Children*.

Narratives of power and oppression in the global South predominantly have been produced by what Kelwyn Sole calls "a culture of the spectacular—the flaunting of material excess cheek by jowl with social poverty, the brutal displays of power and victimhood."[11] They have come to dominate perceptions of sites of postcolonial nationhood with a suspicious easiness, precisely because they have "allowed readers only an aesthetics of recognition, indictment, and ideological confirmation."[12] The predominance of such perceptions indicates what I would call an ethnographic naïveté in the reading of power relations of colonial domination and anticolonial struggle. Not only is the production of the spectacular contingent on its dialectic with the quotidian, but the quiet folds of the everyday, usually invisible because of their very pervasiveness, contain ebbs and flows of power and resistance that do not always run parallel to the narratives of mainstream history. Instead, I focus on an alternative tradition of fiction where the relation between the ordinary and the dramatic comes to represent the troubled global modernity that for Clifford has called for a merging of the ethnographic and surrealist worldviews. There is a quotidian, homespun texture of local life—often tucked away in the intimate folds of the private sphere—where the turbulence of colonial intrusion is refracted in a complex and subdued manner. This is the texture of life that is easily overlooked in the more dramatic modes of narration that in effect end up privileging the macronarrative of power and resistance over every other aspect of indigenous experience.

It is not at all surprising that one of the most politically urgent of colonial contexts, that of twentieth-century South Africa, has been a major site for these cultural contestations. The definition of South Africa as a colonial context, however, is a complex historical affair. British colonial rule in South Africa came to an end, if not in 1910, when the Union of South Africa ceased to be a British colony and became a dominion of Great Britain, then in 1931, when the union was granted independence from Britain with the passage of the Statute of Westminster. However, apartheid rule, long considered a form of colonial domination, intensified in South Africa when the Afrikaaner-led National Party was elected to power in 1948. Viewed this way, colonialism in South Africa does not end until 1994, when the dismantling of apartheid is formally celebrated by the election of the African National Party and the presidency of Nelson Mandela. Within this historical framework, much of twentieth-century South Africa would appear to be both colonial and postcolonial at the same time. In the following pages, I focus on Anglophone literature that derives its cultural legacy from the British colonial domination of South Africa as well as the central public events concerning apartheid and the antiapartheid movement.

The South African text where the protagonist's fate stands most unequivocally for the fate of the nation in the manner of the national allegory is—perhaps unsurprisingly—Nelson Mandela's autobiography, *Long Walk to Freedom*. But it is probably the genre of "protest literature" that has become the more recognizable literary context to the struggle against apartheid and also the dominant narrative paradigm in twentieth-century South African literature. Going back at least to Sol Plaatje's chronicle of internecine warfare in *Mhudi* (written in 1919 and published in 1930), the first novel published by a black South African, the genre of protest literature includes a range of important South African works, such as Lewis Nkosi's novel *Mating Birds* and his play *Rhythm of Violence* and Miriam Tlali's novel *Muriel at Metropolitan*.[13] A concern with the traumatized public sphere remains a consistent feature of most works of "protest literature," whether it assumes thematic centrality, as in *Rhythm of Violence*, or whether it is expressed through a metaphoric reflection on the microcosm of the private sphere, as in Tlali's autobiographically driven novel *Muriel at Metropolitan*. It is perhaps as a historical inevitability that in South Africa the need to narrativize the past to understand and redress its injustices and human rights violations under apartheid has been established as a vital one, as Derek Attridge and Rosemary Jolly argue in their introduction to their critical anthology *Writing South Africa*. This need was institutionalized in the establishment of the South African Truth and Reconciliation Commission in 1995, chaired by the

Nobel laureate Archbishop Desmond Tutu. The commission provided a forum of grievance, amnesty, and justice for the witnesses, victims, and perpetrators of crimes sponsored by the state under the apartheid regime. Under such a historical climate, the narrativization of the most dramatic stories of oppression, violence, and resistance have understandably come to constitute one of the most significant literary paradigms.

However, the dominance of such narrative paradigms have also been the subject of a sustained critique in South Africa, not only for the aesthetic limitedness they pose but also for their inadequacy in helping to understand a historical situation that far transcends any form of simple Manichean opposition. One of the most openly polemical of these critiques from the aesthetic standpoint was articulated by the South African activist and lawyer Albie Sachs, who insisted, in the 1989 African National Congress seminar on culture, that claims of culture as a weapon of struggle should be banned, at least for a period of time. Academic critics have also taken note of this crucial conflict. "Perhaps for obvious reasons," Elleke Boehmer writes, "the heat of opposition to apartheid caused writers to favour certain formal decisions over others, to adopt an upfront, hard-hitting, mimetic aesthetic, and therefore to pay less attention to form as such, to experiment, nuance and the play for ambiguity for its own sake."[14] Brian Macaskill also identifies this as "a tension common to recent South African literatures" and summarizes it as "perhaps only an ostensible disparity, of demands for revolutionary struggle on the one hand and aspirations for a more private aesthetic on the other."[15] Such arguments concern a large number of interrelated issues. Admittedly, a straightforward opposition between revolutionary political concerns and aesthetic experimentation is not necessarily the concern of the postcolonial national allegory, which can be quite radical in its experimental poetics. But the specific aesthetic component that I am concerned with here—the production and the celebration of the texture of ordinary life—seems to be absent from the fantastically structured national allegory well as from the overt macropolitical concerns of South African protest literature. Instead, both offer a celebration of the grand, the traumatic, and the spectacular moments of national history.

The black South African writer Njabulo Ndebele famously criticized the insistent privileging of what he calls the "spectacular" events of the public domain in South African "protest" literature as a means of apprehending the ethics and politics of racial oppression under apartheid. Opening his essay

"The Rediscovery of the Ordinary," Ndebele writes: "The history of black South African literature has largely been the history of the representation of spectacle. The visible symbols of the overwhelmingly oppressive South African social formation appear to have prompted over the years the development of a highly dramatic, highly demonstrative form of literary representation." Following Barthes' analysis of the wrestling match, Ndebele identifies the "manifest display of violence and brutality" as central to "the highly organised spectacle of the political wrestling match of the South African social formation,"[16] which has dominated the narrative politics of South African fiction. This culture of spectacle, consequently, is governed by a binary aesthetic: the dramatic juxtaposition of power and disenfranchisement, what Kelwyn Sole calls "an aesthetics of recognition, indictment and ideological confirmation."[17] In a related essay, "Redefining Relevance," Ndebele elaborates on this binary aesthetic:

> We were shown in this literature the predictable drama between ruthless oppressors and their pitiful victims, ruthless policemen and their cowed, bewildered prisoners; brutal farmers and their exploited farm hands; cruel administrative officials in a horribly impersonal bureaucracy, and the bewildered residents of the township, victims of that bureaucracy; crowded trains and the terrible violence that goes on in them among the oppressed; and a variety of similar situations.[18]

In contrast to this public spectacle of violence, Ndebele advocated the minute details of the "intimate knowledge" embedded in private, internal consciousnesses, which go beyond the binary nature of this spectacular aesthetics and for which the "rediscovery of the ordinary" was an essential precondition.[19] Thoba, Ndebele's young protagonist in some of the stories in the collection *Fools*, gets tentative access to this intimate knowledge from the textured atmosphere of the domestic everyday around him and through his relations with his playmates, family members, and other members of the local community within which he grows up. As a black male, however, Thoba enjoyed a privileged status within the dominant traditions of anticolonial nationalism that has furnished the ideology of protest literature, even though Ndebele's own work lies outside this genre. Instead, the work I explore disavows the certitudes of masculine liberation struggle and the monolithic confidence of Black Nationalism, which has often tended to set itself up in a binary opposition to Afrikaaner Nationalism. I focus on a linked collection of short stories by the first female South African writer of mixed racial heritage—"coloured" under the apartheid classification—whose discomfort with mainstream anticolonial narratives is traceable to her racial and gendered identity.

Zoë Wicomb's *You Can't Get Lost in Cape Town* spans the mid-1950s to the mid-1980s, coinciding with nearly the entire period of apartheid rule in South Africa. The book resembles Ndebele's collection in many ways but pushes much further this polemical attempt to rediscover the ordinary in the midst of a racially, politically, and ethically embattled South Africa. Wicomb's text exemplifies this important alternative narrative wherein the minute texture of the ordinary is foregrounded in a striking critique of the grand and dramatic narratives of colonial domination and its public resistance. The child of somewhat similar middle-class parents, Wicomb's young narrator-protagonist, Frieda Shenton, is a "coloured" female and perhaps a slightly more articulate version of Ndebele's Thoba.[20] In the opening story, Frieda is a child under ten, and in the last couple of stories, she is a woman around forty. Her psychological, emotional, intellectual, and physical growth is the subject of this linked collection of stories, which sometimes appears to be a loosely structured novel. This growth takes place in the private and domestic realms of family and close friends, through the persistent weaving of an ordinary everyday. This everyday is both shaped and periodically punctured by the extraordinary upheavals rocking the public life of the nation under apartheid. Such is the intrusion of the English colonizer in the everyday routine of the local community ("Bowl Like Hole"), the political assassination of Prime Minister Hendrik Verwoerd in 1966 that perturbs the predictable routine of work and play in Frieda's school ("A Clearing in the Bush"), and the abortion that becomes a watershed moment in Frieda's life ("You Can't Get Lost in Cape Town").

Among Ndebele's contemporaries, it is Zoë Wicomb whose work—especially the present collection—represents one of the most successful and sensitive fictionalizations of the "rediscovery of the ordinary." Carol Sicherman writes, in her literary afterword to the Feminist Press edition of *You Can't Get Lost in Cape Town*:

> In fact, despite obvious differences in subject matter and perspective, many aspects of Wicomb's stories can be described in the same terms as Ndebele's own: they are, Lokangaka Losambe notes, "internal and deeply rooted in

the daily life of the oppressed," manifesting, as Ndebele himself writes, a "dialogue with the self" that features "the sobering power of contemplation, of close analysis, and the mature acceptance of failure, weakness and limitations."[21]

However, Wicomb's "rediscovery of the ordinary" takes place in a context that is arguably more complicated than that of Ndebele's *Fools*. Her linked stories form a fractured female künstleroman in the context of a creolized South African community. They offer an alternative to the dominant narratives of the postcolonial public sphere that have been predominantly masculine and embedded in a Manichean black-white binary. Writing from a self-imposed exile in Scotland, Wicomb provides a delicate ethnography of the community she left behind in a manner reminiscent of another exiled writer, James Joyce. Her künstleroman evokes Joyce's more tenuously linked stories about the mundane lives of ordinary Dubliners, which provide a similar literary ethnography about the community left behind and a similar skepticism about mainstream anticolonial struggle. The growing Frieda, in her sensitive observation of the nuances of quotidian life, comes to us through a portrait of the artist as a young girl that recalls Joyce's own autobiographically inflected künstleroman. In the end, there is in fact something about Frieda's abiding, intricate interest in the banal and the marginal that resonates with the complexity and indirectness of the modernist artist's relationship to political upheavals in the public sphere. Graham Pechey's pithy summary of Ndebele's important and crucially timed invitation attends to this engagement with the ordinary that in turn becomes a complex and implicit venue of history:

> Njabulo Ndebele . . . in the dying apartheid years . . . called so eloquently for a post-heroic culture of irony, the local, the ordinary: that is to say, a culture, or a literature, preoccupied not with the polar conflicts of "the people" versus "the state" but with textures of life which have eluded that epic battle and have grown insouciantly in the cracks of the structures that South Africa's fraught modernity has historically thrown up.[22]

Kelwyn Sole has also called for the continued relevance of Ndebele's plea on behalf of the ordinary in postapartheid South African poetry in his aptly titled essay "Quotidian Experience and the Perspectives of Poetry in Postliberation

South Africa." The relevance, Sole points out, is most immediately apparent in poetry by women, which displaces questions of power from the spectacular public sphere into private domains of quotidian domesticity. Indeed, since 1990 and continuing into postliberation South Africa, Ndebele's vision of the rediscovery of the ordinary has been realized most sensitively by a number of women poets who had been active in the struggle against apartheid. This position would closely approximate Wicomb's as well as that of her fictional protagonist Frieda Shenton. Sole provides the examples of the Durban poets Nise Malange and Boitumelo Mofokeng, who cast into their poetry the multilayered oppressions endured by women through the nexus of race, class, and gender in the course of the daily burdens of the workaday. Such is the quotidian experience of suffering, for instance, tellingly articulated in Mofokeng's poem "With My Baby on My Back," lines from which form the epigraph to this chapter.

The growing Frieda, too, experiences the realities of apartheid not through grand public-sphere spectacles but through the domestic domain, where the complex hierarchies of class are played out in the "coloured" community of Namaqualand and Cape Town. More importantly, the ordinary, workaday sites of oppression shape her consciousness of liberation struggle, just as they shape the worldview of the postliberation poets of the quotidian. In many ways, therefore, both Wicomb and Frieda share this small but significant emerging counterculture of the ordinary that Ndebele had envisioned.

My exploration of Wicomb's linked stories, in certain ways, looks back to the delineation of similar motifs in the short stories of Katherine Mansfield. Wicomb, like the late colonial modernist Mansfield, locates the narrative consciousnesses of her fictions within the realm of the domestic. When the narrator-protagonists of such works set foot in the public sphere and acquire a sense of its turmoil, their knowledge of the public events and forces of mainstream history are refracted through the resolutely private nature of their consciousness.

Unlike the personality, consciousness, and kinship structures associated with Saleem Sinai in *Midnight's Children* or the spirit-child in *The Famished Road*, the private and the domestic experiences that shape Frieda do not turn into allegories or mimetic metaphors for the public life of the nation-state. The linked short stories *In You Can't Get Lost in Cape Town* create a certain hesitant, gradual unfolding of the magical banality of the everyday that rarely preoccupies other eloquent chronicles of the sub-Saharan female experience, such as Tsistsi Dangarembga's riveting bildungsroman *Nervous Conditions* or the novels of Bessie

Head or of Ama Ata Aidoo. Both Head's *A Question of Power* and Aidoo's *Our Sister Killjoy*, for instance, demonstrate a far more intense and direct involvement in the turbulent macropolitical history of the colonial or postcolonial nation-state, as does, for that matter, Wicomb's own novel, *David's Story*, published in 2000. In *David's Story*, set in 1991 after the release of Nelson Mandela, Wicomb fuses the personal narrative directly to a larger historical trajectory of anticolonial struggle, not only through the main characters' involvement with the liberation movement spearheaded by the African National Congress but also through the ancestry of the protagonist David Dirkse, which includes some of the most significant leaders of the Griqua people, most notably Andrew le Fleur in the late nineteenth and early twentieth centuries. David's exploration of his own role in the contemporary liberation movement is critically entwined with his research into le Fleur's life and his leadership of the Griqua people. It is not only the spectacle of anticolonial struggle but, perhaps more crucially, the larger arc of historical inquiry that takes this novel farther away from an immediate apprehension of quotidian life, a narrative movement that also marks Wicomb's more recent novel, *Playing in the Light*. This powerful and remarkable novel, while originating in the quotidian pattern of the life of the protagonist, Marion Campbell, quickly upsets its initial quotidian rhythm through Marion's discovery of the racial secrets of her own family lineage.

You Can't Get Lost in Cape Town, therefore, is significant in its persistent attachment to quotidian life not only in the larger context of the cultural history of Anglophone South African fiction but also in the more immediate context of Wicomb's own writing. The form of the short story seems to provide a generically intimate space within which the tentative but curious subjectivity of the growing girl is meaningfully situated in a subtle and idiosyncratic relation with that history. However, even though *You Can't Get Lost in Cape Town* shares some features with a modernist collection such as *Dubliners*, the celebration of the ordinary in late-twentieth-century Anglophone fiction from the global South differs from the representations of banality, boredom, and the ordinary in canonical modernist texts from the early decades of the twentieth century in some crucial respects. While banality and boredom are represented in the earlier texts predominantly as a marker of the sociopsychological consequences of colonial rule, in certain Anglophone texts from the global South, they are primarily revealed as a mode of understanding postcolonial reality missed by the urgent constructions of fictional historiography in the late colonial or postcolonial public sphere. If a significant seed of high modernism's idiosyncratic elevation of the banal fragments of life can be found in its impatience with the functional deployment of such fragments by Edwardian realism, a small minority of Anglophone writers from the global South point to spaces neglected by the valorized genres of postcolonial narration, ironically because of their very embeddedness in the clear light of the mundane everyday.

Banality, Grandeur, and the Clash of Historiographies

This is exactly why Wicomb's *You Can't Get Lost in Cape Town*, even more than anything else she has published subsequently, has a seminal importance in this polemical tradition that rediscovers the ordinary at a crucial moment of Anglophone culture politics in the global South. It appeared in the critical last years of apartheid, when the contention surrounding the ethics of representing South African reality had attained a critical momentum, not least because of Ndebele's controversial intervention. Wicomb's collection was published in 1987, during the years between Ndebele's own fictionalization of the intimate ordinary in the short-story collection *Fools* (1983) and the book in which his polemical essays were brought together (1991).[23]

You Can't Get Lost in Cape Town reinvigorates the conflicted interaction of the ordinary and the dramatic that has historically shaped important parallels between modernity, colonialism, and literary modernism. Wicomb uses the perspective of the growing child to encapsulate reality marked by the colonial conflict as a striking interaction of the ordinary and the extraordinary. In these linked stories, the power of this interaction often depends on the narrator's impressionability to the foreignness represented by the colonial intrusion. The consciousness of a maturing female child serves Wicomb well in this portrayal, as it turns out to be singularly impressionable not only to the strange and transformative force of colonial intrusions but also to the rootedness and regularity of everyday domestic lives perturbed by such intrusions. Especially within the amorphous consciousness of the early stories, the ordinary and the extraordinary enter into a mutually disruptive relationship that echoes the violence of the colonial encounter, especially the rude force with which Western modernity makes its incursion into the communal life of rural Namaqualand. To the village children, this intrusion is a striking and magnificent affair, as we see in the very second paragraph of the opening story, "Bowl Like Hole":

> A vehicle swerving meteor-bright across the veld signalled a break in the school day as rows of children scuttled out to hide behind the corner, their fingers plugged into their nostrils with wonder and admiration. They examined the tracks of the car or craned their necks in turn to catch a glimpse of the visitor even though all white men looked exactly the same. Others exploited the break to find circuitous routes to the bank of squat ghanna bushes where they emptied their bowels and bladders. On such occasions they did not examine each other's genitals. They peered through the scant foliage to admire the shiny vehicle from a safe distance. They brushed against the bushes, competing to see, so that the shrivelled little leaf-balls twisted and showered into dust. From this vantage point they would sit, pants down, for the entire visit while the visitor conducted his business from the magnificence of his car.[24]

It is a classic scene, one made memorable from the earliest of colonial expeditions into undiscovered rural terrains of non-Western countries, where the paraphernalia of the European traveler is examined eagerly by a troupe of local dark-skinned children. The key difference, however, is that the perspective describing this event is autoethnographic. If the entry of the magnificent car (a Mercedes, we learn soon) into the daily life of the village symbolizes the abruptness of colonial intrusion into indigenous life, the intrusion is narrated, significantly, as a conflict of the ordinary and the dramatic as such values are configured *within* local culture. The cross-cultural implication of this conflict, even though represented within this autoethnographically structured fiction, is not lost upon the reader situated outside this culture. That the very appearance of the vehicle is an exciting interruption of ordinary life is made clear not only by the use of flamboyant adjectives such as "meteor-bright" but also by the fact that the incident is potent enough to signal "a break in the school day" and bring out "rows of children" who plug their fingers "into their nostrils with wonder and admiration." The wonder and surprise impel them to crane "their necks in turn to catch a glimpse of the visitor," who is dramatic and extraordinary because of his whiteness but is also, ironically, indistinguishable individually for the very same reason. So fascinating is the phenomenon of the white man and his "shiny vehicle" that whether they continue to stand there or run off to empty "their bowels and bladders," they keep their eyes riveted on the visitor and his car "for the entire visit."

The very dramatic quality of this intrusion, on the other hand, is highlighted by the materiality and solidity of the ordinary everyday that the intrusion ruptures. Frieda displays an ethnographer's commitment to the most marginal and quotidian of details, which sometimes appear ordinary, other times grand, in her burgeoning consciousness. In this scene, the daily routine contains "circuitous routes to the bank of squat ghanna bushes," where the children empty "their bowels and bladders," and the expected mutual examination of "each other's genitals" occurs. The last is a routine practice that is apparently left out in the dramatic scheme of things, as the view of "the shiny vehicle" makes stronger claims on the children's attention at the moment. To the reader located outside the immediacy of this culture, the figuration of the mutual examination of genitals as an ordinary, everyday practice becomes a commentary on the very local nature of the value systems that construct the dualities of the ordinary and the dramatic. It is this value system that portrays the swerving vehicle as an extraordinary event and the social examination of genitals in this community of schoolchildren as an entirely ordinary practice that loses interest before the more magnificent spectacle of the white man and his shiny car. The Malinowskian duality of the "coefficient of weirdness" and the "coefficient of reality," while shaping each other, easily change places with the corresponding change of perspective from culture to culture as the ethnographic gaze moves back and forth between them. They continue to jostle and shape each other, as local and foreign, the familiar and the alien persist in the final contestations of their evaluation of the spectacle:

> Children tumbled out from behind the schoolroom or the ghanna bushes to stare at the departing vehicle. Little ones recited the CA 3654 number plate and carried the transported look throughout the day. The older boys freed their nostrils and with hands plunged in their pockets suggested by a new swaggering gait that it was not so wonderful a spectacle after all. How could it be if their schoolmaster was carried away in the Mercedes? (6)

The very fascinating power of the situation depends on the complete exclusion of all local peoples from its constituent elements, all of which are quickly and clearly established as representing a foreign, white, and, by implication, imperial force. Its claim as an exceptional event is seriously damaged by its inclusion of a local person, even if it is the schoolmaster, who, at any event, has a distinct and superior status within the community. The dramatic force of the incident is contingent on the preservation of its utter difference, its existence on a completely different world order. It is this difference that enthralls the locals.

The local in this incident from Wicomb's story is synonymous with the pattern of ordinary life and linked to the tired iterations of the banal, while the foreign is coincident with the grand and the extraordinary. This value system entails a reversal of the ethnographic gaze. "The master narrative of ethnographic authority," James Buzard points out, "features a controlled submission to alien ways, a demonstration that the self is uniquely positioned with regard to the culture that it penetrates while never losing its footing in Western rationality."[25] The ethnographer's gaze comes from outside and tries, as Malinowski insists, to read pattern, significance, and, most importantly, the culture's rootedness in quotidian life, in customs and institutions that initially appear strange and alien. Wicomb shows the gaze directed by the locals (significantly, children) toward the Englishman, with one of their more privileged and articulate representatives, Frieda, offering an autoethnographic account of the foreign intrusion into the local life of the village. Within this autoethnographic gaze, not only do we witness the reversal of the alien and the familiar as they might have been framed in the ethnographer's gaze but also the eagerness of the local children to preserve the alien quality of the intruding phenomenon as essential to its value as a grand spectacle. If the ethnographer, motivated by Western rationality, is invested in making sense of what they see as alien and strange and therefore reading them as ordinary and everyday, the local children are invested in preserving the utter foreignness of the foreign, in *not* reading them as ordinary.

The interaction of the ordinary and the extraordinary has a certain representational effect that is the persistent feature of the stories that I discuss in this chapter. Beyond that, however, it is the symptom of a larger historiographic conflict that is characteristic of post-Renaissance European colonialism. This disjuncture of meaning, of life-worlds, is symptomatic of the incompatibility of colonial and indigenous modes of imagining history. More importantly, however, as demonstrated by the scene with the man in the Mercedes, this incompatibility of local and colonial historiographic modes has been undone to a certain extent by the very force of colonialism, and a clear relationship of hierarchy has been established between the two models. Consequently, social events can now be evaluated on a common scale, and the result is obvious, as for instance from the "wonder and admiration" preserved for the white man and his car and the barely disguised disdain for their own schoolmaster, a local. In *Provincializing Europe*, Dipesh Chakrabarty identifies historicism to be the epistemological force that had enabled European domination of the world in the nineteenth century. It is at such moments of colonial and local encounters that the power—and the simplicity—of such an argument become clear. The ideological success of colonial domination depends on the degree to which the colonized people have internalized the primacy of European historiography and the "backward" location of their own culture within that European model. "Wonder and admiration" are reserved for the shiny Mercedes because in the context of rural Namaqualand, it represents an "advance" within the European historiographic framework that the locals have internalized as their own. The schoolteacher, in spite of his position within the local community, is not seen as a credible participant in this "advance." Ironically, in the very next sentence, his daughter (the narrator-protagonist Frieda) makes a case for her father's importance and of his inclusion in the "shiny" vehicle of European modernity by reiterating the fact that "Father was the only person for miles who knew enough English" (6): that is, on the basis of his command of the language that has undisputed privilege within this hierarchy.

The interaction of conflicting values and meanings in the stories I discuss in this chapter reflects not only the initial incommensurability of local and colonial historiographic modes but also the hierarchy of power between the two modes that is ideologically established in both indigenous and European minds. This ideological power structure has "coloured" many traditional ethnographic accounts and travel stories, as postcolonial theorists—most famously, Edward Said in *Orientalism*—have argued. Moreover, as Johannes Fabian argues in *Time and the Other*, anthropology provided significant justification to the colonial enterprise by strengthening the West's belief in "natural" or evolutionary time, which eventually became a political and economic legacy. Progress could now be universalized and easily measured:

> It promoted a scheme in terms of which not only past cultures, but all living societies were irrevocably placed on a temporal slope, a stream of time—some upstream, others downstream. Civilization, evolution, development, acculturation, modernization (and their cousins, industrialization, urbanization)

are all terms whose conceptual content derives, in ways that can be specified, from evolutionary time.[26]

Political and economic value judgments, such as those encapsulated in the terms "primitive," "savage," and "Third World," imply hierarchized locations along this unidirectional, linear slope of time. The conceptualization of the banal and the extraordinary, the ordinary and the dramatic is also done with reference to this time slope. As this scene from Wicomb's story shows, what is branded as banal and what is considered striking depends on who is speaking and to what extent they have internalized the ideology of the time slope. Banality is the aesthetic form of incomplete or subaltern modernity—a state of not-yet-there-ness where excitement and eventfulness can only be seen at a distance, not experienced within one's immediate reach. The natural venue for the conflict of the banal and the striking, therefore, is the contact zone of the colonial encounter.

The banalization of one's life is one of the most damning markers of backwardness. The sense of the banality of life in the village as realized in the sensibility of the children corresponds to the boredom that anthropologists have recently demonstrated to be a powerful affective malaise afflicting people in parts of sub-Saharan Africa well into the early years of the twenty-first century. "In Ethiopia," Daniel Mains points out, "the inability to experience progress, in the sense of actualizing a future that is different from one's present, caused time to expand rather than contract for many youth, producing a sensation that was akin to Western notions of boredom." It is "akin" but not identical to boredom (or, more accurately, "ennui") as embodied in the context of "romantic individualism" of the metropolitan West, since it is molded not by the failure of the realization of "individual humanity" but by the inability "to actualize their expectations of progress." Boredom is the apparently unlikely but immediate affective consequence of lack or absence: "the absence of entertainment, the absence of health, and the absence of modernity."[27] The result is a sense of the endless prolonging of empty time ironically comparable to Western-metropolitan versions of boredom. Such is the natives' relationship with their sense of their own lives and habitat in Jamaica Kincaid's *A Small Place*, where their "crushing banality and boredom and desperation and depression" evolves not only from their desire for the distant metropolis but also through the arrival of metropolitan tourists who derive aesthetic pleasure from the same cultural and historical contexts that seem to imprison the sadly immobile natives.

In Wicomb's story, the white man and his Mercedes become, as objects of unfulfilled colonial desire, markers of grandeur and excitement that form a disruptive contrast with the banality in the collective life of the local community. Following the ideological interpellation of such a desire into the collective mind of the colonized, the quotidian everyday of indigenous life waits for the continual intrusions of colonial force to provide the narrative drive essential to both the life and the fictions that depict it. As Spacks points out repeatedly in her study of boredom, the banal and the boring defy the possibility of narrative. It is hardly coincidental that Wicomb's story—and the book itself—opens its narrative at the moment the white man in his Mercedes appears in the rural community. This dramatic event puts the local children into motion, and it does the same to the narrative. Following the ideological overpowering of indigenous historiography, both narrative and historiographic progress will now be dictated on colonial terms.

The Praxis of Refusal

For the eventfulness of progress, then, the colonized has to wait. Waiting, in fact, is the recognized historiographic trope that characterizes the colony's relation to Western modernity. It is a trope that takes on added complexities in the historical context of twentieth-century South Africa. At several key points throughout Wicomb's book, waiting defines the temporality of these stories, shaping and drawing out the oppressive, iterative quality of time that hangs heavy as characters wait for something to happen, even for something as seemingly private and apolitical as the train's arrival or one's turn with the doctor. The German word for boredom, *langweiler*, evokes an unpleasant prolonging of time, and few motifs consolidate the social and psychological impact of painfully prolonged time with those of boredom as seamlessly as the trope of waiting. In the story "When the Train Comes," it is the oppression of prolonged time no less than the disturbing presence of the boys close by that Frieda's father hopes to fight with tricks that seem sadly banal to his teenage daughter. However, if the final fringes of adolescence reveal to Frieda the banality of childhood distractions, it is in the mature sensibility of an adult Frieda that the act of waiting assumes a disturbing political immediacy. This becomes clear in the doctor's waiting room in the story "Behind the Bougainvillea."

The management of quotidian temporalities, this story reveals, is a revealing index of localized modernity. When Frieda, back from England for a visit with her family, plans to make an appointment to see the doctor, her father says, "I don't think you can make appointments, not yet. This isn't Cape Town, you know. You just go along and wait" (106). But if provincial South Africa is denied the modernity of arranging appointments, it is at least granted the consolation modernity of a waiting room, as her father points out: "But there's a lovely waiting room with a modern water lavatory" (106). What he *neglects* to mention is that the modern amenity of the waiting room, like all facilities in the segregated nation, is not available to everyone. Occupying the indoor waiting room for white patients, the "coloured" Frieda (who passes as white fairly easily) is unable to experience even the private discomfort brought about by waiting without being drawn into a gnawing awareness of such discomfort as a racially uneven experience. "It is in any case absurd to pretend," she knows well, "that I have assumed this as my position for waiting. I turn and meet the thousand eyes of those squatting in the yard. They have been watching" (106). Aware of the segregated spaces to which the lightness of her skin allows an ethically ambiguous access, she watches the nonwhite patients waiting out in the yard, haunted by the feeling that they've been watching her in turn. The most private and idiosyncratic gestures of boredom are revealed in terms of their relation to race and class. Ways of resisting the boredom of waiting, meanwhile, depend on one's political identity and, crucially, one's cultural literacy: "They register the tension of the moment by shifting and scratching as people do who ease the discomfort of waiting. I settle on my haunches against the wall and open my bag for a book but cannot bring myself to haul it up. Such a display of literacy would be indecent" (106). Nothing is private in this racially charged world where hierarchies are not only blatant but also institutionalized, branded on every single quotidian experience. Abandoning the more socially pretentious act of reading, which would further demarcate her from those waiting out in the sun, Frieda chooses instead an appropriately uncouth bodily gesture: "Instead I draw up a paper handkerchief and ostentatiously blow my nose" (106).

Empty time, such as that embodied in the act of waiting, is a loaded motif for Wicomb, as it is for her autobiographical protagonist, Frieda Shenton.

The moment of reckoning where the writer, the narrator, and the protagonist become indistinguishable from one another comes in the last story of *You Can't Get Lost in Cape Town*, where Frieda's mother lashes out at the vacant temporality of the stories: "'Stories,' she shouts, 'you call them stories? I wouldn't spend a second gossiping about things like that. Dreary little things in which nothing happens'" (171). The lack of events is as much an internal problem in these stories as it is a metafictional commentary on the aesthetic worldview that shapes them. Moreover, the aesthetic of vacant, banal time has a larger political significance.

If the various lures of excitement, modernity, and progress spring from the edifices of racial and colonial power, Zoë Wicomb's insistent aestheticization of banal temporality is a critical refusal of such power structures. Frieda persistently subverts this spectacle of dramatic action with intricately plotted production of humdrum inertia, through which she transports select moments of the everyday to the affective extreme of the banal. Beyond this deceptive subversion of the ideological structures of colonialism, her celebration of the banal also marks a highly effective resistance against the totalizing historiography of the national narrative. The political import of what I call the counternarrative of the banal becomes fully clear against our awareness of the national public sphere that forms the historical context to *You Can't Get Lost in Cape Town*. This is in fact a phase of South African political history replete with dramatic events and issues, mostly related to apartheid and the struggles against it. Many of them cast direct or indirect shadows on the stories, such as the assassination of Prime Minister Hendrik Verwoerd, the Black Consciousness Movement and the leadership of Steve Biko, the formation of the United Democratic Front, strikes, constitutional changes, and the formation of Zimbabwe.

Some of these events catalyze personal crises in Frieda's life, either directly or indirectly. However, it is striking and, on the surface, quite inexplicable that often during moments of such crises, Frieda's narrative sensibility demonstrates a sensual and psychological immersion in objects or situations of daily life that would normally appear to be trivial and marginal. A perfect example is the bus ride in the title story, "You Can't Get Lost in Cape Town." For the longest time, we are not told (though there are very delicate hints that become fully meaningful only after we have access to the facts) that Frieda is on her way to Cape Town to get an abortion, illegal under the laws of the time. This is not only a highly unusual situation in the life of a teenage girl from Frieda's class, race, and cultural background but a racially "guilty" one, and one that is literally criminalized under the then current Immorality Act, since her boyfriend and the father of her child, Michael, is white. Moreover, for her abortion, Frieda is going to a private residence in the white part of segregated Cape Town, where, as it turns out, she has to pass as white. Michael, who is to meet her in Cape Town and accompany her to the abortionist's home, utters the richly ironic sentence that is to become the title of the story and the book. "A look at my anxious face compelled him to say, 'You can't get lost in Cape Town' " (73). The sheer comfort and ease with which he makes the assertion is clearly rooted in his privileged race and gender. Moving around in the city with a clear sense of direction, just like the relatively aimless indulgence of flânerie, illustrates a physical and political agency that is easily available to him but not to Frieda. Michael overlooks his "coloured" girlfriend's exclusion from this confident and knowledgeable mobility, which is what ensures that one never gets lost in Cape Town.

However, it is part of Wicomb's narrative irony that most of the information regarding the planned abortion is withheld from us for the first several pages of the story, during which time Frieda's mind seems to be a strange amalgam of boredom and distraction. She shows only the faintest concern about the journey she has embarked on and on the thought whether one can or cannot "get lost in Cape Town." Her mind instead hovers distractedly over trivial details, such as the leather bag of the bus conductor, the tumbling coins in his hand, the five-rand note in her own, the chatter of the two women in front of her, the pieces of roast chicken they are sharing, the half-eaten drumstick and the bare bone in their hands. Next to the life-changing situation she is soon to face, it seems that her mind deliberately takes refuge in banalities. In hindsight, the pervading sense of banality seems to affirm indirectly the sweeping significance of the pregnancy and its abrupt termination—a significance that is almost concealed, not unlike the way the staccato exchanges and the overarching boredom seem to overshadow a similar preoccupation in Ernest Hemingway's "Hills Like White Elephants." Some things in life are urgent to the point where they perhaps do not bear talking or even thinking about. Both stories demonstrate that banality and boredom are not only conscious strategies but also particularly ironic ones. In Frieda's case, this strategy is not merely a protective effort to rid her mind of the enormity of the situation or distract it from the reality of her fears and concerns. This becomes clear not only from a careful reading of this story but of comparable situations in other stories.

In "Home Sweet Home," in the midst of the larger, urgent concerns about emigration, family, and clan, as Frieda prepares to leave a restless, rapidly changing South Africa for a new life in England, her mind follows a similar whimsical pattern, focusing on trivial, marginalized details that are only occasionally epiphanized into larger significances. Such is her sudden fascination with the raindrops falling on the iron roof of the sitting room of her house: "And inside, below, always the tap-tap of the roof as the iron contracted, tap-tap like huge drops of rain falling individually, deliberately. But drops of rain would sizzle on the hot iron and roll off evaporating, hissing as they rolled. So merely the sound of molecular arrangement in the falling temperature of the iron" (101). In the very next moment, her eyes and mind drift toward Aunt Nettie brushing with her duster: "She dusts well, with a practised hand—that is, if the criteria for dusting are indeed speed and agility. Her right wrist flicks the duster of dyed ostrich feathers across surfaces, the left hand moving simultaneously, lifting, before the duster flicks, and then replacing ornaments" (102).

Such moments abound in Wicomb's book, creating an abiding chain of engagement with the delicate materiality of the minute and the trivial. The eccentric Jan Klinkies emerges as a metafictional figure, a conscious architect of marginalia. He is the sensitive arranger of discarded tin cans, whose design is so subtle that it is easy to miss:

> But I suspected that careful aesthetic considerations had been at play. The cans so callously shoved aside might have been placed one by one, interrupted by the stepping back to appraise from a distance and perhaps replace or reposition. There is the business of balance, for instance; the wrong shape could bring the lot toppling down and you'd have to tap sliding cans carefully back into place. And a starting pattern can gradually lose its regularity until a completely new one is formed. It is perhaps only the beginning, the first small mound that you step back from, that is totally pleasing. With such a great number and variety of cans the permutations of summit and slope must be endless. Perhaps it was precisely that consideration that made Jan Klinkies appear a detached observer. (16)

This story, too, encapsulates the sensibility of a young child, albeit written in the retrospective vision of the adult. But its conclusion marks the protagonist's development toward the more mature years of adolescence. It ends with the magical sight of a constellation of discarded tin cans: "The tree barely moved, but the branches stooping heavily under the hundreds of cans tied to them with wire rattled and sent off beams of blinding light at angles doubtlessly corresponding to a well-known law" (20).

The preoccupation with the banal is especially noticeable when it arises at times of emotional and psychological crisis. There is an element of irony in the emphasis on banality as a conscious narrative impulse during such moments. Rummaging in her bag for the letter from Uncle Hermanus, where he writes about the extraordinary experience of the snow-covered Canada to where he has emigrated, Aunt Cissie's hand touches a banal but reassuring reminder of her domestic life and its rootedness in the local: "Her eyes caper at the secrets awakened by her touch in that darkness, secrets like her electric bill, so boldly printed in words and figures, protected from their eyes by the thin scuffed leather" (83). If immigration poses something of a dramatic crisis for the immigrant as well as for those left behind, the crisis also offers a rich moment for introspection offered by a banal detail. In "Behind the Bougainvillea," Frieda recollects how in England, far from home and family, the pouring rain and the intricately shaped raindrops come to metaphorize her emotions of longing and the pain of exile:

> From the window I had been watching the lurid yellow of oil-seed rape sag like sails under squalls of rain. On the beam in the kitchen drops of rain lined up at regular intervals, the bright little drops meeting their destruction in an ache for perfection, growing to roundness that the light from the bare electric bulb would catch, so that the star at the base grew into a bright point of severance and for a second was the perfect crystal sphere before it fell, ping, into the tin plate and splattered into mere wetness. But then, before the fall, the star would spread into an oval of reflected light, pale and elliptical on the shadowed beam, an opal ghost escaping. (112)

Frieda's preoccupation with the carefully wrought banal detail at moments of crisis is not merely the creative caprice of a fiercely original, artistically inclined sensibility in a state of crucial personal, cultural, and historical transition—it is also an intensely political act. Naomi Schor's arguments for the delineation of the minute detail as feminine as opposed to the grand, sweeping structures of abstract knowledge are important here:

To focus on the detail, and more particularly on the *detail as negativity*, is to become aware, as I discovered, of its participation in a larger semantic network, bounded on the one side by the *ornamental*, with its traditional connotations of effeminacy and decadence, and on the other, by the *everyday*, whose "prosiness" is rooted in the domestic sphere of social life presided over by women.[28]

Schor argues that within Western aesthetic and epistemological traditions, the masculine suspicion of the minute detail has been recycled from classicism into neoclassicism and the Enlightenment, culminating in Hegel's organicist aesthetics: "The contempt Hegel flaunts for 'the little stories of everyday domestic existence' and 'the multiform particularities of everyday life'—in short, for all he lumps under the dismissive heading 'the prose of the world.' "[29]

In this light, I would read Frieda's persistent preoccupation with the loaded trivialities of intricately shaped raindrops, tiny chicken drumsticks, delicately jingling coins—in sum, the nontranscendental prose of the world—as a refusal to be drawn into the masculinized abstraction of grand, national conflicts. Such an idiosyncratic withdrawal into the erratic and the marginal indicates an active participation in what Graham Pechey calls "the textures of life which have ... grown insouciantly in the cracks of the structures" of "South Africa's fraught modernity."[30] The spectacular, when it makes its disruptive appearance in the context of the local and the familiar, immediately establishes itself as an intrusion by alien forms of power structures and knowledge systems.

However, we would do well to remember that Ndebele had warned against a possible criticism of the model of contemplative interiority defining both Frieda's and Wicomb's character. "It will lambast interiority in character portrayal as bourgeois subjectivity."[31] While the identification of psychological interiority as necessarily bourgeois is itself indicative of the kind of problematic politicoaesthetic climate Ndebele criticizes, the kind of interiority celebrated by Wicomb and Frieda, admittedly, does not escape this criticism entirely. Throughout the book, the contemplative celebration of the quotidian and its banal extremes remains a personal privilege for the educated, upwardly mobile, creative Frieda. Such contemplation remains noticeably outside the conscious reach of disenfranchised figures such as Tamieta and Skitterboud. It is indicative of Frieda's growth and maturity that the young Frieda ignores Tamieta, while the older Frieda, returned from England, listens with attention to Skitterboud's story.

A sense of banality can just as soon be an index of inadequacy as it can be a gesture of refusal and resistance. In fact, it has been the argument of this book that the inadequate and fractured nature of subaltern modernities finds aesthetic expression in the banal. The transformation of the banal into a radical narrative instinct requires a kind of creative agency that might be available to Frieda but is unavailable to more deeply disenfranchised figures *within* colonial society. The character of Tamieta, the cook from Namaqualand in the university cafeteria in "A Clearing in the Bush," is a telling example. As an uneducated, rural woman of an underprivileged class, Tamieta in many ways approximates the position of the indigenous subaltern, occupying a social position distinct from that of the educated, middle-class Frieda. Tamieta's position is characterized by her lack of access to knowledge provided by education and social privilege, which is available to Frieda and her friends at the university. This lack of access also implies an exclusion from the national public sphere and, more crucially, the anticolonial movements that are usually defined and shaped by the nation's elite. It is obvious that even within the educated, politically aware student community there is a gendered hierarchy through which knowledge and, subsequently, the ability to participate is transmitted. Thus Frieda and her friend Myra sit wondering what is going on, observing the irregular behavior of the boys in the school—including that of their close friend, James—till James comes and informs them of the planned boycott of the memorial service for the assassinated prime minister, Hendrik Verwoerd, to be held in the afternoon. In Tamieta's case, of course, no one tells her anything at all. This exclusion culminates in the sad irony of the last scene, where Tamieta sits puzzled in the memorial service, the only person of color to attend, the rows of empty chairs stretching like a confusing questionnaire before her. None of the student activists—not even the veteran Mr. Johnson, who goes from class to class to inform the students of the planned boycott and invite their participation—thought it worth their while to include Tamieta in their plans or even to share any information with her. Moreover, it is doubtful how she might have responded even if she had been informed, not necessarily sharing their subscription to an anticolonial movement clearly dominated by the educated elite.

Lack of knowledge, which coincides with the inability to participate in the macropolitics of anticolonial movements in the public sphere, not only prevents an intellectual and political transcendence of the everyday but rather molds the everyday with an overarching sense of emptiness and banality in the lives of those excluded. Those left out are stranded in the solitary confinement of a private consciousness that is affected by the upheavals in the public sphere but that fails to grasp the significance of such upheavals. Such subjects are also excluded from the masculinized public sphere of macropolitics that decisively shapes the private and domestic lives to which women are confined but that declines to share knowledge or participation across gender lines. Frieda and Myra sit wondering over the inaction and the vacuum suddenly created by their exclusion from the visibly important and exciting activities occupying the boys:

> James always sits with us. We have learned to make allowances for the filtered version of friendship that boys offer; nevertheless his behaviour today is certainly treacherous. Why has he gone without explanation to join the dark tower of boys peering down on to the table at the back? It is clearly not the klawerjas game that holds their attention. Someone screened from our vision is talking quietly, then bangs a fist on the table. The voices grow more urgent. We watch James withdraw from the inner circle and perch on the back of a chair shaking his head, but he does not look across at us. (51)

Egged on by a sense of urgency by her obvious exclusion from the excitement at the boys' table, Myra suggests that she and Frieda try to find out what is happening: "'I think,' says Moira, 'we should go and join them. If they've got something important to discuss then it's bound to affect us so ought to go and find out'" (52). Eventually, James provides the withheld information at Myra's request: "We're organizing the action for this afternoon's memorial service. We must make sure that nobody goes" (53). Carol Sicherman, in her literary afterword to the Feminist Press edition of the book, points out that the male students are unfortunately right in their sexist assumption that they can exclude the female students from the conversation and nevertheless obtain their compliance. She draws attention to Wicomb's declared challenge to the patriarchal structure of anticolonial leadership exemplified in the university boycott in this story. "I can think of no reason," Wicomb writes, "why black patriarchy should not be challenged alongside the fight against apartheid."[32]

It is in this manner that in Wicomb's stories those domains of everyday life filled with dramatic upheavals are repeatedly brought into pointed and often polemical contrast with banal and empty moments. An immersion into the latter is, for Frieda, often a personalized site of refuge or a consciously articulated gesture of protest or resistance. But that this capacity of resistance or refusal is uneven is demonstrated by the fact that Tamieta does not have access to the liberating potential of banality enjoyed by Frieda. Nevertheless, it is significant that the story opens with an event of quotidian materiality—the itch on Tamieta's back and her inability to remedy or understand its symbolic meaning except through a nameless sense of foreboding: "Tamieta, leaning against the east-facing walls, rolls her shoulders and like a cat rubs against the bricks to relieve the itching on her back. Which must mean something ominous, such a sudden and terrible itch, and as she muses on its meaning, on its persistence, the rebellious flesh seems to align itself with the arrangement of bricks now imprinted on her back" (37).

If Frieda, Myra, and the other female students are excluded from conscious agency vis-à-vis the masculinized protest movement, Tamieta exists much farther down in this hierarchy of power and knowledge. The materiality of her body that opens her story is in fact expressed through a rhetoric of animality that is telling—we are told that she "rolls her shoulders and like a cat rubs against the bricks to relieve the itching of her back." She is fully aware of her significant social difference from Frieda, who comes from Little Namaqualand just like Tamieta herself, and that awareness is laced with irony and resentment: "She casts a resentful look at the girl just sitting there, waiting for her coffee with her nose in the blinking book. She too is from the country. Tamieta knows of her father who drives a motor car in the very next village, for who in little Namaqualand does not know of Shenton?" (46).

Just as gender is an important determinant for involvement in liberation movements, class affiliation and education, too, significantly affect participation. For Tamieta, not only is the students' gesture of protest beyond all understanding or awareness, but upheavals in public history are of no concern to people like her or Charlie, whom she rebukes for showing an interest in such history: "It's because you listen to other people's conversations that you forget the orders hey. You'll never get on in this canteen business if you don't keep your head. Never mind the artitex; clever people's talk got nothing to do with you" (43). Her lot is with the mechanical production and preservation of the slice of everyday life left in her charge. In the university cafeteria she is neither privileged nor empowered to understand the meaning of the interruption of this quotidian order by dramatic events such as protests and boycotts. Her exclusion from political agency in the public sphere is therefore both willed and forced. It leaves her with the conviction that politics is none of her concern. Suspended in the vacuum of a disenfranchised private sensibility, she lacks the political and aesthetic agency of the socially and educationally privileged Frieda to turn the exclusion into a finely honed critique of the inequalities perpetuated by the liberation movements themselves.

The fact that the story opens with the unexplained, unremedied itch and closes with another confusing and embarrassing situation whose meaning Tamieta does not understand is therefore a clever structural choice on the author's part. The spectacle of the liberation movement is, as always, claimed by the privileged. Exclusion and deprivation from meaning and knowledge can only deepen her enslavement to an everyday that, in the end, lends itself to an oppressive banality. While the few present members of the audience maintain the ritual silence of grief at the end of the meeting as the story comes to a close, Tamieta cannot focus her mind on the significance of the incident, nor on the meaning of the boycott. Instead, her mind wanders, as it did in the opening of the story, to a relatively trivialized affliction of her body and to sundry domestic needs: "The heads hang in grief. Tamieta's neck aches. Tonight Beatrice will free the knotted tendons with her nimble fingers. She does not have the strength to go into town for the wool, but Beatrice will understand" (61). She leaves the memorial service confused and full of questions but finds herself only thinking of the wool she needs to get—"the parcel of clothes tucked under her left" arm—and the rain she needs to avoid, rather than the day's events. Her day, for her no different from yet another ordinary day, notwithstanding its dramatic political significance, ends with her affective immersion into the banal.

With the requisite space made for this important criticism about differential empowerment *within* the racial groups oppressed by apartheid, there is still no denying the radical political implications of Frieda's preoccupation with the minute, the fragmentary, and the ordinary precisely at such moments of crisis. Making deserved allowances for Wicomb's personal aesthetic ethos, I would suggest that the impetus behind her troubling of the dramatic nature of the "polar conflicts"[33] is rooted within the dimensions of her identity as a woman and a "coloured" person. Aspects of these identities not only resist the structures of apartheid and colonialism but also refuse to fit neatly into struggles *against* such structures. Frieda's recourse to the minute and banal detail located within the domestic everyday can be read as a feminist critique of the masculinized sphere of macropolitics that have often sought to keep the women out of its domain just as much as it can be read as a commentary on the complicated relation that people of mixed racial heritage have had with black nationalism.

In the story "Ash on My Sleeve," the adult Frieda and Myra reflect on the past and the present of the racial confusion and disowned identities of interracial peoples. The story is set in the 1980s, well after the United Democratic Front had established the solidarity of all races classified as "nonwhite" in segregated South Africa under the crucial influence of Steve Biko's Black Consciousness Movement. "Just think," Myra says, "In our teens we wanted to be white, now we want to be full-blooded Africans. We've never wanted to be ourselves and that's why we stray" (156). In her essay "Shame and Identity: The Case of the Coloured in South Africa," Wicomb draws attention to the negative recognition accorded to the "coloured" in South Africa, through the negativity of its demographic definition under the Nationalist Government's Population Registration Act of 1950: "not a White person or a Black."[34] Officially recognized as a negativity and often ignored between competing models of nationalism, being "coloured" was a matter of shame not only because of its undefined location but because of the violation that defines its origins: "Miscegenation, the origins of which lie in a discourse of 'race,' concupiscence, and degeneracy, continues to be bound up with shame, a pervasive shame exploited in apartheid's strategy of the naming of a Coloured race, and recurring in the current attempts by coloureds to establish brownness as a pure category, which is to say a denial of shame."[35]

Her keen awareness of her identity as a "coloured" person, complicated further by her education and middle-class origins, shapes the unpredictability of Frieda's behavior, sensibility, and metafictional consciousness at every step. This behavioral and imaginative unpredictability works not only with respect to anticolonial nationalism but also in terms of her place in her community (a community that is often upwardly mobile and desires to be seen as white) and finally, within her own intimate relations. If in a flush of youthful romanticism and creativity she writes a clichéd poem as an effort to symbolize race relations in South Africa, she recognizes its imaginative poverty immediately, but her white boyfriend Michael is obtuse about it and admires it in a patronizing way. If, as Lewis Nkosi argues, "in South Africa there exists an unhealed . . . split between black and white writing, between on the one side an urgent need to document and to bear witness and on the other the capacity to go on furlough, to loiter, and to experiment,"[36] Frieda's "coloured" identity seems to bind her to both urgencies at the same time.

"Coloured," female, educated, and creative, growing up in a middle-class community that demonstrates a complex mix of Anglophilia and an undertaking of upward social mobility, Frieda has to assert her unique, individual agency through private and idiosyncratic acts ranging from the smallest of behavior patterns, reveries, and whims to the larger radical decisions of life. Her creative immersion in the banal moments, marginalized objects, and the unusual minutiae of details helps to shape an aesthetic ethos that responds consistently to her unique personal location and destiny as an educated "coloured" woman in the given milieu. It is little wonder that through her intriguing investment in the banality of the everyday around her, she emerges as singularly ill suited to the dramatic historiography of anticolonial nationalism that dominates models of protest literature and the national allegory of the time. *You Can't Get Lost in Cape Town* shares ethnography's valorization of the ordinary and trivial detail of life as sites of critical knowledge production. But in the end, a strategic representation of the heightened banality of such details inscribes something of a counterethnography. It embodies a worldview that not only refuses to take part in the valorized and predominant anticolonial struggles but that also provides a significant if overlooked alternative to the more visible and acclaimed modes of postcolonial narration.

• CHAPTER 4 •

Amit Chaudhuri and the Materiality of the Mundane

The peculiar excitement of poetry that Ramanujan, Arvind Mehrotra, or Dom Moraes (to take only three examples) wrote in the 1960s and 70s derived not so much from their, to use Rushdie's words, "chutnification" of the language, but in part, from the way they used ordinary English words like "door," "window," "bus," "doctor," "dentist, " "station, " to suggest a way of life. This was, and continues to be, more challenging than it may first appear; as a young reader, I remember being slightly repelled by the India of post offices and railway compartments I found in these poems; for I didn't think the India I lived in a fit subject for poetry.

—Amit Chaudhuri, "The Construction of the Indian Novel in English"

The National Allegory and the Fetishization of the Fantastic

More than a quarter-century after its initial publication, Fredric Jameson's controversial essay "Third World Literature in the Era of Multinational Capitalism" retains something of an unfortunate relevance to Anglophone fiction from India. The central claim in that essay—that all Third World cultures are characterized by a fusion of private and public lives and that this fusion ensures that all narratives (especially the novel) from such cultures are structured on the paradigm of the national allegory—still continues to resonate with an overarching trend of Indian English fiction. Ever since the publication of Salman Rushdie's *Midnight's Children*, the novel many consider to be the seminal national allegory for postindependence India, the genre has continued to prosper and to gather critical and commercial momentum on a global scale.

Jameson's essay has provoked heated debate on several fronts—not only in the literary contexts where it makes its most obvious intervention but equally notably in the application of Hegelian and Marxist frameworks to understand cultural phenomena. Responses structured around Jameson's literary archive have been critical of the sweeping nature of his argument, while discussions of his theoretical approach have been more ambivalent. The methodological issue, moreover, has caused considerable ideological unrest between Western and non-Western Marxists. Aijaz Ahmad's celebrated critique, in "Jameson's Rhetoric of Otherness and the 'National Allegory,'" however, finds the essay lacking on both empirical and theoretical grounds. As Michael Sprinker sums it up, Ahmad faults the essay on: "(1) the level of political and social theory (the three worlds), (2) the level of empirical cultural description (postmodernism vs. national allegory), (3) the level of cultural politics and ideology."[1]

Ahmad refutes the empirical validity of Jameson's argument through a consideration of archives both in South Asia and the United States. Sprinker deepens Ahmad's critique through a discussion of American cultural texts, including those produced by minority writers, where politics is far from being "pushed into the recesses of the unconscious,"[2] as Jameson claims it to be. Ahmad's criticism of Jameson's methodology is also acute at the level of political and territorial classification, significantly the stratification of the First, Second, and Third Worlds, which for Ahmad is an inconsistent way of conceiving the world. It is at the methodological level, however, that Jameson's supporters have concentrated their efforts, even when they have withheld support from the empirical content of his claims. Imre Szeman, for instance, is enthusiastic about Jameson's use of the Three Worlds theory, which, as he sees it, seeks "to develop a system by which it might be possible to consider these texts *within* the global economic and political system that produces the third world as the third world."[3] Szeman argues that such a system serves the useful purpose of providing a cultural cartography that is linked to "totality as a central concept in social and political criticism," upon which Jameson has consistently insisted and for which he has been so often misunderstood.[4] Nicholas Brown similarly points to Jameson's flawed general assumptions about literature produced at the periphery of capitalism but reminds us of the essay's important theoretical insight, namely, its use of the Hegelian Master-Slave dialectic to understand world literature. Within this dialectic, "Third World" literature, in the manner of the superior consciousness of the slave, possesses "materialistic consciousness" of the situation that produces it.[5] The presence of this materialistic consciousness in Third World literatures indicates its political and epistemological superiority to their First World counterparts. The means of deciphering this consciousness is, for Brown, not fundamentally different from "the mode of interpretation as 'socially symbolic act' that he recommends for European texts in *The Political Unconscious*."[6]

My concerns in this chapter, however, have far less to do with an entry into this old but still vigorous debate than with the peculiar resonance that Jameson's generic claims have had for the Indian-English novel since *Midnight's Children*. As Ahmad has successfully shown, especially through the examples of Urdu literature, it is very clear that there is no significant preoccupation with the paradigm of the national allegory in the indigenous-language literatures of the Indian subcontinent. However, the greater problem with Jameson's essay—which, it seems to me, none of its interlocutors have indicated so far—is not that Jameson is wrong but that he is right. Here I'm in agreement with him—and a sad agreement it is—over the empirical aspect of his claim inasmuch as it applies to the specific literary archive on which I focus in this chapter, rather than the philosophical structure of his methodology, which is not my subject here. As Ahmad and others have pointed out, the biggest weakness of Jameson's argument lies in its sweeping nature, in its claim to cover "all third world literature," a large claim that has nonetheless found occasional support among scholars even in the subcontinental context. For instance, in her multigeneric reading of modern Indian art forms, Geeta Kapur reads the convergence of the private and the public in late colonial and postcolonial aesthetic texts—including the novels of Rabindranath Tagore and the films of Satyajit Ray and Anand Patwardhan—as bearing out the relevance of the Jamesonian claim about the "national allegory being the pre-eminent paradigm of Third World literature."[7] While I have my own differences with Kapur's position, what I'm concerned with is the peculiar applicability that the Jamesonian argument seems to have when it is confined to a specific discursive field within the vast, multilingual, and multicultural domain of South Asian literatures—that of the Indian-English novel from the 1980s on. Following Rushdie's celebrated novel, the national allegory has indeed become a privileged narrative paradigm in popular and critical discourse. The fact that Jameson is correct when it comes to this specific segment of Third World literature indicates not, as Jameson suggests, a revelation of the political consciousness of the genre but rather, as I would like to argue, a serious limitation. My empirical agreement with Jameson therefore comes at the expense of a deeper ideological disagreement with his claim. To elaborate this ambiguity, let me turn to post–*Midnight's Children* Indian-English fiction to consider it in some detail.

Midnight's Children was published in 1981. The years following its publication, leading up to the mid-1990s, were perhaps the richest for novels that aspired to the model of national allegory in Anglophone India. (Jameson's essay, it might be noted in passing, appeared in 1985, in the journal *Social Text*.) The decade following this period, leading up to the present day, has seen the publication of significant novels deviating from this dominant public-historiographic norm. These include Booker-winning novels by two women, Arundhati Roy's *The God of Small Things* and Kiran Desai's *The Inheritance of Loss*, both of which engage in a far more immediate and sensual apprehension of private, regional sensibilities, existing in greater independence from the nationally constructed public space that the national allegory allows. In 2008, the Booker again went to another Indian writer, Aravind Adiga, for *The White Tiger*, a novel that troubles the middle-class national narrative from a very different angle—from the dark underbelly of crime and violence hidden by the postmillennial climate of economic boom that has increasingly come to define the domestic and global image of India in the twenty-first century. These significant novelistic achievements notwithstanding, the shadow of the national allegory still looms large on the wider horizon of Anglophone Indian literature and still dominates critical discussion about it. One must acknowledge, however, that a preoccupation with the ideas and problems of nationhood, especially in its relation with colonialism and its legacies, is not unique to the post-1980s Indian-English novel. Such concerns are reflected in earlier Indian-English fiction, probably most famously in the Gandhian-socialist novels of Mulk Raj Anand or Raja Rao's 1938 novel *Kanthapura*. As some critics have suggested, there is a possible link between the position of English as a national language in a country of more than forty major regional languages, on one hand, and English-language fiction's engagement with pan-Indian issues, on the other. In a comparable situation, Chinua Achebe had claimed that the title of the "national literature" of Nigeria properly could only be claimed by literature written in English, while those in the various regional languages could only be considered "ethnic literatures."[8] It is possible to see the urge to project a "national literature," working within the English-language literatures of Anglophone Commonwealth nations, leading to an emphasis on national motifs over those relating to regional specificities. However, much of this projection, from both within and without, is a function of the way the chronology of literary history is constructed. Since the modern literatures of most developing nations have, in one way or another, been affected by post-Renaissance European colonialism, this chronology and, accordingly, the literary canon itself get constructed around defining history of that colonialism and are consequently interpreted in "colonial" and "postcolonial" terms.

A large number of novels in the literary canons of developing nations tend to be based upon a certain vision of history. Within the archive of Anglophone Indian national allegories, this vision of history coincides with what Fernand Braudel has identified as the history of the event, understood as both the major marker and determinant of human life. The thrust of narrative is on events that have appeared to be unique, sensational, and disruptive, moving farther and farther away from what Stanley Cavell calls the endlessly repeated conditions of human life. And it is hardly surprising that the canon of events, in this narrative vision, is constructed primarily around the defining moments of colonialism, anticolonial struggle, and liberation, as Amit Chaudhuri argues in his essay "Modernity and the Vernacular": "The only way India enters history is, evidently, via colonialism."[9] Under the predominance of narratives of the national public sphere, what gets left out are the spaces enclosed by not only the ordinary but also the private and the regional sensibility, which are rarely reducible to an allegory of the national public sphere.

However, the separation of a national public sphere from the domain of private or domestic life remains problematic in the Indian context. Modern conceptions of the public sphere in the West significantly derive from the sociological model developed by Jürgen Habermas.[10] In Habermas's formulation, the public sphere is primarily a space for discursive exchange that originates in eighteenth-century Europe as a venue for critical debate on aesthetic matters. Soon, however, the nascent public sphere comes to enable the possibility of crucial debates on the functions of the state, though it remains limited to men of a certain social and economic status. Another influential Western theorist of the private-public divide, Hannah Arendt, looks back to the Greek *polis* instead of eighteenth-century Europe but also identifies the public sphere as a space where humanistic discourse comes to constitute political praxis.[11] For Habermas, the rise of mass culture in the twentieth century essentially pushes the public sphere from the Kantian model of public reason, turning it into a space for passive consumption rather than of rational-critical debate. For Arendt, a comparable erosion of the critical-discursive function of the public sphere happens through the rise of the social, by which capitalism broadens the scope of economic labor to emancipate it from the realm of the household to a new public space.[12] None of these formulations, however, effectively aligns with South Asian society, especially considering local customs and social practices, such as that of arranged marriage, which shapes private and intimate kinships according to collectively decreed criteria such as caste, religion, and the position of planets on individual horoscopes. South Asian historians like Indrani Chatterjee and Sumit Guha have convincingly argued this disjuncture with Western conceptions of the public-private divide.[13] At the same time, however, the reality of an inner or spiritual domain of national culture as opposed to that of the outer or practical domains of the professions, economy, and statecraft have also been theorized by historians and cultural anthropologists of the Subaltern Studies Collective, notably by Partha Chatterjee.[14] In his study of anticolonial resistance in nineteenth-century India, Chatterjee distinguishes between the inner and the outer domains, into which national culture was split by the narratives constructed by such resistances.[15] Admittedly, the spiritual domain is not exactly the same as, or wholly coincident with, the private self, and the public self is also more than a sum total of "economy and . . . statecraft . . . science and technology." [16] On the other hand, something like a public narrative of spirituality and religion has also been dominant in India. But even so, the parallels between the two models has to be at least partially clear, most notably when Chatterjee identifies the home and the family as crucial sites of the inner domain of national culture.[17] On the other hand, as Chatterjee writes, "the history of nationalism as a political movement tends to focus primarily on its contest with colonial power in the domain of the outside, that is, the material domain of the state."[18] It is at moments like this that the affinities come to the surface—between the conception of the public-private divide, on one hand, and, on the other, that of the separation of the inner and the outer domain that has been a crucial aspect of anticolonial struggle.

This same emphasis on spheres of culture that coincide with the public and the outer domains has also been the privileged subject of the national allegories. To follow Chatterjee's arguments, which he bases on an elaborate archival study of nineteenth-century Bengal, the inner domain, in spite of its marginalization in the official histories of the nation, was, in fact, a crucial if indirect site of national culture—in this case, of anticolonial resistance. "The home, I suggest," writes Chatterjee, "was not a complementary but rather the original site on which the hegemonic project of nationalism was launched."[19] Chatterjee's claim here is something of an exact reversal of the paradigm of the national allegory. Rather than the story of the private self reflecting the embattled public history of the nation, the private self constitutes a crucial site of anticolonial struggle. The agents of this struggle are at pains to maintain the private sphere's distinction from the struggles in the outer, public sphere, as indeed the success of the struggle is contingent on the maintenance of this very distinction.

It is not fully clear whether Jameson is theorizing the realities of postcolonial, precolonial, or colonial cultures, but the novelistic national allegories clearly foray into all three directions. *Midnight's Children* tells the story of the nascent republic from the moment of independence onward, and I. Alan Sealy's *Trotternama* does something similar, whereas Shashi Tharoor's *The Great Indian Novel* and Mukul Kesavan's *Looking Through Glass* go back at least to colonial times, and Vikram Chandra's *Red Earth and Pouring Rain* looks back even further. But either way, these novels reiterate celebrated public narratives that are recognizable to a national middle class and even to readers in the metropolitan West by dint of the dramatic markers of history, such as the partition of the colonial nation, the moment of independence, communal riots and parliamentary crises in the independent state, and recognizable figures such as Gandhi and Nehru. The inner, private life is present only as an allegorical reflection of the outer, public domain. Such a construction, even if it doesn't produce "third world writing" as "narratively simplistic or overly moralistic," as Imre Szeman argues in his defense of Jameson, "it necessarily and directly speaks to and of the overdetermined situation of the struggles for national independence and cultural autonomy in the context of imperialism and its aftermath."[20] With the outer domain of national culture thus weighed down by the primary story of the embattlement with colonialism and the formation of a national identity following decolonization, the novelistic national allegory tends to flatten out the individual nuances and the regional idiosyncrasies of the inner domain for the sake of an essentialized version of the public sphere. As the new nation-state forges out its nascent identity following decolonization—the secular, socialist, democratic republic that India has set out to be—the dominant mode of its self-imagination is most visibly carried out on a national scale, that is, by a pan-Indian middle class that shares a common historical education about colonialism, decolonization, and postcolonial development, an education that dominates the bourgeois consciousness. The most significant narratives about postcolonial identity emergent during the post-1981 period often reflect this imagination. The fate of the fictionalized child born on the very stroke of India's independence cannot be his own but must instead belong to the nation. Such allegorical conflations implicitly construct a hierarchy of binaries where constructions of the public are more significant than the private, and the latter's reality, notwithstanding its private idiosyncrasies, is made to fit into certain perceptions of the former.

Sensational events, Nadia Seremetakis argues, "are almost pre-selected as narrated history, and certainly there is an ensemble of cultural, economic and political institutions and technologies devoted to their ongoing recitation."[21] By embodying the national-bourgeois version of history and the Nehruvian vision of the secular socialist republic, the thriving subculture of the novelistic national allegory adds to this narrative ensemble. There is, moreover, an alliance between the dramatic events of history foregrounded by the national allegory and a corresponding narrative-technical investment in the fantastic, the fabulist, and the dramatic. The loud and extroverted narrative style of these novels dramatically disrupts realism and corresponds with a preoccupation with the boldest lines of mainstream historiography, which necessarily provides a telescopic vision of the nation. Formal subversiveness, in other words, comes to frame the historiographic conservatism at the heart of the genre. Shashi Tharoor's *The Great Indian Novel*, both in its title and its thematic scope, epitomizes the magnitude of ambition represented by the post–*Midnight's Children* Anglophone Indian novel. The epic dimension of *The Mahabharata*, from which the novel takes its title and narrative framework, is envisioned as the necessary scale of narration, while the more ambivalent term "great" becomes an alibi for the grand, the spectacular, and the supernatural disruption of ordinary reality. The radical leaps through public-historical time become an index of a mythicized Indian consciousness of temporality. A disruptive and experimental formal structure, therefore, curiously enables the transhistorical space within which an easily recognizable version of India takes shape.

Sara Suleri has warned that the perceived irreducibility of "Otherness" as a privileged category in colonial and postcolonial cultural epistemologies too easily reinforces the "exotic," whose inscription in Orientalist studies such epistemologies had originally set out to displace. "Alterism" thus replicates the "exotic" in such approaches. "As such," Suleri writes, "contemporary rereadings of colonial alterity too frequently wrest the rhetoric of otherness into a postmodern substitute for the very Orientalism that they seek to dismantle, thereby replicating on an interpretative level the cultural and critical fallacies that such revisionism is designed to critique.[22]

I would argue that the various novels that claim the dimension of the national allegory, different as they are from one another, end up catering to such essentializing and "alterizing" theoretical approaches to Indian literature. The disruptive spectacularity of their narrative technique catalyzes such approaches and constructs the genre as an object of colonial alterity. At the same time, this "alterizing" narrative approach forms an ironic, if less readily observable contrast to the mainstream political vision upheld by the genre. The curious marriage of a postmodernist skepticism of realist narration to the supposed "alterity" of Indian discourse and reality, to a great degree, enables the construction of this overarching genre. But the national allegory also receives foundational support from an unlikely ally, the stabilizing vision of a secular-socialist India, which it successfully conceals under its formal subversiveness. In the process, the genre marginalizes several other planes of consciousness that are not only central to the sociohistorical realities of India but also to their literary representations.

The domestic space enclosed by the home and the family, for instance, offers a segment of reality that I think gets overshadowed in the end not only by the dramatic historical content of the national allegories but also by its accompanying generic investment in the grand, the fantastic, and the supernatural. The reality offered by this marginal space is that of the banal and mundane aspects of the domestic everyday, which often disappear because of their very ubiquity. In spite of their supposed interest in the marginal, the quirky, and the idiosyncratic, the major national-history novels, such as those by Rushdie, Tharoor, and Kesavan, are filled with the tremors of the dramatic transformations in its public history. True to the principles of magic realism, in both *Midnight's Children* and *Looking Through Glass*, the quotidian reality of the domestic domain simply forms the backdrop of realism against which the fantastic erupts.[23] The disruptive appearance of the fantastic, moreover, reflects the dominance of the grand public-sphere narratives that ultimately shape the contours and texture of private sensibility in such novels. Such is the event, as in Kesavan's novel, of a physical fall transporting the protagonist through time to a moment of the past that is central to national history—the Quit India movement of 1942.

As recently as in May 2008, in a talk given at Stanford University, Salman Rushdie reiterated one of the convictions that shape the worldview of many of his novels, probably nowhere more importantly than in *Midnight's Children*:

that the possibilities for a distinct private sphere in the contemporary world are increasingly limited by the ever-expansive influence of the public sphere and its turbulent upheavals. According to Rushdie, the quotidian domestic sphere such as that in Jane Austen's novels was insulated from dramatic public-historical events such as the French Revolution and the Napoleonic wars. Such insulation is no longer possible in the present moment of global history, where the private is increasingly determined by the public. The question as to whether an individual private sensibility today is less or more independent from public-historical events is not my subject here, nor is Rushdie's reading of the supposed insulation of the domestic domain from macropolitical history in Austen's fiction, both of which could be subject to more debate than Rushdie's talk allowed. The important point here is that it is precisely this conviction that has, through the seminal influence of *Midnight's Children*, come to define the ethos of the national allegory in Anglophone Indian literature.

However, both the private sphere of consciousness and the regional evocation of reality figure prominently in the vernacular literatures of India, as well as in the discourses of cultural nationalism from the colonial period. Thus, the predominant emphasis placed by the Anglophone novel on the spectacular macropolitics of colonial rule, anticolonial resistance, and the development of the postcolonial nation-state is somewhat curious. There could be any number of reasons behind this shift toward the primacy of a nationally conceptualized historiography, including the coming of age of a certain generation of novelists. Possibly a certain length of time had to pass after 1947—after Indian independence and the trauma of Partition—to make fictional conceptualization of the national self in pan-Indian spaces politically exigent. Moreover, the fact that most of these novelists worked in the English language possibly drew them toward nationalized public spheres as opposed to the quirks of the local and the private. As some have argued, the complex national political situation in the late 1970s, leading to what is considered by many as the end of Nehruvian India, was perhaps occasion enough for its insistent formulation or its questioning in fiction.[24] "The publication in 1981 of *Midnight's Children*, a Nehruvian epic," writes Amit Chaudhuri, "coincided, oddly, with the beginning of the end of Nehruvian India."[25] In calling Rushdie's novel "a Nehruvian epic," Chaudhuri undermines the subversive potential claimed by the formal techniques of the national allegory. Jon Mee, on the other hand, is more optimistic about the subversive appeal of the genre:

Various economic and social pressures have led to the end of the so-called Nehruvian consensus in India. The idea of unity within—so central to the years of nationalist struggle and the building of the new nation state—has been displaced by an urgent need to question the nature of that unity. The issue of imagining the nation, the issue of the fate of the children of the midnight hour of independence, has become a pressing one throughout India. . . . The better novels in English in the past twenty years participate in this larger debate. If Rushdie has ushered a new era of Indian writing in English, it has to be acknowledged that he was more a sign of the times than their creator.[26]

Even a cursory glance at the range of well-publicized novels published during this timeframe reveals the predominance of the national narrative mode and, with it, a preoccupation with the ideas of nationhood as valorized in public historiography. One of the earliest national narratives of this generation, I. Allan Sealy's *Trotternama*, was published soon after Rushdie's novel, and like *Midnight's Children*, it was originally conceived with a narrator born on the midnight hour of India's independence—an idea Sealy decided to drop after reading *Midnight's Children*. Even so, in keeping with the paradigm of the national allegory, in Sealy's novel the fate of the narrator mirrors that of the nation. Shashi Tharoor's *The Great Indian Novel* (1989), probably one of most direct formulations of the genre, retells the Sanskrit epic *The Mahabharata* in the landscape of colonial and postcolonial India, beginning with the Congress-led anticolonial movements and continuing into political intrigues and rivalries in the independent nation, all on a national scale. Vikram Chandra's *Red Earth and Pouring Rain* (1995) uses tropes and devices associated with magical-realist narrative modes and traditions of Indian oral storytelling to narrate another version of this pan-Indian story, this time beginning with the fading glory of the Mughal dynasty and simultaneously the rise of the British East India Company. Chandra's narrator in this novel, Sanjay, is a figure somewhat similar to Rushdie's Saleem. Reincarnated after death as a monkey, he tells the entertaining tale in order to stave off Yama, the god of death. Published the same year, Mukul Kesavan's *Looking Through Glass* similarly employs magical-realist narrative reversals, and it recounts the final years of the Indian struggle for independence, this time from the perspective of a Muslim family in 1940s Uttar Pradesh. Clearly, apart from the fact that the proliferation of such fictions gestures toward a critical juncture of Indian history and historiography, the influence of Rushdie's text remains overwhelming. This influence is made clear not only in the thematic concerns but the narrative and stylistic methodologies of these novels. As Rajeshwari Sunder Rajan points out, "to write fiction in English in India today is to write in the shadow of Salman Rushdie's *Midnight's Children*."[27] It is abundantly clear that this influence ends up operating in a theoretical complicity with Fredric Jameson's valorization of the Third World national allegory.

The pan-Indian public domain, in most of these novels, overcomes the regional topographies that are often admittedly inscribed in these fictional spaces. Bombay is important in Rushdie's work, and Sealy's protagonist comes from a Parsi background; the topos of Tharoor's *The Great Indian Novel*, however, is pan-Indian to the point of being unrecognizable. By an act of a magical geographic conflation, a country (sometimes, the entire subcontinent) with a billion people and a plethora of major regional languages and cultures are presented in a unified topos that is best recognizable to the metropolitan theorists of the postcolonial novel as well as to the Anglo-American literary marketplace. Meenakshi Mukherjee argues that the anxiety of Indian-English fiction to portray a pan-Indian milieu contrasts with the vernacular literatures' focus on the local and the concrete. Her argument echoes Achebe's conferral of the status of Nigerian national literature on only what is written in English but without, it seems to me, the affirmative, indeed, celebratory force of Achebe's observation. In her essay on *Midnight's Children*, Bishnupriya Ghosh sums up Mukherjee's point: "Writers in English always create a unified imaginative topos out of Indian heterogeneity, while bhasha (literally, "language," but here implying the vernacular) writers are more tuned to local and regional specificities."[28] Indeed, in their focus on concretely evoked regional specificities, the social-realist as well as the fabulist modes of vernacular narratives indicate a commitment to what Amit Chaudhuri calls "cultures and localities that are both situated in, and disperse the idea of, the nation."[29] That many of these localities are not even within the physical boundaries of India is indicated in the range of examples Chaudhuri provides, which includes the Bengali village Nischindipur of Bibhuti Bhushan Bandopadhyay as well as the Africa he had never been to; the London, Sylhet, or Lucknow of Quarratulain Hyder's Urdu short stories; and the Czechoslovakia of Nirmal Verma's Hindi fiction. The spatial, demographic, and historiographic practice of the national allegories, on the other hand, is, to a large extent, an imaginative creation of the urban, liberal elite from a pan-Indian middle class; it reflects the homogenizing urge that these novels conceal under their surface disruptiveness. The model of the national allegory therefore creates the "imagined community" par excellence, a trope that finds increasing resonance in a postmodern world where globalization and diaspora are overarching realities for larger and larger numbers of immigrant populations. That the center of the commercial reception and critical recognition of this narrative model is often the diasporic intellectual community is hardly surprising, but the resultant canonicity of the genre does not do justice to the plenitude of alternative imaginations of time and space that have gradually come to be overshadowed under their predominance.

Dallying with Dailiness: Amit Chaudhuri's Flâneur Fictions

The predominant literary climate in India following the publication and canonization of *Midnight's Children* in some significant ways resembles that of South Africa in the late apartheid years, in its preoccupation with the upheavals in the public spheres, especially those of a certain spectacular significance. Just as an urgent concern with a traumatized public sphere has defined the dominant genre of South African protest literature, a valorization of the Nehruvian model of the secular socialist nation has determined the novelistic national allegory in India. While the limitations of fetishizing the spectacle in literary narratives have been pointed out by a number of South African activists, critics, and writers, Njabulo Ndebele's "Rediscovery of the Ordinary" most clearly lays down the terms of this critique by calling for an engagement with minute, mundane details of "intimate knowledge" as opposed to the "spectacular" events of the public domain. If the uneventfulness of the ordinary has been understood by twentieth-century theorists of the ordinary to enable a perspective from which to better appreciate events, Ndebele has richly demonstrated this understanding within the embattled cultural politics of the global South, where the relation between the ordinary and the event does in fact form the subject of some of the most vital debates.

Within the domain of Anglophone Indian literature, the writer who bears an intriguing affinity to the polemical position once occupied by Ndebele in South African literary culture is Amit Chaudhuri. Chaudhuri has been the most articulate voice in expressing a persistent critique of the ethos of the national allegory that had, at one point, come to be nearly synonymous with Anglophone Indian literature. The clearest enunciation of this critique has been *The Picador Book of Modern Indian Literature*, which he has edited, in particular, the essays that form the editorial introduction to the volume.[30] In these essays, Chaudhuri points out that notwithstanding the national allegory's claims to a subversive and experimental narrative form, the genre is driven by an ideological conformity to the Nehruvian vision of modern India. Like Ndebele, therefore, Chaudhuri has been the most significant dissenting voice amid the general narrative valorization of the dramatic events of mainstream history. Intriguingly, like Ndebele, Chaudhuri is a critic who is also a well-known writer of fiction. Like Ndebele's *Fools*, moreover, Chaudhuri's fiction has been an implicit critique of the existing preoccupation with the valorized notions of postcolonial nationhood. Chaudhuri explores the ordinary and the idiosyncratic in a private sensibility, refusing, in the process, its easy alliance with the mainstream public sphere. While Chaudhuri does not directly use Ndebele's term "the ordinary," his own novels focus on the same theoretical problematic that the "ordinary" delineates. His fiction illustrates how the revelatory power of the mundane in the everyday life of private individuals troubles the constructions of spectacular nationhood that shape the narrative model of the national allegory.

Thus, like Ndebele, Chaudhuri provides a valuable alternative tradition of contemporary postcolonial writing that deserves far greater attention than it has received so far. The publication of his anthology in 2001 is a pivotal moment in the articulation of this tradition. Chaudhuri makes this clear most strikingly at a talk he gave at Columbia University in the fall of 2002. In that talk, he described his anthology as his best work of fiction so far. The oxymoronic appeal of such a claim overshadows the statement's indirect hint at an ideological conflict, which indicates why this claim is especially striking. Not only has this conflict affected the disciplinary paradigms of world Anglophone literary studies, but it has also decisively shaped the evolution of English studies on the whole, especially within its institutionalized spaces, which have increasingly been rent apart by the conflicting ideologies of literary theory and creative writing. Among other things, the strain of deconstructive irreverence initiated in the 1970s, more often than not, still keeps theory and criticism at an unfriendly distance from each other. A version of the liberal humanist impetus in literature that had produced poet-critics in the 1930s and 1940s—on both sides of the Atlantic—on the other hand, continues to be a relative rarity, more so within the academy.

It is, however, an odd mixture of this poststructuralist skepticism and a mistrust of this very skepticism that shapes the ways in which the role of writer and critic come together in the career of Chaudhuri, who has, since 1991, published five novels, a collection of short stories, a volume of poetry, the anthology mentioned above, a collection of essays, and a critical study of D. H. Lawrence's poetry, based on his Oxford doctoral thesis. Clearly, it is the very importance of deconstructive criticism in the significantly titled *D. H. Lawrence and "Difference"* that impels Terry Eagleton to crystallize the conflicted relationship between theory and creative writing in acrid sexual satire. "A male theorist in a roomful of male poets," Eagleton writes in his review essay on Chaudhuri's book, "is usually made to feel, spiritually speaking, that he is decked out in spangled tights and a tutu."[31] Chaudhuri, on the other hand, he rightly argues, "finds Derrida's theories congenial not in spite of being a distinguished fiction writer and poet himself, but because of it."[32]

But a more comprehensive reading of Chaudhuri's works shows us that Eagleton is only half right and that Chaudhuri can be notably uneasy about deconstructive methodologies as well. In the preface to his book on Lawrence, Chaudhuri writes:

> My suspicion of theory came from being the kind of writer I was, and still am to a certain extent; the writer who believes that language can transform reality. As post-structuralist theory questions the independent existence of a "reality" outside signification, and endlessly delays the connection of signifier to signified, sign to meaning, it is easy to see why a writer who believed what I did would be in conflict with it. At the same time, curiously, critical theory liberated my quest to articulate my own "difference" as reader and writer, and the "difference" of my historical relationship with English literature. It enabled me to transfer my own "difference" to that site of unity and wholeness, "Englishness."[33]

This ambivalence toward poststructuralism goes not only to the heart of Chaudhuri's fiction but also shapes his complementary role as a novelist and a critic. In his case, moreover, such roles together enact a striking critique of some of the most dominant narratives—again, in both fictional and theoretical senses of the term—of postindependence Anglophone Indian fiction.

In his introduction to *The Picador Book of Modern Indian Literature*, Chaudhuri objects to the application of poststructuralist critiques of notions of realism and authenticity in the context of Indian cultural production. Within the discursive space of twentieth-century Western philosophy, poststructuralism critiqued such notions as they were modeled during the European Enlightenment, though some philosophers like Derrida trace such notions back to the origins of Western metaphysics. The radical rupture of reality enacted by the Anglophone Indian novels modeled on the frequently magic-realist, national allegoristic tradition of Salman Rushdie's *Midnight's Children*, Chaudhuri argues, reproduces this poststructuralist skepticism of "realism" and "authenticity" within an Indian context.[34] This reproduction of poststructuralist unease, he suggests, should itself be taken with skepticism, as it often does violence to indigenous traditions where notions of "realism," "authenticity," and "truth" have not always had the same uneasy position they have held in many Western traditions. Perhaps unsurprisingly, Chaudhuri's concern here reveals a humanistic faith that shapes the depiction of the mundane through a certain investment in realist narration that poststructuralist theory, and postmodernist fiction following it, has severely ruptured. In his introduction to a collection of his essays and reviews put together in 2008, he writes: "My own explorations in tracing a trajectory, an arc of Indian 'reality' and the mundane—especially in the face of epic and fantastic narratives that Indian literature has been made synonymous with—attest, hopefully, to the fact that the humanism I speak of is a critical resource, partly because its own true location is now peripheral and ambiguous."[35] Such a humanism, and the realism that embodies it, according to Chaudhuri, "has been a fundamental and unquestioned component of Indian art, from classical dance to the epics of Valmiki and Vyasa, the court poetry of Kalidasa, and the modern lyrics of Tagore," unlike, what he calls the uneasy centrality of realism in Western culture.[36] As controversial as these large claims may be, they deserve critical attention not only in their demonstration of an alternative ethos to the category of the postcolonial national allegory but also with respect to a reading of Chaudhuri's distinctive oeuvre of fiction, which has been largely marginalized in critical studies of Anglophone Indian literature.

Chaudhuri's own fiction is less driven by a nationally ambitious political or historical narrative than by the literal evocation of the everyday lives of people in specifically evoked regional settings. More often, in fact, Chaudhuri is less interested in such larger narratives than he is in their odd, local variations, not in the public sphere but within idiosyncratic spaces of the domestic domain. There is a moment in his first novel, *A Strange and Sublime Address*, when during a relaxed morning at home, the uncle of the novel's ten-year old protagonist, Sandeep, comes across three young boys from his family occupied in a game of role-playing, in which they pretend to be "freedom-fighters." Suddenly, the uncle is provoked by the fact that Sandeep has chosen to impersonate Mahatma Gandhi. Excitedly, he champions the Bengali nationalist Subhas Chandra Bose over Gandhi, delivering a passionate tirade against Gandhi, which becomes both politically meaningful and circumstantially hilarious: "By a magical suspension of disbelief, he forgot that he was talking to Sandeep and Abhi and Babla; he saw, in front of him, three conservative, pro-Congress intellectuals."[37]

A moment such as this has symbolic importance in Chaudhuri's fiction. It is not so much a trivial moment itself (indeed, its political implications mark it as anything but trivial) as it is a metaphor for the power of the trivial in the face of the grander political narratives of anticolonial struggle. It is, as such, a metafictional moment, in which something as idiosyncratic and private as a children's game reveals the place of a significant motif in the national anticolonial narrative, namely, the reception of its key figure, Mahatma Gandhi. The incident of the role-playing game, moreover, illustrates the interdependent relationship between everyday life and the configuration of locality. In his passionate articulation of a "local teleology and ethos"—to borrow Arjun Appadurai's phrase in his essay "The Production of Locality"—Chhotomama (literally, "youngest maternal uncle") exemplifies a local subject, a crucial concept in the tradition of fiction embodied in Chaudhuri's work. Local knowledge, Appadurai argues, is inextricably linked to the production of local subjectivities and local neighborhoods, wherein they are recognized and organized, as Chhotomama's subjectivity here organizes itself through its interpellation into regional political ideologies.

Gandhi, while considered the most significant national leader of modern India and the celebrated champion of nonviolent resistance globally, has often been the subject of intense criticism in India, for a range of reasons, from his role—or the lack of it—in the sensitive issue of partition of India to his championing of certain groups and individuals in the course of the freedom struggle. This is not the place to elaborate on such controversies, but some of the fiercest criticisms of Gandhi have been regional; in Bengal, this has sometimes taken the form of the near-fanatical deification of the Bengali nationalist Netaji Subhas Chandra Bose and a subsequent criticism and occasional vilification of Gandhi. Gandhi was known to have favored Nehru over Bose in national politics, which contributed to Nehru's rise to prominence. Bose eventually formed his own militant movement of freedom struggle, with alliances that remain somewhat controversial. In the rather comical behavior of Sandeep's uncle, we have a very realistic example of this political regionalism.

The location of a larger political narrative in a site of familial behavior not only resonates with the immediate textures of quotidian life, but it also has a special significance from the perspective of revisionist historiography. Some South Asian historians have recently argued that even revisionist histories have ignored the family even while integrating other peripheral categories and voices. "The history of the family," Indrani Chatterjee writes in *Unfamiliar Relations: Family and History in South Asia*, "has long been the poor relation in the great household of South Asian history, which enthusiastically adopted the study of colonialism and nationalism, and has increasingly made room for peasants, women and the environment."[38] While the family occupies a central place in many of the national allegories with regard to their plot structures, more often than not the private and the familial turn out to be allegorical reflections of national structures and political events and lack significance in their own right. Chaudhuri's fiction, however, places an almost exclusive emphasis on such familial spaces, through which the tangible texture of locality is woven.

The provincial, for Chaudhuri, is a rich and unique space where the banal is produced in a kind of immediate materiality. In *A Strange and Sublime Address*, through the young eyes of Sandeep, we see middle-class Calcutta, a city caught between the opposing forces of the metropolitan and the provincial; suffering economic and political stagnation, it is still suffused with a unique cultural flavor. The short novel describes Sandeep's stay in Calcutta, which he and his parents visit from their home in Bombay to spend a summer with the family of his mother's relatives. The everyday life of this family is the subject of this novel, but through Sandeep's eyes, the very banality of this life is rendered magical. The novel opens with an affirmation of the unattractive banality of this ambience and marks Sandeep's first glimpse of this world: "He saw the lane. Small houses, unlovely and unremarkable, stood face to face with each other."[39] The "unlovely" and "unremarkable" houses are synecdochic of the protagonist's experience of Calcutta on the whole. In his evocation of the subdued magic of the drearily provincial, Chaudhuri shows a strong aesthetic affiliation with the major regionalists of European modernism, especially Joyce. The "strange and sublime address" in the novel's title is a trope that foregrounds the porous borders of the provincial, through which it miraculously blends into the universal. It is the address Sandeep finds written on the first pages of his cousin Abhi's book:

> Abhijit Das
> 17 Vivekananda Road
> Calcutta (South)
> West Bengal
> India
> Asia
> Earth
> The Solar System
> The Universe[40]

It is an address strikingly reminiscent of what Stephen Dedalus writes on the flyleaf of his geography textbook in Clongowes Wood College:

> Stephen Dedalus
> Class of Elements
> Clongowes Wood College
> Sallins
> County Kildare
> Ireland
> Europe
> The World
> The Universe[41]

The provincial, in both these instances, is on the periphery of the British Empire (in Chaudhuri's case, the *former* British Empire); intensely aware of its status as peripheral, the provincial shows a longing for the center, which is implicitly identified with the realm of wider possibilities, of the exciting and the extraordinary. But just the way the extraordinary fails to transform fully the banal in the epiphany, the provincial, even in its longing for the metropolitan, does not abandon its paradoxical centrality within this strange and sublime address. The banal materiality of the provincial, in a state of perpetually unfulfilled longing for the metropolitan, energizes the regionalist aesthetics in such fictions, in late-twentieth-century Calcutta as much as in late-nineteenth-century Dublin.

A colonially inflected local literary culture offers, for Chaudhuri, one of the richest spaces for this dialectic of the provincial and the metropolitan. Perhaps the most fully developed illustration of this curious model of what one might call cosmopolitan provincialism is to be found in the figure of the private tutor in the story "Portrait of an Artist," a story with a noticeably Joycean title. The "mastermoshai," a title that is roughly translated as the tutor (more literally, the reverend master), is a classic figure of banal Bengali provincialism inflected by a colonially inherited model of cultural cosmopolitanism. He personifies a culture where the banality of the provincial and the excitement of the cosmopolitan exist in a kind of symbiosis without intruding upon each other's authority. There is a historical logic to this apparent contradiction, to be sought in the nineteenth-century phenomenon of the Bengal Renaissance, a movement of social reform and cultural production unprecedented in the history of the province. It is a movement that ushered a colonial modernity and a culturally hybrid middle-class sensibility, a quotidian version of which we see in mastermoshai. Provincial cosmopolitanism is the defining feature of his social persona as well as his cultural sensibility. On his very first meeting with the autobiographically modeled narrator, who writes poetry, mastermoshai asks, "in an English accent tempered by the modulations of Bengali speech: 'Are you profoundly influenced by Eliot?' "[42] The odd friendship that develops between the sixteen-year-old boy and the middle-aged man grows through the mutual cultivation of a literary imagination informed by the aesthetics of European modernism reshaped in the provincial Bengali sensibility. Thus Sartre, Camus, and Heidegger shape their discussions, which are punctuated by assertions such as "Every writer needs his Pound." Their relationship, which also sees itself as emulating that of Leopold Bloom and Stephen Dedalus in Joyce's *Ulysses*, grows around this unique dialectic of the provincial and the cosmopolitan, becoming:

> a friendship that could have formed only in a country with a colonial past. Even more provincial, and marginal to Europe, than Dublin was in the early twentieth century, was Calcutta at the century's close. Trams, rickshaws,

markets, office buildings with wide, creaking stairs, bookshops, little magazines, literary critics, uncles, aunts, created this Dublinesque metropolis of which mastermoshai was a part.[43]

"Metropolis" is something of a paradoxical word to describe such a cultural setting. Part of Calcutta's "metropolitan" nature, in fact, hinges on its inherent cultural longing for worlds outside its spatial and temporal frontiers, its perpetual dream of the dramatic in the middle of its banal, local reality. Such is the peculiarly resolved synthesis of the banal and the dramatic through which the narrator gets the final glimpse of this world, of his cousin literally on stage, "dressed in silk and costume jewelry as a medieval king," but who is, in the end, shaped by his awareness that "Calcutta is his universe; like a dewdrop, it holds within it the light and colours of the entire world."[44]

The dialectic of the cosmopolitan and the provincial also appears in his second novel, *Afternoon Raag*, which consists of a series of sketches about the life of an Indian graduate student in England moving back and forth between Oxford, where he studies, and Bombay, where his parents live. The ways in which representations of the ordinary and the dramatic, the local and the global, are placed in an almost dialectical relation with each other is heightened not only by the "foreignness" of the novel's Oxford locale but also through subdued reminders that this particular "foreignness" has a special relevance to the colonial history that shapes the protagonist's character. It also reminds us that definitions of the "local" are never absolute, just as the way banality, even though it is frequently conceptualized universally, can only be concretely apprehended at a local level. This is how disparate forms coexist and even merge in the Oxford room of another student:

> The books had significant titles on their spines, narrating stories of crises in faraway countries, conjuring the exciting imaginary worlds that graduates inhabit. Yet the global concerns expressed in the titles fitted in quite unremarkably with the marginal life in Shehnaz's room, with its teacups and electric kettle, and with the green, semi-pastoral life in Oxford.[45]

Such a celebration of the duality of the ordinary and the exceptional, the local and the distant, the crucial and the marginal, puts each side in perspective. It critically defines the spirit and ethos of student life—and in a larger sense, the contradictory life-worlds inhabited by intellectuals. What remains understated, however, is the transcultural significance of this duality, wherein "the green, semi-pastoral life in Oxford" is an object of colonial desire for the upper-middle-class Indian student. So are "the exciting imaginary worlds" of "faraway countries," whose awareness has been historically instilled through the cultural and ideological effects of imperialism, which have radically reoriented the spatial imagination of the colonial subject. While life in Oxford constitutes in the subject's immediate present, the faraway countries remain elusive, shaping the duality of fulfillment and deferral of desire that in turn molds the movement between the dramatic and a banalized everyday. The dialectical nature of this relationship is evident in the way the public and the private, the ordinary and the grand, the near and the distant, curiously become the most distinct at the very moment they seem to merge into one another, as in the description of the magazine seller in the Bombay neighborhood where the protagonist takes leisurely walks:

> In the midst of all this, there was a bit of unexpected picturesque detail, an intrusion of rural India, in the magazine-stall, bamboo poles holding up a canopy of cloth, which sheltered a long sloping table.... The magazines were filled with speculations about politicians who looked a little like the magazine seller, but lacked his sense of time and place. Together, they composed an unending Hindu epic, torn apart by incest and strife and philosophy. While the political magazines were like minutely detailed family histories, there was another kind of magazine that spoke exclusively of individuals, and described a happy secular life of evening parties and personalities that seemed as remote from government as the wood-fire-lit lives of villages. But, from time to time, the two kinds of magazines would merge into one another.[46]

The fragment of quotidian detail is not only the space where private sensibilities and subjectivities are constructed, but it also creates the venue where the relation of the private with the public—always idiosyncratic and ambivalent—is spectrally etched. The banality and triviality of the details motivate both the quest for meaning and the perpetual deference of that very meaning. Isolated glimpses of quotidian reality occupy the peripheries of the aesthetic canons of traditional realist narratives that string such realities together in functional or referential forms to construct stories with beginnings, middles, and ends.

In his essay on Chaudhuri, Terry Eagleton identifies Chaudhuri's involvement with Derridean textualities "as a play of traces, revisions, supplements, erasures, repetitions and the like."[47] The deconstructive strain is marked in Chaudhuri's fiction through the endless fractured strings of whimsically culled ordinary details, intermittent views of daily rituals, ruptured characterizations and subjectivities, and, most of all, in the endless play of difference that continually places affective imaginations of the banal and the extraordinary in a dialectical relationship with each other. In *A Strange and Sublime Address*, as the evenings bring the daily power cuts and the city is immersed in darkness for an hour or two, Sandeep's uncle takes his sons and nephew for a walk along the streets. The stray glimpses into people's lives, from windows and house porches, seems to Sandeep to contain infinitely interesting stories that were, however, never destined to completion or fullness:

> But why did these houses seem to suggest that an infinitely interesting story might be woven around them? And yet the story would never be a satisfying one, because the writer, like Sandeep, would be too caught up in jotting down the irrelevances and digressions that make up life, and the life of a city, rather than a good story—till the reader would shout "Come to the point!"—and there would be no point except the girl memorizing the rules of grammar, the old man in the easy-chair fanning himself, the house with the small, empty porch that was crowded, paradoxically, with many memories and possibilities. The "real" story, with its beginning, middle and conclusion, would never be told, because it did not exist.[48]

Such stories—or rather the promise of them—are the very stuff of Chaudhuri's fiction. They are, moreover, metafictional in the way they foreground the ethos of his work. Unlike many introspective writers, who delve deeper into the human psyche, for Chaudhuri the deepest wonders of life seem to lie on its very surface, on the quotidian materiality of its daily texture, indeed, in the banality of their aesthetic. Implicit in this vision is a certain impatience with what Michael Taussig calls the "ideational." This vision moves away from conceptual depths, staying rather on the more immediate plane of the "imageric and sensate."[49] Different from a determined linear or vertical intellectual pursuit, it is, as Taussig describes it, a "flitting and barely conscious peripheral vision perception unleashed with great vigor by modern life," the vision that has as its ideal archive "the modern everyday."[50] The sense of interiority generated in this vision is much too fickle, much too distracted to believe that any one fragment of this fabric contains a sustained significance that is worth a deep pause. This is where the roving eye becomes something of a deconstructive reader who believes that there is no single monolithic text to be read but rather an endless number of fragmentary texts, equally pleasant and subversive. Like the stories Sandeep suspects are contained in the houses he sees, they never quite add up to a comprehensive whole, even though they teasingly promise wholeness.

It is no coincidence that one of the most notable paradigms of South Asian revisionist historiography, the Subaltern Studies Collective, has used poststructuralist, especially deconstructive, reading strategies to retrieve figures and spaces marginalized by both colonial and bourgeois-nationalist models of history writing. As Vinayak Chaturvedi argues in his introduction to an anthology of subaltern historiography, Subaltern Studies has transitioned from a collective producing Marxian histories of colonial India to one practicing poststructuralist readings crossing temporal, regional, and disciplinary boundaries.[51] However, it is in the work of Dipesh Chakrabarty that we witness the most intriguing version of the collective's relation with deconstruction. Deconstructive reading strategies are crucial in Chakrabarty's identification of a specific kind of disciplinary crisis, or aporia, within the professional discourses of history: "Subaltern pasts thus act as a supplement to the historian's pasts. They are supplementary in a Derridean sense—they enable history, the discipline to be what it is and yet at the same time show what its limits are."[52]

I would suggest that the isolated fragments of the quotidian foregrounded in Chaudhuri's fiction approximate the effects of such subaltern pasts, not only with respect to the dominant canons of historiography but also with those of novelistic aesthetics, especially in postcolonial Anglophone Indian contexts. The deconstructive aspect, however, remains only a subdued undertow in Chaudhuri's work. The consequent narrative of delicate "supplementarity" in his work, in fact, echoes the strand of subaltern history theorized by Chakrabarty in an earlier essay, which appears to be something of a theoretical predecessor to the "time-knots" and "subaltern pasts" in *Provincializing Europe*. The "fragmentary and episodic" model of history he had proposed in his 1995 essay "Radical Histories and Question of Enlightenment Rationalism" seems very much to be the historiographic equivalent of what Chaudhuri achieves in his fictional narration.[53] Chakrabarty's essay, however, is a negotiation of the somewhat contesting worldviews of Marxism and deconstructive philosophies.

Certain Marxists may object to such parallels between models of subaltern history and Chaudhuri's fiction, which often demonstrate many of the social and intellectual elitisms of European modernism. Nevertheless, I insist on the parallels, encouraged by Chakrabarty's assertion that subaltern pasts constitute a disciplinary and not an identitarian issue—that is, they are more intimately tied to crises in the discipline of history than to marginal identities. As Chakrabarty puts it, subaltern pasts can very well belong to privileged groups, specifically to theoretically intractable moments and situations in their lives. Chaudhuri's fiction is a perfect example of this, in its preoccupation with the marginal moments of the everyday in the lives of the middle and the upper-middle class of urban India. It is the banality of these moments that his fiction celebrates so lyrically, as opposed to the fully developed narrative significance in fiction that places more weight on its realist mission.

Naomi Segal argues that banal objects exist in naturalist and symbolist fiction in radically different capacities. In naturalistic fiction, they are strictly functional and referential, thus contributing to the creation of setting or the depiction of characters. They are located, in most cases, in their positions of conventional material utility. Symbolist fiction culls a few objects from everyday life and elevates them into transcendental metaphoric grandeur, ironically heightening their banality by this paradoxical act. The anonymous banality of the quotidian object or practice that is resistant to either modes of meaning making therefore comes into existence only when the two modes clash, "when objects which have no place in the poet's world intrude and make their claim."[54] The transformation of elements of the everyday into the banal is thus a narrative act, one that creates a paradoxical aesthetic value.

A roving eye such as Sandeep's in *A Strange and Sublime Address* or the young graduate student's in *Afternoon Raag* takes in a profusion of marginal details: fish and chicken bones on discarded dinner plates, swirls of dust on city pavements, the random collection of magazines hung up on jute strings in magazine shops. All of these exemplify "un-poetic" objects that intrude "in the poet's world," here represented with a lyricism rarely associated with them. Moreover, none of these details is integrated within the referential order of naturalistic fiction, but neither are they quite elevated into symbolic grandeur. The only meaning that materializes is through this very difference or deferral, whereby the reader always moves on to the next detail, toward a promised wholeness that never materializes. Chaudhuri's fiction, however, does not enact a drastic break with realism, as magic-realist narratives are likely to do. The idiosyncrasies of his fictional choices are not that of a man physically slipping into the past or a child possessing the powers of radio transmission but of the odd, momentary gaze on an old, cracked table in an English pub or of the careless lines of music sung by a man in his shower. Like the peripheral textual fragments of texts with which deconstruction is preoccupied, such as a footnote, a parenthesis, a punctuation mark, or a casual allusion, such markers of the quotidian remain perpetually supplementary, never adding up to a coherent narrative. The cross-cultural milieus of the fictions, moreover, make it clear that banality is not only a predominantly local construct but is also an important precondition for the evocation of the local.

The awareness that ordinariness—or, for that matter, extraordinariness—is a cultural construct is never far removed from Chaudhuri's fiction. It is striking how often the conflicting production of such categories becomes a subject itself, not only within the culturally fractured subjectivities of diasporic characters like Sandeep, Jayojit, and the nameless Oxford graduate student but also within the ostensible unity of a given culture, where the identification of the ordinary and the dramatic, the familiar and the unfamiliar, is shown to be a historical act. The imagination of the growing child is a rich ground for the mutual interaction of the fantastic and the familiar. Shobha mami, the aunt in the story "Beyond Translation," is such a comforting source of familiarity to the children. Her presence frees up their minds to run wild in the realm of fantasy: "My aunt—whom I will call Shobha mami—hovered around as we sat with our books in our hands; her presence brought us comfort while our minds raced with demons, usurped kingdoms, seashores, and collapsing houses."[55] In *A Strange and Sublime Address*, the description of Sandeep's uncle's daily busy preparation before he rushes off to work hinges on a similar conflict of the banal and the mythical, creating a curious mood of comic urgency:

> He would become an archetype of that familiar figure who is not often described in literature—the ordinary breadwinner in his moment of unlikely glory, transformed into the center of his universe and his home. Over and over again, he would shout, "I'm late!" in the classic manner of the man crying "Fire!" or "Timber" or "Eureka!" while Saraswati and mamima scuttled around him like frightened birds.[56]

Ironically, the sole breadwinner of the family is bereft of this grandeur not because of his peripherality but in fact because of his very centrality—the essential and everyday nature of his business, which is the economic life of the whole structure. Within the larger spaces of public historiography, the juxtaposition of the uncle's anxious utterances with the same celebrated exclamations associated with some of the most phenomenal inventions of human civilization amounts to a sly commentary on the cultural value system that has left banality and grandeur to be such overdetermined categories.

But Sandeep's imagination is always ready to disorient, indeed, reverse such overdetermined categorization. If his uncle's breadwinning duties have been banalized by their regularity, Sandeep is eager to confer a mythical grandeur on his business activities, which cultural canons have reserved for bestowal elsewhere.

> He liked listening to his uncle talk about business. He liked it because his uncle's account of the small-business world always seemed like a suspense story or a myth or a fairy-tale, full of evocative characters that worked themselves slowly into his imagination; cheats, sophisticated two-timers, astringent moralists, clever strategists, heroic fighters, risk takers, and explorers. Each new business venture sounded like a new military onslaught, each new product like a never-before weapon capable of conquering the world added to a nameless arsenal.[57]

The staid, the ordinary, and the quotidian are in fact not just mythical on this plane of existence; they are the very source of life and its prime means of sustenance. When the most out-of-the-ordinary event in this novel—Sandeep's uncle's heart attack—upsets the routine pattern of the everyday, it is the familiar constellation of ordinary objects that reassures that all is not disrupted, that normalcy is still a possibility:

> The room, with its ancient, brown furniture, the clothes hanging from the clothes-horse, the timeless wall-lizard, the clock and the radio on the cupboard, the photographs and portraits of grandfathers and grandmothers, surrounded them, giving them a sense of objects and things that lived always in the present; it was a relief for them that there were so many things in the room that did not possess a past or a future.[58]

The immediacy of life asserts itself over the transcendental unreality of death through the familiar banality of the sociophysical space of the home. The assertion of social and physical immediacy can, in Chaudhuri's world, just as easily banalize death at the very moment that seeks to ritualize its sublimity, as in the Shraddh ceremony, something of a Hindu counterpart to the memorial service. This is what happens to Mr. Mitra, the middle-aged protagonist of the story "Real Time," in such a ceremony: "He felt bored; and he noticed a few others, too, some of whom he knew, looking out of place. Shraddh ceremonies weren't right without their mixture of convivial pleasure and grief; and he couldn't feel anything as complete as grief."[59] Boredom is the ultimate anticathartic emotion; it resists the social and psychological catharsis that the ritual of the Shraddh is ideally meant to achieve. The failure of this catharsis and the banalization of experience that it brings, however, constitute the very reality of the experience of living, which is defined by a longing for this affective catharsis as much as it is marked by the frustration of such a longing.

The delicate dialectic of the banal and the dramatic as constituent of the texture of everyday life becomes particularly vivid in the metafictional sensibilities of Chaudhuri's autobiographically inflected protagonists, whose engagement with the world effectively reflects on the way his fictional worlds are created in the author's mind. In *The Immortals*, the protagonist Nirmalya dreams of the sea. The Arabian Sea, which fringes the city of Bombay and lies adjacent to his family's residence, in these dreams takes on all-engulfing proportions, entering a cinematic frame that stretches the quotidian into the surreal: "But the balcony had become the front rows of a movie theatre, and the flat itself was like the inside of a cinema; a cinema that was elegant and in business, but strangely empty."[60] Yet this surreal world that visits him in the reality-stretching moments of his dream never entirely loses its familiar banality, a sense that stays with him as he wakes up in the morning: "Next morning, he woke up with a sense of the other world he'd visited still upon him, of having gone and returned from an elsewhere that was familiar, banal, and yet, unexpectedly, magnificently on the brink of destruction: he knew no one survived the flood."[61] Neither the banal nor the magnificent, in Chaudhuri's flâneur sensibility, is quite complete without the other, and if real life has a dreamlike quality about it, dreams, too, are magically haunted by the banality of the familiar.

Flânerie, however, in these novels is not a mere metaphor for the way the observant sensibility slides through the textures of quotidian life. As it is in texts by Baudelaire, Joyce, Woolf, and Eliot, flânerie is literalized in the way urban neighborhoods are evoked in Chaudhuri's fiction through the simultaneously attentive and distracted sensibility of its protagonists. Like Joyce's and Woolf's urban fictions, walking in the city plays a significant role in Chaudhuri's work. Sandeep walks through Calcutta during routine blackouts, Nirmalya meanders through Bombay, and there are the endless perambulations of the older protagonists in *Afternoon Raag* and *A New World*. In *Afternoon Raag*, it is the sensibility of the modernist urban flâneur that shapes the protagonist's sense of the city's spatiality: "There is no centre in Oxford, only different points of reference, from each of which the conception of the city is altered slightly."[62] For Jayojit in *A New World*, who comes from Iowa with his young son to visit his parents in Calcutta, the habit of flânerie provides something of a concrete remooring into the city's environment. Neighborhoods initially appear more alien and bewildering but eventually materialize through a familiar ordinariness:

> He felt somewhat conspicuous as he turned back; he didn't know why. Perhaps because people don't wander about and not go anywhere; perhaps this was what made him feel strange and doubtful and that he stood out. Everyone else, whatever they looked like, had somewhere to go to, or seemed to; and if they were doing nothing or postponing doing something, as some of these people squatting by the pavement, who seemed to be in part-time employment, were doing, it was for a reason. But the small journey—in the heat, constantly assailed by traffic on the small arc back had somewhat settled his thoughts.[63]

Flânerie has been read not only as a significant aesthetic experience of urban modernity, as it clearly is to the variously displaced characters in Chaudhuri's fiction, but also as one that reveals the cartography of power within such a modernity. While cultural anthropologists like Michel de Certeau have provided foundational theorizations of "everyday practices" such as walking, feminist critics like Rachel Bowlby and postcolonial readers like Enda Duffy have located specific modes of power politics within the modernist literary practice of flânerie.[64] In Chaudhuri's fiction, flânerie, perhaps more significantly than any other everyday practice, sets into motion the semiotic play of differences that not only define a deconstructive narrative aesthetic but also mark the fragmented nature of postcolonial subjectivities. It is this empowering play of differences that enables the Indian graduate student to conceive a decentered vision of the city of Oxford, the proverbial center of the intellectual and academic authority of the British Empire. For Jayojit, this play of differences revealed through his aimless walking stakes out both the startlingly unique color of the urban neighborhood and his own dislocation within it.

Chaudhuri's critical writing also reflects an intense awareness of the political significance of flânerie. He speculates on conditions that make the existence of the flâneur possible in the milieu of postcolonial Calcutta. Chaudhuri's writing on flânerie and its significance within modernist culture constitutes part of his reading of Dipesh Chakrabarty's "Meditations on the Limits of Western Notions of Modernity and History." It is an interesting place to find Chaudhuri's thoughts on flânerie because Chakrabarty's arguments about disciplinary crises of history writing, as I have tried to show above, resonate with the epistemological significance of the quotidian fragment in Chaudhuri's own work.

"In the Waiting Room of History," a review essay of Chakrabarty's *Provincializing Europe*, Chaudhuri identifies in the figure of the flâneur and the streets of Paris Walter Benjamin's conceptualization of "an alternative version of modernity and space" opposed to the paradigms of speed and progress set up by Hitler's autobahns. The flâneur, Chaudhuri argues, is a subversive reader of history, one who "deliberately relocates its meanings, its hierarchies."[65] This reading of the subversive flâneur assumes a pointed significance as Chaudhuri tries to locate the flâneur in colonial cities—Dublin and Calcutta. The possibility of the flâneur's existence in Calcutta, he argues, is related not only to the internal crises of Western notions of modernity but also to the manner in which such notions were valorized in nineteenth-century Bengal. His identification with one of the most celebrated quotidian activities in modern urban literature clearly resonates with his protagonists' penchant for bored, lazy flânerie as a way of mooring themselves within local and foreign cityscapes. But more importantly, it reflects, through the languorous, wandering quality of the fictions, the estranging effect of cross-cultural encounters. In a more recent essay on the Indian poet Arun Kolatkar, Chaudhuri invokes Benjamin's essay "The Return of the Flâneur." Benjamin's flâneur, he reminds us, is happy to trade grand historical monuments for "the scent of a single weathered threshold or the touch of a single tile."[66] Rushdie's *Midnight's Children* has inaugurated what he calls the "monumental view of Indian history in literature," celebrating "the great reminiscences, the historical frissons, everything that was so much junk to the flâneur."[67] Chaudhuri's own work, like that of Kolatkar, whom he so admires, points to an alternative tradition of Anglophone Indian writing, that of the flâneur's fascination with the fragments of dailiness.

Even though certain quotidian objects, habits, and practices continue to be important in Chaudhuri's fiction—such as that of walking in the city—the general texture and orientation of the quotidian transform themselves in his later work, partly because of shifts in the nature of the worlds they depict. The worldview of his fiction begins to change as it begins to depict the rapidly changing India of the 1990s, when drastic economic restructuring and shifts in political ideologies begin to cause noticeable alterations in people's values, attitudes, personal habits, and lifestyles. This movement becomes clear from his third novel, *Freedom Song*, onward. This novel is set in the Calcutta of the 1990s, caught between a decadent Communist government and the incoming forces of globalization. The narrative moves through the day-to-day incidents in the lives of a few families, whose members occupy such diverse roles as members of the local Communist party, organizers of Marxist street theater, and corporate troubleshooters for dying public companies. The novel marks a wistful, even nostalgic moment of the gradual passing away of the older, more organically connected, humanistic world of Chaudhuri's first two novels, whose lyrical style emanated from some essential quality of the life they portrayed. The new world is defined by globalized capitalism and advanced technology, with the disturbing rise of religious fundamentalism as the backdrop. In his first novel, the tantalizing sense of the everyday was produced by objects such as the maidservant's broom, "swiping away dust in an arc with its long tail," and "the tranquil bedsheets on the old beds." In "Real Time," a story in his 2002 collection, a call on a cell phone represents the intrusion of the banal, everyday reality of business and officialdom into the mournful sublimity of a memorial service.

Even though the politics of the shifting public sphere seem more urgent in some of his later work, his primary focus continues to be on the ambivalent nature of individual lives: on the fractured aggregations of private whims, desires, and ideals that are always held in unpredictable relationships with larger public ideologies and behavior patterns. What remains crucial in such portrayals is the subtle tension between the concrete, peculiar individuality of private lives and the collectivities they form, communities that are often imagined into existence. Such a coming together of individual, private selves from within the concealing folds of larger collectivities is exemplified in the Indian custom of arranged marriage between two people who, until the marriage proposal, have been strangers to each other. In *Freedom Song*, Bhaskar is about to have his life knotted to a stranger culled out of such an imagined community.

> And now a link was sought to be made between one person and another, between Bhaskar and a girl, who had been growing up all the while in the city secretly, while Bhaskar had been wearing half pants, and going to Gariahat market with Robi da to buy a water bottle and riding in trams, his shirt clinging to his back with sweat—someone, somewhere else, was growing up as well in a random and unpredictable way in a little self absorbed world of day-to-day desire.[68]

Chaudhuri is sociologically insightful in choosing a key ritual of Indian society that troubles Western conceptions of the public-private split. Even the most private and intimate of kinships, that of marriage, is organized not on the basis of preexisting personal relationships between individuals. Rather, it is contingent on the collective parameters of such kinships as decreed by society and religion, including the matching of caste and subcaste and the planetary positions on the prospective bride and groom's horoscopes. The social rite of arranged marriage is not only a very familiar one in the given cultural context but is, in fact, one of the defining customs of this society and its vital kinship structures. Yet it is a custom that comes as alien to many outside cultures, notably to the individualistic West. In his lyrical description of this custom, Chaudhuri retains an ambivalence that enfolds a sense of an outsider's wonder into the familiarity and the knowledge of an insider. It was not so much the "growing up" of the girl that was "secret" or "random and unpredictable" by itself. Rather, it is the suddenly conjured possibility of her being wedded to Bhaskar that has highlighted the strangeness of the fact that her past has been so utterly alien and anonymous to Bhaskar and his family, in spite of the insignificant physical and communal distance between them. But this sense of surprise and wonder sounds only an undertone in an otherwise unsurprised, detailed description of the entire social processes framing the arranged marriage from the vantage point of someone familiar and knowledgeable about such processes.

"The auto-ethnographic self," argues James Buzard, "makes omniscience its project, painstakingly representing its cultures in order to be seen to be absent from it: depicting the culture and erasing the acculturated self are the same enterprise."⁶⁹ A necessary ambivalence must therefore mark the autoethnographic self, whose literary exponents might include a writer such as Amit Chaudhuri as well as James Joyce, the figure who provided the immediate context for Buzard's argument. When the authorial consciousness represents a diasporic sensibility—be it the modernist artist in exile or a mobile, cosmopolitan novelist from the globalized present—such a sensibility becomes a natural vehicle of this ethnographic ambivalence. Brought up in Bombay but having spent eighteen of his adult years in England and living in Calcutta since 1999, Chaudhuri inhabits this ambivalence not only in relation to India but also, more specifically, to the Bengali culture and community that he writes about, whether in Bombay, Calcutta, or Oxford. If the "master narrative of ethnography," imperial in character, never loses "its footing in western rationality" even as it chronicles alien cultures,⁷⁰ the autoethnographic self necessarily troubles this clear schism between subject and archive, ethnographer and community. Inasmuch as Chaudhuri's fiction possesses traits of autoethnography, it must, as it does, refuse to commit itself fully either to the outsider's wonder or to the insider's easy familiarity.

The consequent perspective, here as well as in those of his novels that have diasporic protagonists, is always fractured. This fracture is doubtlessly accentuated by the description of Indian, indeed, regional cultural realities in a colonial language that has become an uneasy but integral postcolonial legacy, as Raja Rao famously articulated in his foreword to his novel *Kanthapura*.⁷¹ This focus on the familiar through this perspective that is almost but not quite familiar is crucial to the creation of the duality of the ordinary and the extraordinary so essential to Chaudhuri's fictions. This duality, articulated via culturally fractured subjectivities, indicates the fragmented, partial, and often subversive relationship of postcolonial cultures with European paradigms of modernity, which draws the attention of a historian like Dipesh Chakrabarty as much as it attracts a fiction writer like Amit Chaudhuri. Chaudhuri often creates the sense of an everyday defined in time and place by focusing on such elements of it that are of deepest familiarity within the culture but foreign and out of the ordinary to those outside it. It is a reminder that the quotidian is, more often than not, a deeply local construct. Yet it is this sense of the ordinary and the familiar as constructed within a culture that becomes the privileged producer of knowledge not only to outsiders but also to those half-insiders with fractured subjectivities that represent the culture's relationship with colonial modernity.

If Malinowskian anthropology had shared with modernist literature the intellectual climate that privileged the quotidian detail, it is fair to say that the valorization of the ordinary assumes new significances within the hybridities of postcolonial life, especially as portrayed through the fractured worldview of Anglophone literatures, which claim some of the most subtle and nuanced legacies of metropolitan modernism. If the very use of English in the literary representation of regional and communal Indian life is an event inseparable from colonial history, a subtle, unresolved tension between the local and the foreign, the ordinary and the striking, is naturally endemic to the linguistic fabric of the fictional worldview that is produced by this representation. Chaudhuri remarks on this in certain Anglophone Indian poets' use of "ordinary English words like 'door,' 'window,' 'bus,' 'doctor,' 'dentist,' 'station,' to suggest a way of life."[72] The slight angle at which everyday English words sat in the crevices of postcolonial Indian life is accentuated in the hybrid consciousness of Anglophone Indian literature, yet this was a subdued, elusive hybridity refusing to draw attention to itself. The space enclosed by this consciousness, Chaudhuri recalls, appeared far from spectacular—if anything, this was a banal, unpoetic world ironically evoked by poetry: "as a young reader, I remember being slightly repelled by the India of post offices and railway compartments I found in these poems; for I didn't think the India I lived in a fit subject for poetry."[73]

This tension between the familiar and the strange, or the narrative dialectic of the banal and the dramatic, constitutes much of the quiet appeal of Chaudhuri's fiction, from the ambivalent cast of its autoethnographic voice to the poetry of his prose. While more and more postcolonial Anglophone novels focus on the dramatic narratives of the development of the postcolonial nation-state, with the very good reason that those are important stories to tell, Chaudhuri, in both his fiction and criticism, provides a lyrical reminder that the aesthetic lack embodied in the quotidian fragments can be deceptive. Such fragments simultaneously enable the larger narratives and reveal their limits.

EPILOGUE
The Uneventful

At the heart of the genre of prose fiction exists a set of fundamental questions about time and narrative. If narrative is inextricably bound up with the category of time, what is—and what should be—the relative importance of the ordinary everyday and that of the major event? Is narrative essentially event bound? Is it embedded in what Franco Moretti calls a Hegelian "teleological rhetoric," wherein "the meaning of events lies in their finality" and where "events acquire meaning when they lead to *one* ending, and one only"?[1] Does the crux of narratives, as Moretti puts the question, rest on events, with the final event defining the grand teleological climax that gives meaning to everything that comes before? Should we make a distinction between the narrative politics pertaining to the ordinary and that attending to the special event? What about the banal? If banality is to be understood as the aesthetic of ideological inadequacy, can it not also be defined as the absence of the event and, by implication, of history?[2]

The same set of questions, repeatedly asked in this exchange, goes to the very heart of narrative as a fundamental category that defines fiction and history alike. Modernist fiction, with its radical reconceptualization of temporality, has been especially invested in this question, as Liesl Olson points out, for instance, in the difficulty faced by Virginia Woolf in the narration of the nonevent, or "the dullness of habitual experience",[3] as opposed to the pointed contours of trauma that stand out more easily in memory and are similarly more easily narratable. But while the sharpness of traumatic experience threatens to take over narrative, one of the great challenges of modernist fiction has been to find a narrative aesthetic of the ordinary and the nonevent, a concern it has intriguingly shared with the methods of historical narration in the twentieth century. The ordinary, therefore, has posed a challenge to both fiction and history, inasmuch as they are both rooted in the category of the narrative. The banal, however, is therefore more than the mere lack of event—it marks a cultural lacuna that, in the final instance, embodies a perceived exclusion from historical progress. Time, in this lacuna, is cyclical and iterative, produced in the sensibility of the marginal subject empty of historical as well as aesthetic significance.

Thomas Dumm suggests that we should maintain a distinction between a reading of the ordinary and a reading of the event. "Because both the normalization of life and the emergence of events entail the control and deployment of representations that originates in the space of the ordinary, we must learn to distinguish a politics of the ordinary from the politics that attends events and norms."[4] Making this distinction, however, is far less simple than it looks on the surface. Dumm's attempt to provide a politics of the ordinary alerts us to the fact that even if a distinction between "a politics of the ordinary from the politics that attends events and norms" is worth making, it is perhaps even more important not to lose sight of the fact that the construction of ordinary life is itself a political act. The social construction of the everyday by Dumm, and by Henri Lefebvre before him, hinges on the very disciplinary and normative function of the political. Yet, as Nadia Seremetakis reminds us, the politics of the ordinary are almost always overshadowed by the more dramatic politics of the event: "The sensory structure of everyday life is experienced as naturalized, almost cosmic time over and against which eruptive, 'sensational events' such as elections, performances, accidents, disasters, are profiled," with the latter as "almost pre-selected as narrated history."[5] When narrative, be it historical or fictional, is seduced into this easy but flawed distinction, the consequence is the recognized polarity between the everyday and the eruptive, the banal and the dramatic: "The polarity between the sensational and the mundane is also the dichotomy between sensational and the sensory in which the latter is left unmarked, unvoiced and unattended to, as a banal element of the everyday. The division distinguishes the anonymous flow of the everyday from that which is culturally, politically and biographically set aside as notable and discursive."[6]

At the heart of this false binary is also a misconstruction of the political, which now inheres exclusively in the sensational, which is understood to make its mark against the supposed apolitical neutrality of the banalized everyday.[7] But while this banalized everyday is imagined as neutral and continuous, what is forgotten is the fact that organic time is itself shaped through a political process.

This debate over the relative importance of the ordinary and the event begins with a provocative statement about the discursive production of history made by Fernand Braudel in his monumental history of the Mediterranean world. Here, Braudel describes the history of sensational events and warns against its seductive appeal: "A history of brief, rapid, nervous fluctuations, by definition ultra-sensitive; the least tremor sets all the antennae quivering. But as such it is the most dangerous of all, the richest in human interest, and also the most dangerous." Contrasted to this is Braudel's celebrated history of the *longue durée*: "there can be distinguished another history, this time with slow but perceptible rhythms."[8] This is the kind of history that, as Seremetakis argues in her reading of Braudel, helps to divert attention away from the sensation of the event and becomes "an analytical tool and empirical description of historical experience in everyday life."[9]

Braudel would have the historian cultivate a certain suspicion of, and intellectual distance from, the event that appears to puncture the gentler, submerged rhythms of time. These rhythms, over a longer period, reveal themselves to be a more reliable index of historical development than the brief, sporadically erupting event possibly can be. "Events are the ephemera of history," he offers his caveat well beyond the middle of his monumental history; "they pass across the stage like fireworks, hardly glimpsed before they settle back into darkness and as often as not into oblivion." The history that takes as its point of departure "the spectacular and often misleading pageant" of events, moreover, "tends to recognize only 'important' events, building its hypothesis only on foundations which are solid or assumed to be so."[10] Such history, however, overinvests itself in moments, which, no matter how spectacular or disruptive they might have appeared to their contemporaries or even subsequent historians relying on available documentary evidence, in the long run turn out to be misleading signposts. They fail to reveal the larger and far more significant patterns that underlie history, which are rarely contained within the framework of events, notwithstanding the aesthetics of spectacle often embodied within that framework.

Seremetakis's participation in the debate about the importance of the event is shaped by her interest in what she calls "modern sensory experience." She sees Braudel's suspicion of an event-driven history as rooted in an allegiance to the textures of everyday life. I hesitate, however, to attribute Braudel's suspicion of the event to a corresponding commitment to the ordinary everyday. The everyday, it would seem, is an ideal alternative space next to the kind of eruptive spectacle Braudel understands the event to be. But I would be careful to maintain a distinction between Braudel's model of *longue durée* and the kind of interest in the ordinary everyday that I myself share with Seremetakis. Braudel, as Paul Ricoeur indicates in his description of the new historical trends, rather emphasizes "a *social time* whose major categories—conjuncture, structure, trend, cycle, growth, crisis, etc.—are borrowed from economics, demography and sociology."[11] Even though a sensual immersion in the quotidian may very well intersect with the longer, gentler patterns of this social history, there is little in Braudel's writing that suggests that the historian actually imagined them as mutually interdependent.

The debate over the relative importance of the ordinary and the event defines the fundamental category of narrative. The narrative theorist Paul Ricoeur's engagement in this argument initiated by Braudel is driven by his belief that a crucial component at the heart of narrative—be it fictional or historical—is time. Any form of human experience, private or public, he reminds us, can only unfold along a temporal scheme. "The world unfolded by every narrative work," he writes at the very beginning of his two-volume *Time and Narrative*, "is always a temporal world." And then, later: "*time becomes human to the extent that it is articulated through a narrative mode; narrative attains its full meaning when it becomes a condition of temporal existence.*" His awareness of time as the central dimension that bridges history and aesthetic narrative leads Ricoeur to observe the historiographic shift from "political history toward social history."[12] If political history frames "the realm where events go off like explosions," the history of deep-lying trends is championed by the historians of the French Annales school, most notably Braudel, to whose preface to *The Mediterranean* Ricoeur refers carefully.

Ricoeur's intervention in the work of the Annales historians on the relation of history and event has influenced what is perhaps the most engaging debate about the epistemological status of the ordinary in the twentieth century. In his response to this debate about whether narrative can or cannot extricate itself from the event, Stanley Cavell refers to an earlier paper by Ricoeur (developed in *Time and Narrative*) and critiques Ricoeur's claim that narrative history cannot make a clean break with the unfolding of events.[13] "My contention here," Ricoeur is quoted in this paper as having said, "is that history cannot be radically eventless because it cannot break its ties with the kind of discourse which is the original 'place' of the notion of the event, i.e. narrative discourse."[14] This is the crucial point where Cavell objects to Ricoeur's argument. Narrative, according to Cavell, need not necessarily remain tied to the notion of the event. Essential to this disagreement is a dispute over the definition of an event. Cavell chooses to depart from the three criteria of an event that he reads Ricoeur as articulating: "that it is of something past, something done by or done to human beings, and something unrepeatable."[15] Clearly, such a definition of an event is rather exhaustive and consequently makes the possible extrication of narrative from the event difficult, if not altogether impossible. Cavell instead defines events as necessarily possessing a certain importance that leads to them being institutionalized, to some degree or the other, in the public sphere: "Obvious examples are the things high schools in my days used to call current events, the things newspapers call news, the things that appear on calendars of events."[16] Cavell's definition of the event here, it seems to me, is closer to Braudel's than to Ricoeur's—both emphasize, among other things, the event's obvious and immediate importance to its contemporaries, as news headlines tend to be. Ricoeur's reading of Braudel has already begun to set up a distinction between that which seeks out the dramatic and that which does not: "Braudel's opposition is evidently to a concept of event, one of whose negative features is that it *theatricalises* human existence."[17] By contrast, Cavell is drawn toward Braudel's interest in the collective, larger structures of history: "toward the long-term, endlessly repeated conditions of human life amounted to history's turning away from attention to the story of individual human beings in favor of attention to more or less anonymous collectivities."[18]

Cavell finally arrives at his own argument about narratives embedded in the ordinary and the marginal via Emerson's and Thoreau's commitment to the ordinary as an insight into immediate sensual experience. Crucial here is Emerson's idea of adjacency, of being in a state of unmediated proximity to the world and the laws of nature as opposed to the grand achievements of human culture and civilization canonized in history. "I embrace the common, I explore and sit at the feet of the familiar, the low," Cavell quotes Emerson as declaring. "Give me insight into today, and you may have the antique and the future worlds."[19] The historical narrative that is extricable from the event, accordingly, would not be the "*eventless*" but rather "the *uneventful*, seeking, so to speak, what is not out of the ordinary."[20] Moreover, the distinction between the history of events and that of the uneventful ordinary is not to be overstated. The ordinary, as Thomas Dumm points out in his reading of Cavell, is not just the small and the unnoticed that is opposed to the event: "the uneventfulness of the ordinary is the inevitable ground from which we may come to a better appreciation of events."[21] An unmediated engagement with the local and the ordinary, as opposed to a narrative fixation of dramatic or "important" events, therefore, not only enables a better understanding of history but also a more nuanced appreciation of the events themselves.

The polemic about the potential of the ordinary in the conversation about fiction in late-twentieth-century Anglophone cultural politics, I would suggest, is a crucial illustration of the relationship between ordinariness and narrative in the field of literary practice. In this context, the celebration of the ordinary is not only indicative of a radical aesthetic but, more importantly, a polemical departure from the national narratives about domination and resistance, which are configured as "events" in the sense Cavell and Braudel define them. Ndebele's project of rediscovering the ordinary not only seeks fiction's liberation from the spectacle of events in the national public sphere, but it also suggests the minute textures of the mundane everyday as the means through which fiction can actualize such a liberation. Added to the dichotomy of the ordinary and the event are two further sets of concerns—the national and the local, and the public and the private. The plea here is to move away from a telescopic view of history as it is shaped by a public consensus, usually in a national space, and toward the local and the immediate as it might be experienced in the immediacy of private sensibilities, often embedded in the quirks of regional cultures that do not add up to this national narrative. Such an immersion in the sensually evoked contours of the local and the immediate recalls Cavell's reading of Emerson, as the latter asks for an engagement with "the common, the low, the near" as opposed to the great and the remote.[22]

If some of the most significant genres of mid- and late-twentieth-century Anglophone fiction from the global South, such as protest literature and the national allegory, have shown an entwinement with history, it is the history of *events*—as variously pointed out by Braudel and Cavell—with which they have been preoccupied. Most of such events, moreover, have been what Seremetakis calls "sensational events"—elections, performances, disasters, wars, riots, and similar eruptions that the contemporary public sphere institutionalizes as "important." The consequence has been a necessary turning away from the ordinary, "endlessly repeated conditions of human life" that constitute a distinctive, if alternative, space for the political. The ordinary is subsequently used only as a passive backdrop against which such major events shape the course of historical narratives and define the ethos of fictional ones, often through a contingent formal investment in the fantastic, the theatrical, and the magical realist. Fiction and history have come closer together than ever in the national allegory, illustrating, in the process, Ricoeur's belief that narrative has to remain exclusively embedded in the temporal unfolding of events. The definition of the "event," moreover, remains predictable in such narratives—it is a canon of public-historic importance with which liberation movements and the postcolonial nation-state pedagogically interpellate its citizens. If, for Cavell, such events are what high-school education canonizes as current events, Amit Chaudhuri has argued that the postcolonial novel in India "rehearses a national narrative that every middle-class Indian child has learnt in school and which every member of the Indian ruling class is defined by: the narrative about colonialism and independence, and the idea of India as a recognizable totality"; that in fact the historiography offered in the Anglophone novelistic national allegory is likely to make some readers "feel that they have gone back to their Indian Certificate of Secondary Education textbook."[23]

Within the cultural politics of the Anglophone fiction from the global South, these arguments constitute a timely and powerful polemic. The more obvious historical burden that appeared to be placed on the postcolonial novel following the spectacular force and intensity of anticolonial movements, the resplendent moment of liberation, and the excitement of postcolonial development makes the fictional articulation of the mundane everyday a morally daunting project. Gestures of attention to the textures of ordinary life signify a large measure of courage for the writer of postcolonial fiction at a time when the novelist's mission still seems inextricably entwined to the still-unfinished business of decolonization and nation building in its full public glare. Ndebele's call for a "Rediscovery of the Ordinary" is, in fact, an undisguised plea for a politicomoral ambiguity in the face of what was arguably the most traumatic and troubling phase of his nation's history. A rediscovery of the marginal narratives of the banal, the quotidian, and the humdrum, often located far away from the din of mainstream History, is, at a moment like this, an act of intense political ambivalence for the postcolonial writer, who is always confronted with the kind of ethical urgency that draws him (usually a "him") farther and farther away from the quotidian materiality of local idiosyncrasies, which are usually hidden in the crevices of the private sphere. Such a rediscovery is, in that sense, politically irresponsible, in the face of the normative definition of the political that emerges in the theater of mainstream political struggle and the imaginary of postliberation progress. This capacity for moral idiosyncrasy not only resonates with Cavell's view of the ordinary as an alternative space for the historical, but it also recalls experimental modernism's radical introspection within the frames of the ordinary everyday at a time when the public sphere, within respective national contexts as well as worldwide, was being ripped apart by the seismic tremors of global war, warring political ideologies, the radical polarity of unforeseen economic prosperity and depression, and the gradual disintegration of colonial empires all around the globe. In my archive of fiction, I have chosen such moments from the early and the late twentieth century as the crucial occasions for the aesthetic celebration of banality in Anglophone fiction in the global British Empire.

In late-twentieth-century and early-twenty-first-century fictions, the focus is less on banality as a trope of colonial lack and desire than on the minutiae of ordinary life as a mark of empowering distance from the narratives of spectacle dominating the public sphere. The move from the affliction of banality to the polemical assertion of the ordinary as a significant site of the historical and the aesthetic charts a narrative that parallels the shift from colonial subjection to the growth and development of postcolonial cultural identity. The late-twentieth- and early-twenty-first-century narrative affirmation of the ordinary begins to consolidate an immensely significant momentum of self-reflection for Anglophone postcolonial literature. But it is an assertion that has gone largely unnoticed in the critical study of such literatures, which, to a great degree, still continues to see postcolonial literature as primarily welded to public historiography and invested, above all else, in mainstream political struggle.

There is a distinguished tradition of intellectuals of radical working-class movements who have warned against the fetishization of the spectacular moment and grand victories, asking instead for a focus on the preoccupations of quotidian life. While Guy Debord has explicitly stated that "the revolutionary proletariat . . . will have to renounce everything that transcends everyday life,"[24] Jacques Rancière has wondered about the implication of the revolutionary working class simply asking for a different everyday life as opposed to the more politically defined claims for better working conditions or for a share in factories.[25] Henri Lefebvre, reading the subservience of the everyday to capitalism, has argued for the centrality of the everyday in the revolution: "A revolution cannot just change the political personnel or institutions; it must change *la vie quotidienne*, which has already been literally colonized by capitalism."[26] More recently, Sonali Perera has urged moving beyond the mythologized spectacular moments of the revolution toward the smaller, quotidian struggles of the everyday, which continue *after* the revolution has taken place.[27] Such a movement, according to her, offers us the kind of understanding of nonmetropolitan working-class literature that is long overdue, dominated as it has been by a single-minded preoccupation with the resplendent moment of revolution celebrated in mainstream history.

Discourses of the minority experience—especially those connected to forms of imperialism—have been associated with overt trauma and dramatic spectacles of oppression for too long, as Ndebele had reminded his fellow citizens during the disturbing years of apartheid. Even from the perspective of liberation struggles, a limited version of art's relevance to politics has often hinged on the degree to which art has directly participated in the dramatic arena of such struggle. "The operative word here," Ndebele writes in his essay "Redefining Relevance," "is 'dramatic.'" And consequently, "what is dramatic is often defined according to the imperatives of *real politik*. According to this definition, the dramatic can easily be determined: strike action, demonstrations; alternatively, the brutality of the oppressive system in a variety of ways."[28] Much of this association, I repeat, is fully justified, as such oppressions worldwide, and the chain of tragic events they have historically unleashed, indeed have had dimensions of the spectacle. One only has to think of acts of colonial genocide, extermination of indigenous groups in settler colonies worldwide, and religious and communal violence in the global South for some of the most obvious examples. But just as the historical recording of such spectacles of oppression has not prevented theorists of working-class struggles from looking into the theoretically intractable moments of the ordinary everyday far from the sound and fury of the public sphere, literary readers should also not hesitate to consider the mundane and the marginal as a pertinent index of subaltern consciousness.

Not doing so would be to run the risk of missing out significant facets of these realities and of equating the entirety of such experiences with a handful of oft-repeated—albeit important—stories that gain cultural centrality both with the indigenous bourgeoisie and in the metropolitan centers of the West. I, for instance, grew up in a large city in postcolonial India. My personal experience of the most oppressive legacies of colonialism and the obstacles to postcolonial development had little to do with spectacles of riots, terrorism, genocides, all of which had wreaked havoc at other times and in other places. It had much more to do with the mind-numbing boredom inspired by functional and dysfunctional bureaucracies alike, a thousand trivial details of institutions not working the way they might have been expected to work, even within local parameters. What was much more real for me was not the spectacle of power but the banality of it. Underlying such power was not brutality but apathy, what Michael Herzfeld has aptly called "indifference," whose "real danger" is "not that it grows out of the barrel of a gun, but that it too easily becomes habitual."[29] The banality of power was the affective consequence of a certain public mindset of indifference, which, as Herzfeld has so eloquently put it, "is the opium of the state drudge."[30] This banality was made up of bureaucratic formalities that made little or no sense; the "predictability of routine" of the failure of public and private institutions; the long empty evenings of daily, repeated power cuts; the long, slow trips in crowded buses that made up the experience of the everyday.[31] I know these failures unleashed far more traumatic consequences elsewhere, and I share all the outrage and anger at such consequences, but it still remains hard to deny that one of the main consequences of these failures—of governmentality as much as of market logic—is inaction; of "unpleasantly extended time," to use Goodstein's words for the German sense of boredom; of the kind of banalizing emptiness that frustrates the private citizen of the postcolonial state caught in a fractured relation to neoliberal capitalism.

Narratives of postcolonial reality can scarcely stop at the rediscovery of the ordinary; they must therefore reclaim banality as an aesthetic form and boredom as the affective structure of everyday lives led far from the glare of the spectacle. Banality and boredom stifle the possibilities of catharsis with the same intensity with which violence, brutality, and trauma drive the suffering subject toward it; the denial of catharsis poses a moral ambiguity before the aesthetic chronicler of the postcolonial experience. The noncathartic is an unconvincing index of suffering. And it is an equally unsatisfying index of the dream and the nightmare of postliberation progress. The spectacle of the event, on the other hand, offers the fullness of catharsis, of trauma as well as celebration, emerging as the normative model of fictional narration for the colonial and postcolonial writer. That the narrative of the spectacle continues to overshadow the prose of the world is therefore scarcely surprising, but it is also, as this study has sought to show, something of a loss for all of us.

Acknowledgments

The innovative imagination of several generous people shaped the conditions under which this book on banality came into its final shape. For its early life, I'm indebted to the English department at Rutgers University, especially my mentors there: Derek Attridge, Abena Busia, Marianne DeKoven, Marc Manganaro; and to Myra Jehlen, for insights into the rich paradoxes of the writing process. The neighboring English department at Princeton offered a great turf to toss back and forth risky ideas; my gratitude goes to Tim Watson, for tireless cheer over the years, and to Diana Fuss, for pushing me to take risky paths whose rewards have become clear to me far beyond the reaches of this particular project.

The book developed into its final shape through deep engagement by a number of colleagues at the English department at Stanford. I'm grateful to John Bender, Michele Elam, Andrea Lunsford, Franco Moretti, Paula Moya, Blakey Vermeule, and Alex Woloch for having read and commented on significant portions of the manuscript. Gavin Jones, Seth Lerer, and Ursula Heise were tireless supporters in its final journey as a book, and Sianne Ngai's careful eyes helped me hone a few key passages at the final stages of the editing process. Ramón Saldívar and Jennifer Summit were generous and supportive department chairs as the book came to grow into present life. Some of the most attentive reading of the chapter drafts came from friends in the department with whom at various times I exchanged work in progress: Andrew Goldstone, Evan Horowitz, Hannah Sullivan, and Karen Zumhagen-Yekplé. Ann Gelder, Nikil Saval, and James Wood provided valuable assistance with copy editing. Allison Rung's meticulous help with bibliographic research, citations, and formatting greatly eased this book's passage into its final form. Alyce Boster and Dagmar Logie have been the source of deeply generous administrative support throughout the process. Similar thanks go to Colleen Boucher, Judy Candell, Katie Dooling, Nelia Peralta, and Nicole Yun for responding promptly to every professional need well before I was able to articulate them fully. Beyond the department, special thanks go to Russell Berman, Elisabeth Boyi, Jim Ferguson, Josh Landy, David Palumbo-Liu, and Ban Wang for their interest in my project and their suggestions for its improvement; to Ximena Briceno and Héctor Hoyos for their friendly support of this work and its author; to Emily-Jane Cohen and Julie Noblitt for their thoughts on the best ways of wishing bon voyage to a book.

In the wider world of the discipline, this project was lucky to get support of several other scholars with whose work it envisions a dialogue. Thanks to Jed Esty, Doug Mao, John Marx, and Rebecca Walkowitz, for reading parts of the manuscript and sharing their thoughts, and to Sarah Brophy, John Bugg, Daniel Coleman, Nadia Ellis, Andrew Griffin, Mike Rubenstein, and Keri Walsh, for the miracle of long-standing friendship over shared passions. Excerpts from the project were presented at talks given at Stanford, the University of California at Berkeley, the University of Delhi, Jawaharlal Nehru University, Jadavpur University, and the Australian National University. To the audience at these talks I owe much provocation of thought; special thanks go to Gautam Premnath, Prasanta Chakravarty, Saugata Bhaduri, Supriya Chaudhuri, Debjani Ganguly, and Shameem Black for inviting me to present my work. Some of the early material appeared in journals: *James Joyce Quarterly* 42/43, nos. 1/4 (Fall 2004/Summer 2006), *Genre* 39, no. 2 (Summer 2006), *Studies in the Novel* 39, no. 4 (Winter 2007), and *Modern Fiction Studies* 55, no. 1 (Spring 2009). I'm grateful to the editors for permission to reproduce the material here. Philip Leventhal at Columbia University Press deserves my gratitude for his unflagging faith in the potential of this project; thanks also to the anonymous readers at the press for their comments.

The publication of this book was partially supported by a grant from my home department at Stanford, and the manuscript was honed into its final shape during a year of sabbatical leave, a semester of which was spent at the Jawaharlal Nehru Institute of Advanced Study, at Jawaharlal Nehru University. My thanks to Jennifer Summit, then chair of the Stanford English department, for providing me with the subvention grant, and to Aditya Mukherjee, the director of JNIAS, for the generous fellowship that supported my stay at the institute.

The writing of any book must owe worlds to the banality as well as the excitement of labor rooted in the everyday, and for sharing this dailiness with me, my special gratitude goes to Subhasree Chakravarty. And just as this book was nearing completion, our daughter Inaya arrived to change our everyday forever; to her I owe a radically new meaning of the quotidian.

Notes

Introduction: Poetics of the Prosaic

1. "In or about December, 1910, human character changed." Virginia Woolf, "Mr. Bennett and Mrs. Brown," in *Collected Essays*, 4 vols. (New York: Harcourt, Brace, and World, 1967), 1:320.
2. Katherine Mansfield, *The Katherine Mansfield Notebooks*, ed. Margaret Scott, 2 vols. (Canterbury: Lincoln University Press, 1997), 111–112.
3. Jeffrey Auerbach, "Imperial Boredom," *Common Knowledge* 11, no. 2 (Spring 2005): 283.
4. Sianne Ngai, *Ugly Feelings* (Cambridge, Mass.: Harvard University Press, 2005), 6. Beginning with Aristotle's category of "aesthetic emotions" in the *Poetics*, Ngai distinguishes "grander passions like anger and fear" and "potentially ennobling or morally beatific states like 'sympathy, melancholia and shame' " from feelings that are "explicitly amoral and noncathartic, offering no satisfactions of virtue, however oblique, nor any therapeutic or purifying release" (6). Such "noncathartic feelings" have been generally marginalized in "major forms and genres like Homeric epic and Shakespearean tragedy" because such aesthetic models tend to rely upon what Philip Fisher calls "vehement passions"—the more recognizable emotions, such as wrath, pity, and fear, that have clearer, more distinct and important places in the canon of values that is constructed socially as well as aesthetically. See Philip Fisher, *The Vehement Passions* (Princeton, N.J.: Princeton University Press, 2002).
5. This argument has gathered significant momentum in recent years through the work of scholars who read literary modernism as a significant point of departure for the cultural

globalization that comes to define the twentieth century, especially through the global expansion of English-language literature. See Rebecca Walkowitz, *Cosmopolitan Style: Modernism Beyond the Nation* (New York: Columbia University Press, 2006); and Jed Esty, *A Shrinking Island: Modernism and National Culture in England* (Princeton, N.J.: Princeton University Press, 2004). The clearest articulation of this specific argument of modernism as the beginning of the globalization of English-language literature is to be found in John Marx, *The Modernist Novel and the Decline of Empire* (Cambridge: Cambridge University Press, 2005).

6. Marx, *The Modernist Novel*, 1.
7. Woolf, "Mr. Bennett and Mrs. Brown," 1:329.
8. Virginia Woolf, "Modern Fiction," in *Collected Essays*, 4 vols. (New York: Harcourt, Brace, and World, 1967), 2:105.
9. Woolf, "Mr. Bennett and Mrs. Brown," 1:331.
10. G. W. F. Hegel, *Aesthetics: Lectures on Fine Art*, trans. T. M. Knox, 2 vols. (Oxford: Clarendon, 1975), 1:150.
11. Ibid., 1:149.
12. Max Weber, *Economy and Society: An Outline of Interpretive Sociology*, ed. Guenther Roth and Claus Wittich, 2 vols. (Berkeley: University of California Press, 1978), 2:956.
13. Max Weber, *The Protestant Ethic and the Spirit of Capitalism*, trans. Talcott Parsons (London: HarperCollins, 1991), 181.
14. Anthony Giddens, *The Consequences of Modernity* (Stanford, Calif.: Stanford University Press, 1990), 12.
15. Woolf, "Mr. Bennett and Mrs. Brown," 1:337.
16. Lars Svendsen, *A Philosophy of Boredom*, trans. John Irons (London: Reaktion, 2005), 47.
17. Liesl Olson, *Modernism and the Ordinary* (New York: Oxford University Press, 2009), 1.
18. Ibid., 60–62, 65–66.
19. Ibid., 66.
20. Heather K. Love, *Feeling Backward: Loss and the Politics of Queer History* (Cambridge, Mass.: Harvard University Press, 2007), 5–6.
21. John Marx, *The Modernist Novel and the Decline of Empire* (Cambridge: Cambridge University Press, 2005), 169.
22. Patricia Meyer Spacks, *Boredom: A Literary History of a State of Mind* (Chicago: University of Chicago Press, 1995), 62.
23. Since the early years of the twenty-first century, critical practice has begun to identify a mechanism of epistemological resistance in a range of what Ngai calls "noncathartic" motifs and objects, in aesthetic and philosophical discourse. While Giorgio Agamben, reading Heidegger, understands "profound boredom" in terms of a refusal of action, communication, or gratification, Bill Brown, John Frow, and Peter Schwenger, writing in the 2001 special issue of *Critical Inquiry* on "Things," theorize the foregrounding of the object and the epistemological resistance embodied in its opacity as part of twentieth-century aesthetics' political and ethical critique of Enlightenment paradigms of reason, subjectivity, and knowledge production. Giorgio Agamben, *The Open: Man and Animal*, trans. Kevin

Attell (Stanford, Calif.: Stanford University Press, 2004), 65; Bill Brown, "Thing Theory," in "Things," ed. Bill Brown, special issue, *Critical Inquiry* 28, no. 1 (Autumn 2001): 1–22; John Frow, "A Pebble, a Camera, a Man Who Turns Into a Telegraph Pole," *Critical Inquiry* 28: 270–285; Peter Schwenger, "Words and the Murder of the Thing," *Critical Inquiry* 28: 99–113. Woolf's impatience with the rationalist deployment of factual details in the meticulous realism of the Edwardians can be read as echoing this critique of Enlightenment modernity that was launched by experimental literary modernism. Edwardian realism appears to assert a faith in the model of rational modernity that is thrown into a crisis by the acceleration of modernism and its experimental narrative methods. In the set of essays put together by *Critical Inquiry*, however, this critique is identified in writing throughout the twentieth century and not merely in literary fiction or poetry. Frow's examples are chosen from Rilke, Williams, Neruda, and Ponge (273), while Brown, in his editorial introduction to the issue, sees formulations of this critique recurring in Heidegger, Lacan, Frank O'Hara, Robert Rauschenberg, Baudrillard, and Claes Oldenburg (14). But for both Brown and Schwenger, it is modernism that is the privileged moment of the disruptive appearance of the object, both in terms of its concrete materiality and of its refusal to be "objectified" and domesticated. For me, too, the point of greatest interest in this branch of material cultural studies that has come to be known as "thing theory" is its identification of modernist literature as the cultural-historical moment when the opacity of the banal object not only finds its most triumphant moment of aesthetic celebration, but also assumes the most striking dimensions of resistance and disruption.

24. "For thinkers and all sensitive spirits, boredom is that disagreeable 'windless calm' of the soul that precedes a happy voyage and cheerful winds. They have to bear it and must wait for its effect on them. Precisely this is what lesser natures cannot achieve by any means." Friedrich Nietzsche, *The Gay Science*, trans. Walter Kaufmann (New York: Vintage, 1974), 108. For Walter Benjamin, boredom is "the dream bird that hatches the egg of experience," the bird who is driven away by "a rustling in the leaves." Walter Benjamin, *Illuminations*, ed. Hannah Arendt, trans. Harry Zohn (New York: Schocken, 1973), 91. Kierkegaard writes: "Those who bore others are the plebeians, the crowd, the endless train of humanity in general; those who bore themselves are the chosen ones, the nobility." Søren Kierkegaard, *Either-Or*, trans. Howard V. Hong and Edna H. Hong (Princeton, N.J.: Princeton University Press, 1987), 1:290.

25. Ethnographic analyses of boredom on the margins of global capitalism include Daniel Mains's work on boredom and shame in the lives of young men in urban Ethiopia, boredom and postcolonial temporality in the Australian Aboriginal settlement of Yuendumu by Yasmine Musharbash, labor and the configuration of time in postcolonial Senegal by Michael Ralph, and Bruce O'Neill's dissertation-in-progress on the relation of boredom and economic instability in postsocialist Romania. I discuss all these analyses in greater detail in subsequent chapters of this book.

26. The sociologist Zygmunt Bauman provides a helpful historical framework through which to identify modernity. Opening the argument of his book *Modernity and Ambivalence*,

Bauman writes: "I wish to make it clear that from the start I call 'modernity' a historical period that began in Western Europe with a series of profound social-structural and intellectual transformations of the seventeenth century and achieved its maturity: (1) as a cultural project—with the growth of the Enlightenment; (2) as a socially accomplished form of life—with the growth of industrial (capitalist, and later also communist) society." Zygmunt Bauman, *Modernity and Ambivalence* (Cambridge: Polity Press, 1991), 3n1. The emergence of this modernity in the seventeenth century and its attainment of cultural and social maturity with the Enlightenment and the formation of industrial society is also the key moment for another of influential theorist of modernity, Anthony Giddens, who similarly privileges this period as the historical sphere of its emergence. Anthony Giddens, *The Consequences of Modernity* (Stanford, Calif.: Stanford University Press, 1990), 1. Beyond its periodicity, however, for Giddens, this modernity has a set of abstract and concrete features, including: "(1) a certain set of attitudes towards the world, the idea of the world as open to transformation by human intervention; (2) a complex of economic institutions, especially industrial production and a market economy; (3) a certain range of political institutions, including the nation-state and mass democracy." *Conversations with Anthony Giddens: Making Sense of Modernity* (Stanford, Calif.: Stanford University Press, 1998), 94. Bauman's understanding of modernism is helpful here not only because of its specification of the movement's historical scope but more importantly because of the clarity with which Bauman distinguishes it from modernity: "Hence *modernity*, as I use the term, is in no way identical with *modernism*. The latter is an intellectual (philosophical, literary, artistic) trend that—though traceable back to many individual intellectual events of the previous era—reached its full swing by the beginning of the current century." Bauman, *Modernity and Ambivalence*, 3–4n.

27. For several theorists of the modern, "modernity" and "modernism" have been mutually continuous. Probably the most influential work that has woven them into a single narrative is Marshall Berman's *All That Is Solid Melts Into Air*, where the experience of modernity extends from Goethe's Faust to New York in the 1970s. Marshall Berman, *All That Is Solid Melts Into Air: The Experience of Modernity* (London: Verso, 1999).In the more recent *A Singular Modernity* by Frederic Jameson, too, the distinction between the two is rarely maintained. Frederic Jameson, *A Singular Modernity: Essay on the Ontology of the Present* (London: Verso, 2002). In *Writing in Limbo: Modernism and Caribbean Literature*, a pioneering study of the relation of European modernism and nonmetropolitan literature, Simon Gikandi also privileges the continuities between modernity and modernism in the context of the metropolitan West. Simon Gikandi, *Writing in Limbo: Modernism and Caribbean Literature* (Ithaca, N.Y.: Cornell University Press, 1992).

28. For an interesting survey of this debate, see Patrick Williams, "Simultaneous Uncontemporaneities: Theorizing Modernism and Empire," in *Modernism and Empire*, ed. Howard Booth and Nigel Rigby (Manchester: Manchester University Press, 2000), 20.

29. *The American Heritage College Dictionary* (Boston: Houghton Mifflin, 2000), 106.

30. The banal "oven" is a good example of this use of this word. Common in medieval France, it was generally the property of the local feudal lord. Since personal ovens were prohibited

by law, people had to pay the ovenmaster a fee for the use of the communal oven. The tradition of the banal oven system seems to have more or less died out during the eighteenth century, though historical remnants sometimes lingered on during community celebrations in later periods, mostly in rural France.

31. Thomas L. Dumm, *A Politics of the Ordinary* (New York: New York University Press, 1999), 13.
32. Michael Hardt and Antonio Negri, *Empire* (Cambridge, Mass.: Harvard University Press, 2000), 71.
33. Henri Lefebvre, *Critique of Everyday Life*, trans. John Moore (London: Verso, 1991), 29.
34. Franco Moretti, "Serious Century," in *The Novel*, vol. 1: *History, Geography, and Culture* (Princeton, N.J.: Princeton University Press, 2006), 376.
35. Catherine Gallagher's argument about the nascent category of fictionality is worth recalling here. According to Gallagher, fictionality liberates early English fiction from the need to portray the adventurous, even the improbable, so as to deflect the accusation that it was trying to depict the untruthful. Catherine Gallagher, "The Rise of Fictionality," in *The Novel*, vol. 1: *History, Geography, and Culture*, ed. Franco Moretti (Princeton, N.J.: Princeton University Press, 2006), 342. Fictionality thus enabled the early English novel to celebrate the verisimilitude rooted in ordinary life, a domain that was not quite available to it before. Also significant is the way Ian Watt brought together the demographic and the aesthetic connotations of the ordinary—the common man and the ordinary nature of his everyday life—to consolidate the narratological texture of Robinson Crusoe, which, according to Watt, "is the first fictional narrative in which an ordinary person's daily activities are the centre of continuous literary attention." Ian Watt, *The Rise of the Novel: Studies in Defoe, Richardson, and Fielding* (Berkeley: University of California Press, 2001), 74. In *The Origins of the English Novel, 1660–1740*, Michael McKeon has drawn attention to the analogy drawn by Watt between "the epistemological premises of formal realism and those of 'philosophical realism,' the modern tradition of realism inaugurated by Descartes and Locke." Michael McKeon, *The Origins of the English Novel, 1660–1740* (Baltimore, Md.: Johns Hopkins University Press, 1988), 2. The philosophical shifts of the time, moreover, were significantly paralleled in comparable generic shifts that were to pave the way for the rise of the novel in its modern form. Most of the significant theorists of the early English novel, in fact, agree that ordinariness and ordinary life were aesthetic and epistemological categories that were integral to the emergence of the genre. The category of the ordinary in the early English novel, however, lies at a slight angle to my reading of banality as an aesthetic form of colonial modernity; the well-theorized history of the former is perhaps best addressed here through ellipsis.
36. Michal Peled Ginsberg and Lorri G. Nandrea, "The Prose of the World," in *The Novel*, vol. 2: *Forms and Themes*, ed. Franco Moretti (Princeton, N.J.: Princeton University Press, 2006), 244.
37. Ibid., 244–245.
38. Elizabeth S. Goodstein, *Experience Without Qualities: Boredom and Modernity* (Stanford, Calif.: Stanford University Press, 2005), 102, 107.

39. Ibid., 407.
40. Moretti, "Serious Century," 378.
41. Dumm, *Politics of the Ordinary*, 14.
42. Ibid.
43. Spacks, *Boredom*, 12.
44. Ibid., 262.
45. Goodstein, *Experience Without Qualities*, 214.
46. Ibid., 228, 232.
47. The tension between the understanding of boredom or ennui as a spiritual condition and as a situation primarily enacted by material causes was also a key feature in post-Enlightenment discourses about these affective states. Goodstein reveals this tension through detailed archival research on the evolution of the concept. The materialist emphasis in the interpretation of the subjective experience that followed the Enlightenment increasingly shifted the explanation of boredom toward psychological and physiological causes, further away from its conceptualization as a spiritual phenomenon. Even then, the question of terminology remained crucial: "Thus, while invocations of ennui initially fell in the category of romantic and idealistic reactions to the attendant historical changes, as the language of boredom spread and evolved, it rapidly came into the force field of materialist modes of reflection" (104). In Maria Edgeworth's novel *Ennui*, the feudal aristocrat Lord Glenthorn appears thoroughly bored with his life, yet the term "boredom" is never used in the novel. Glenthorn's insistence on the French term, ennui, to describe his affective state, I would suggest, not only indicates his internalization of his aristocratic position but also a refusal to give up the "romantic and idealistic reactions to the attendant historical changes" and tune his sensibility to "materialist modes of reflection." "Ennui," as such, seeks to retain its elevated position over "boredom" on at least two levels—in terms of the understanding of the affect as a spiritual malaise as opposed to a materially driven phenomenon, and with respect to the superiority of aristocratic subjectivity over more plebeian sensibilities. It is the identification of boredom as an "'aristocratic' sentiment . . . out of place in Balzac's and Stendhal's nineteenth-century classics of upward mobility" that forms part of Bruce Robbins's reading of the emotion as what he calls "an alternative gamut of class-related feelings" that are either "political or politicizable." Bruce Robbins, *Upward Mobility and the Common Good: Toward a Literary History of the Welfare State* (Princeton, N.J.: Princeton University Press, 2007), xii–xiii. Though Robbins uses the term "boredom," the more appropriate term for this aristocratic emotion might be the more philosophically elevated "ennui," as Goodstein's analysis of the emergent tension between the spiritual and the secular implication of the affect in question makes clear: it is a tension that is at least partially rooted in the politics of class itself. Glenthorn's refusal, therefore, can be seen as a representative gesture—whether conscious or unconscious—of the dominant class's refusal to give up the claim to ennui as the exclusive "plight" of the aristocratic subjectivity.
48. Lefebvre, *Critique of Everyday Life*, 8.
49. Ibid., 10.

50. Dumm, *Politics of the Ordinary*, 1. Probably the most perfect example of the ideological prowess of ordinary consumerism was displayed, as Karal Ann Marling has demonstrated, in the 1959 American Exhibition in Moscow, where everyday consumer goods and durables from the domestic domain such as dishwashers, stoves, and refrigerators were displayed to establish U.S. affluence and power at a time when the superpowers were waging the far more spectacular struggle for nuclear and global supremacy. Karal Ann Marling, *As Seen on TV: The Visual Culture of Everyday Life in the 1950s* (Cambridge, Mass.: Harvard University Press, 1994), 243–250.
51. Dumm, *Politics of the Ordinary*, 2, 3.
52. Thomas Blom Hansen and Finn Stepputat, *States of Imagination: Ethnographic Explorations of the Postcolonial State* (Durham, N.C.: Duke University Press, 2001), 9.
53. For an interesting reflection on the disciplinary relation of anthropology and cultural studies, see James Clifford, *On the Edges of Anthropology* (Chicago: Prickly Paradigm Press, 2003), 15–19.
54. See, for instance, apart from James Clifford's *The Predicament of Culture: Twentieth-Century Ethnography, Literature, and Art* (Cambridge, Mass.: Harvard University Press, 1988), Buzard's *The Beaten Track: European Tourism, Literature, and the Ways to Culture, 1880–1918* (Oxford: Clarendon, 1993) and Pratt's *Imperial Eyes: Travel Writing and Transculturation* (London: Routledge, 1993).
55. Michael Taussig, *The Nervous System* (New York: Routledge, 1992), 142, 143.
56. Bronislaw Malinowski, *Argonauts of the Western Pacific: An Account of Native Enterprise and Adventure in the Archipelagoes of Melanesian New Guinea* (New York: Dutton, 1961), 18.
57. Clifford, *The Predicament of Culture*. It is not coincidental that Clifford's book offers one of the most persuasive readings of this relationship. The book itself a classic of anthropology's so-called literary turn (Clifford, *On the Edges*, 105–106) in the 1980s, implying, this time, the impact of poststructuralist literary theory on anthropological thought and methodology.
58. "The anthropology of colonialism," Peter Pels has summarized succinctly, "is always an anthropology of anthropology, because in many methodological, organizational, and professional aspects the discipline retains the shape it received when it emerged from—if partly in opposition to—early twentieth century colonial circumstances." Peter Pels, "The Anthropology of Colonialism: Culture, History, and the Emergence of Western Governmentality," *Annual Review of Anthropology* 26 (1997): 165.
59. Mary Louise Pratt, *Imperial Eyes: Travel Writing and Transculturation* (New York: Routledge, 1993), 6.
60. Throughout the twentieth century, both literary criticism and ethnographic discourse have acknowledged their mutual affinities, beginning with Malinowski, the pioneer of the British "functionalist" school of anthropology, and continuing to the present day. Among the notable recent interlocutions in this subject, Jed Esty's *A Shrinking Island: Modernism and National Culture in England* (Princeton, N.J.: Princeton University Press, 2004) examines late modernist and midcentury British literary texts in terms of their autoethnographic

exploration of English national culture. John Marx's *The Modernist Novel and the Decline of Empire* (Cambridge: Cambridge University Press, 2005) considers the ethnographic implications of high modernist novels, especially those by Lawrence, Woolf, and Joyce.

61. One of the most sustained and significant critical engagements with Enlightenment modernity is to be found in Paul Gilroy's *The Black Atlantic: Modernity and Double Consciousness* (Cambridge, Mass.: Harvard University Press, 1993), 1–40. A significant examination of this engagement in literary discourse is Simon Gikandi's *Writing in Limbo: Modernism and Caribbean Literature*. Gikandi makes a persuasive case for the contradictory relation Caribbean writers share with the historical vision and aesthetic structures embodied in European modernism. "Caribbean writers," he writes, "cannot adopt the history and culture of European modernism, especially as defined by the colonizing structures, but neither can they escape from it because it has overdetermined Caribbean cultures in many ways" (3). The result is the striking process of literary and historical revisionism in which Caribbean writers engage with respect to the paradigms of European modernity and modernism, two terms that Gikandi appears to read as more or less continuous with each other. More recently, a compelling reading of the colonial life of European modernity is provided by Aamir R. Mufti's *Enlightenment in the Colony*. In this book, Mufti makes a persuasive argument about the articulation of power and knowledge that the European Enlightenment comes to embody in the colony: "The larger problem of Enlightenment in the colony is that it brings to an auratically hierarchized social space, to an 'enchanted' world, a dialectic whose context proper in the metropolis is precisely the dissolution of heterogenous subjectivities and the social spaces they inhabit. The objective substratum here is not an unfinished or incomplete progress, however, but rather the distinct articulation of power and knowledge under conditions of colonial capitalism, whose logic Ranajit Guha has identified, in a succinct formulation, as 'dominance without hegemony.'" Aamir R. Mufti, *Enlightenment in the Colony: The Jewish Question and the Crisis of Postcolonial Culture* (Princeton, N.J.: Princeton University Press, 2007), 25.

62. Andrew Gibson, *Joyce's Revenge: History, Politics, and Aesthetics in* Ulysses (Oxford: Oxford University Press, 2002); Enda Duffy, *The Subaltern* Ulysses (Minneapolis: University of Minnesota Press, 1996); Emer Nolan, *James Joyce and Nationalism* (London: Routledge, 1995). Some of the most stimulating approaches to the relation between Joyce and colonialism are collected in Derek Attridge and Marjorie Howes, eds. *Semicolonial Joyce* (Cambridge: Cambridge University Press, 2000).

63. John Marx, *The Modernist Novel and the Decline of Empire* (Cambridge: Cambridge University Press, 2005), 1.

64. Ibid.

65. See ibid., 169. Marx cites Robert Crawford's earlier argument about the complementary rather than antithetical relation between the metropolis and the periphery that characterized modernism. Crawford argues that in its attempt "to outflank the Anglocentricity of established Englishness through a combination of the demotic and the multicultural, Modernism was an essentially provincial phenomenon." Robert Crawford, *Devolving English*

Literature (Oxford: Clarendon Press, 1992), 270, quoted in ibid. Marx goes on to make a significant point about modernism's export of provincialism to the metropole "in the form of dialect and regional idiom punctuating modernist prose and poetry" (ibid.). An exciting recent example of such a "provincial" approach to modernist cosmopolitanism is to be found in Matthew Hart's *Nations of Nothing but Poetry: Modernism, Transnationalism, and Synthetic Vernacular Writing* (New York: Oxford University Press, 2010). Hart points out the global nature of the vernacular, bringing out, at the same time, the vernacular nature of the global. His key concept is that of synthetic vernacular discourse in poetry, which hinges on the deconstruction of not only the local and the global but also that of high and low cultures, providing an alternate model of transnational poetics in the process. "Synthetic vernaculars," he writes, "operate in the gray area between ethnonational languages and the macaronic linguistic constructions of cosmopolitan modernism" (ibid., 7). Along with Hugh MacDiarmid, T. S. Eliot, and Edward Kamau Braithwaite, Hart reads the poetry of Basil Bunting, Melvin Tolson, and Mina Loy by way of demonstrating the productive mutual dialectic of the vernacular and the transnational.

66. See Casanova's *The World Republic of Letters*, trans. M. B. DeBevoise (Cambridge, Mass.: Harvard University Press, 2005). For a detailed discussion of cosmopolitanism and its relation to twentieth-century British fiction, see the introductory chapter of Walkowitz's *Cosmopolitan Style*.
67. Wicomb's fiction generally avoids continental Europe and England. Even Edinburgh and Glasgow, where she has spent much of her adult life, occupy only a marginal place in her fiction, and that only in her more recent work, most notably toward the end of her 2006 novel *Playing in the Light*. Apart from the depiction of student life in Oxford in part of one novel, *Afternoon Raag* (1991), England has rarely figured in Chaudhuri's fiction so far.
68. Ralph Waldo Emerson, quoted in Stanley Cavell, *Themes out of School: Effects and Causes* (San Francisco: North Point Press, 1984), 193.
69. Jamaica Kincaid, *A Small Place* (New York: Farrar, Straus and Giroux, 1988), 18–19.
70. The particular text by Wicomb that is my focus in this book was first published in 1987, seven years before the end of apartheid rule in South Africa. She has, of course, continued to publish fiction well beyond the end of apartheid.
71. Kelwyn Sole, "'The Deep Thoughts the One in Need Falls Into': Quotidian Experience and the Perspectives of Poetry in Postliberation South Africa," in *Postcolonial Studies and Beyond*, ed. Ania Loomba et al. (Durham, N.C.: Duke University Press, 2006), 182. Sole has significantly extended Henri Lefebvre's reading of the everyday in terms of desire and power to the postcolonial spaces of the global South, where the interplay of such desires points to the disparity of global distribution of material resources and the colonial history that shapes such disparities. "Amid banality and repetition in those spaces," he writes, "where constraints and boredom are produced, in a global arena where abundance and lack occur side by side, dissatisfaction and unfulfilled desires emerge as natural consequences" (185).
72. Ibid., 182, 185.

73. It would be naïve, however, to read all fiction produced from locations in the colonial or postcolonial global South as overarchingly preoccupied with the aesthetics of the spectacle. The major narrative thrust in a novel like Chinua Achebe's *Things Fall Apart*, in many ways the representative early novel immediately following the midcentury wave of decolonization, is the paradigmatic story of colonial intrusion in all its spectacular intensity, notwithstanding its immediate location within the everyday rural life of an Igbo village. This dramatic historiography of the colonial encounter, however, does not exhaust the midcentury repertoire of fiction even if it dominates the narrative paradigm emerging from the (newly) former colony. A significant counterexample to this model, from the same period of postcolonial literary history, might be V. S. Naipaul's *A House for Mr. Biswas*, which chronicles the unfolding of the quotidian within a private sensibility and far away from the din and bustle of the mainstream public sphere.
74. Njabulo Ndebele, *South African Literature and Culture: Rediscovery of the Ordinary* (Scottsville, South Africa: University of KwaZulu Natal Press, 2006), 31.

1. James Joyce and the Banality of Refusal

1. James Joyce, *Dubliners* (New York: Dover, 1991), 68; further references to this work will be cited in the text.
2. Hannah Arendt, *The Human Condition* (Chicago: University of Chicago Press, 1998), 84.
3. Ibid., 176–177.
4. James Joyce, *Ulysses*, ed. Hans Walter Gabler (New York: Vintage, 1986), 6; further references to this work will be cited in the text.
5. Joyce, "Drama and Life," in *The Critical Writings of James Joyce*, ed. Ellsworth Mason and Richard Ellmann (Ithaca, N.Y.: Cornell University Press, 1989), 45.
6. Quoted in Richard Ellmann, *James Joyce*, 2nd ed. (Oxford: Oxford University Press, 1982), 163.
7. James Joyce, *Stephen Hero* (New York: New Directions, 1963), 79; further references to this work will be cited in the text.
8. Rebecca Walkowitz, *Cosmopolitan Style: Modernism Beyond the Nation* (New York: Columbia University Press, 2006), 64.
9. James Joyce, *A Portrait of the Artist as a Young Man* (New York: Garland, 1993), 190; further references to this work will be cited in the text.
10. Garry Leonard, "The History of Now: Commodity Culture and Everyday Life in Joyce," in *Joyce and the Subject of History*, ed. Mark Wollaeger et al. (Ann Arbor: University of Michigan Press, 1996), 22.
11. Naomi Segal, *The Banal Object: Theme and Thematics in Proust, Rilke, Hofmannsthal, and Sartre* (London: University of London Press, 1981), 2.
12. Ibid., 25.
13. Criticism arising from developments in literary and cultural studies that within the last decade have become known as "Thing Theory" has occasionally pointed to the opacity of

objects as a kind of resistance. Most significant of such approaches are the essays collected in the 2001 special issue of *Critical Inquiry* on Bill Brown, ed., "Things," special issue, *Critical Inquiry* 28, no. 1 (Autumn 2001). In his essay, for instance, John Frow quotes the poem "Pebble" by the Polish poet Zbigniew Herbert. The pebble, in this poem, "has a scent which does not remind one of anything"; it "does not frighten anything away does not arouse desire." John Frow, "A Pebble, a Camera, a Man Who Turns Into a Telegraph Pole," *Critical Inquiry* 28 (2001): 271. Through the isolated banality of its existence, the pebble seems to resist meaning making, a resistance that renders parodic the courtly and romantic idiom of the poem that makes the pebble the center of its intense gaze. "The paradox of any fascination of the thingness of things," Frow writes, is "that things posited in themselves, in their distinction from intention, representation, figuration, or relation, are thereby filled with an imputed interiority and, in their very lack of meaning, with a 'pebbly meaning' which is at once full and inaccessible" (272). In the end, the anonymous banality of the pebble defeats all subjective effort to assume epistemological control: "—Pebbles cannot be tamed / to the end they will look at us / with a calm and very clear eye" (ibid.).

14. Liesl Olson, *Modernism and the Ordinary* (Oxford: Oxford University Press, 2009), 35.
15. Douglas Mao, *Solid Objects: Modernism and the Test of Production* (Princeton, N.J.: Princeton University Press, 1998), 4.
16. Ibid., 7.
17. Leonard, "The History of Now," 14. In his later "Hystericising Modernism: Modernity in Joyce," in *Cultural Studies of James Joyce*, ed. R. B. Kershner (Amsterdam: Rodopi, 2003), Leonard makes the argument that "in the 20th century commodified objects began to replace the subject as a guarantor of 'inner being' as the rise of commodity culture paralleled the decline of the 'Imperial Subject'" (183). Joycean studies of the object have in fact mostly tended to see it as a commodity, that is, in its relation to consumer capitalism. See Jennifer Wicke, "Modernity Must Advertise: Aura, Desire, and Decolonization in Joyce," *James Joyce Quarterly* 30/31, no. 1 (Summer–Fall 1993): 593–613; and Garry Leonard, "Joyce and Advertising: Advertising and Commodity Culture in Joyce's Fiction," *James Joyce Quarterly* 30/31, no. 1 (Summer–Fall 1993), 573–592.
18. Dipesh Chakrabarty, *Provincializing Europe* (Princeton, N.J.: Princeton University Press, 2000), 101.
19. Patrick Williams, "Simultaneous Uncontemporaneities: Theorizing Modernism and Empire," in *Modernism and Empire*, ed. Howard Booth and Nigel Rigby (Manchester: Manchester University Press, 2000), 20.
20. Naomi Schor, *Reading in Detail: Aesthetics and the Feminine* (London: Routledge, 1989), 3.
21. John Bishop, "The Banal, the Boring, and Ulysses," paper presented at the Nineteenth International James Joyce Symposium, Dublin, June 12–19, 2004.
22. Segal, *The Banal Object*, 10.
23. Ibid., 14.
24. Catherine Gallagher and Stephen Greenblatt, *Practicing New Historicism* (Chicago: University of Chicago Press, 2001), 112.
25. Ibid., 112–115, 117.

26. Robert Martin Adams, *Surface and Symbol: The Consistency of James Joyce's* Ulysses (New York: Oxford University Press, 1962), xviii.
27. Olson, *Modernism and the Ordinary*, 35.
28. Georg Lukács, quoted in Schor, *Reading in Detail*, 59.
29. Georg Lukács, "Realism in the Balance," in *Aesthetics and Politics: The Key Texts of the Classic Debate Within German Marxism*, trans. Rodney Livingstone (New York: Verso, 1980), 33.
30. Schor, *Reading in Detail*, 60.
31. It is interesting that Erich Auerbach's objections to *Ulysses*, in his book *Mimesis*, are very much comparable to Lukács's position with respect to Joyce—especially to what Auerbach considered incomprehensible symbols in Joyce's work.
32. Lukács, "Realism in the Balance," 37.
33. Marjorie Howes, "Joyce, Colonialism, and Nationalism," in *The New Cambridge Companion to James Joyce*, 2nd ed., ed. Derek Attridge (Cambridge: Cambridge University Press, 2004), 268.
34. By totality, I imply the structure within which Marxist theory perceives the relationship of the cultural and the material, moving beyond the simpler determination of the base-superstructure model usually derived from Marx's preface to *A Contribution to the Critique of Political Economy*. Probably the best illustration of the way in which the totality model of understanding society emerges as a significant theoretical sophistication of the vulgar Marxism of the base-superstructure model is to be found in Raymond Williams's essay "Base and Superstructure in Marxist Cultural Theory," where he writes: "The totality of social practices was opposed to this layered notion of a base and a consequent superstructure. The totality of practices is compatible with the notion of social being determining consciousness, but it does not understand this process in terms of a base and a superstructure." Raymond Williams, "Base and Superstructure in Marxist Cultural Theory," *New Left Review* 82 (November–December 1973): 7.
35. Daniel Moshenberg, "A Capital Couple: Speculating in Ulysses," *James Joyce Quarterly* 25 (1988): 345.
36. Leonard, "Hystericising Modernism," 183.
37. Bill Brown, "The Secret Life of Things: Virginia Woolf and the Matter of Modernism," *Modernism/Modernity* 6, no. 2 (1999): 1–2.
38. Marc Manganaro, *Culture, 1922: The Emergence of a Concept* (Princeton, N.J.: Princeton University Press, 2002), 111.
39. James Buzard, "Culture and the Critics of *Dubliners*," *James Joyce Quarterly* 37, nos. 1–2 (2000): 55.
40. See James Buzard, "Mass-Observation, Modernism, and Auto-Ethnography," *Modernism/Modernity* 4, no. 3 (September 1997): 93–122.
41. Ibid., 94.
42. Robert Deming, ed., *James Joyce: The Critical Heritage* (London: Routledge, 1970), 1:265, quoted in Manganaro, *Culture, 1922*, 105.
43. Manganaro, *Culture, 1922*, 105.

44. Bronislaw Malinowski, *Argonauts of the Western Pacific: An Account of Native Enterprise and Adventure in the Archipelagoes of Melanesian New Guinea* (New York: Dutton, 1961), 18.
45. For an identification of this disciplinary turn in anthropology with special attention to Joyce, apart from Manganaro, see Buzard, "Culture and the Critics." Buzard reads Dubliners "in connection with the growth of another of the twentieth century's influential new disciplines: modern ethnographic science, in contrast to its Victorian antecedents, was centered around a plural, holistic, and relativistic 'culture-concept' and based upon the ethnographer's personal "immersion" in fieldwork" (45). In his interview with Jose Reginaldo Goncalves, Clifford also points to this shift away from the Frazerian comparativist model around the turn of the century: "At the end of the nineteenth century, culture was still thought of in the singular: people had higher or lower degrees of culture. It was a very important change when it became possible to say 'cultures' in the plural—a specific moment, in English at least, toward the end of the nineteenth century." James Clifford, *On the Edges of Anthropology* (Chicago: Prickly Paradigm Press, 2003), 2.
46. Manganaro, *Culture, 1922*, 135–136.
47. Ibid., 136.
48. Michel de Certeau, *The Practice of Everyday Life* (Berkeley: University of California Press, 1984), 97.
49. Enda Duffy, "Traffic Accidents: The Modernist Flâneur and Postcolonial Culture," in *The Subaltern* Ulysses (Minneapolis: University of Minnesota Press, 1996), 53–92.
50. Ibid., 63–64, 67–69.
51. Rachel Bowlby, *Feminist Destinations and Further Essays on Virginia Woolf* (Edinburgh: Edinburgh University Press, 1997), 191–220.
52. Walter Benjamin, "The Storyteller: Reflections on Works of Nikolai Leskov," in *Illuminations*, ed. Hannah Arendt, trans. Harry Zohn (New York: Schocken, 1973), 91.

2. Katherine Mansfield and the Fragility of Pākehā Boredom

1. Katherine Mansfield, "Prelude," *Selected Stories*, ed. Angela Smith (Oxford: Oxford University Press, 2002), 99; all further references to Mansfield's stories in this chapter come from this volume and will be cited in the text.
2. Jeffery Auerbach, "Imperial Boredom," *Common Knowledge* 11, no. 2 (Spring 2005): 304.
3. Ibid., 300.
4. Robert Young, *Postcolonialism: An Historical Introduction* (Oxford: Blackwell, 2001), 354.
5. While still far from the radical sense of inadequacy and nonmodernity instilled in the indigenous mind by the ideological enterprise of European colonialism, the settler colonial tedium here in some ways approximates another kind of boredom that recent anthropological research has brought to the surface. This is the boredom that afflicts decolonized peoples in the global South whose quotidian life is pervaded by the loss and shame of being excluded by the hegemonic narrative of modernity and capitalism. In such locations,

boredom emerges variously as the overarching experience of everyday life and as an affective marker of the lack of progress that becomes measurable in contact with dominant colonial or neocolonial powers. For the Warlpiri people in the Australian Aboriginal settlement of Yuendumu, Yasmine Musharbash argues, boredom emerges as a concept only after contact with the European settlers. In its contemporary form, boredom pervades the everyday experience of the Warlpiri people, who are caught between the polarities of "neither-there-anymore (the boredom-free presettlement past) and a not-there-at-all (the mainstream)" that leaves them in the aggravating presence of modernities that exclude them. Yasmine Musharbash, "Boredom, Time, and Modernity: An Example from Aboriginal Australia," *American Anthropologist* 109, no. 2 (June 2007): 315. The disenchanting temporality that follows this feeling of exclusion eventually turns into boredom, as it also does with a very different social group likewise haunted by lack of progress: urban youth in contemporary Ethiopia living in the global shadow of neoliberal capitalism. Daniel Mains, whose ethnographic research chronicles this experience of neocolonial boredom, reveals that the solution sought to this affective problem posed by unrealized temporality is ironically, but perhaps unsurprisingly, spatial—in terms of migration to the perceived centers of economic progress in the West, which is also seen as enabling a social freedom unimaginable in Ethiopia. Daniel Mains, "Desire and Opportunity Among Urban Youth in Ethiopia," (PhD diss., Emory University, 2007), 668.

6. Claire Tomalin, *Katherine Mansfield: A Secret Life* (New York: Knopf, 1988), 8.
7. Ibid. The effort to replicate English landscape and architecture in the colonies, though intended to create a "something like a home feeling," Jeffrey Auerbach argues, only helped to further conceal the unique local appeal of the colonial world that "is such an essential component of a satisfying touristic experience." "Imperial Boredom," 294. This further deepened the tedium of life in these locations. Examples of such attempts at replication include the government house in Calcutta, a brick copy of Kedleston Hall in Derbyshire, and the general design of the Indian hill stations, intended to replicate English villages (294). Elleke Boehmer also points to the striking architectural resemblances across the major cities of the global British Empire, including Adelaide, Toronto, Calcutta, Sydney, Victoria, Wellington, Kingston, Harare: "Not only the architectural motifs and street names, but also the urban layout and the statuary, the sandstone or bluestone World War memorials, the societies, banks and other institutions that stand squat and large on Main Street or High Street, all are repeated or find their resonance in urban centres thousands of miles apart." Elleke Boehmer, "The Worlding of the Jingo Poem," in "Nineteenth Century Globalization," ed. Pablo Mukherjee, special issue, *Yearbook of English Studies* 41, no. 2 (July 2011): 41–57.
8. Witi Ihimaera, *Dear Miss Mansfield* (Auckland: Viking, 1989), 32.
9. Quoted in Tomalin, *A Secret Life*, 8.
10. Ibid.
11. Quoted in Antony Alpers, *The Life of Katherine Mansfield* (New York: Viking, 1980), 216.
12. Kate Fullbrook, *Katherine Mansfield* (Bloomington: Indiana University Press, 1986); Claire Hanson, "Katherine Mansfield," in *Gender of Modernism*, ed. Bonnie Kime Scott (Bloom-

ington: Indiana University Press, 1990); Sydney Janet Kaplan, *Katherine Mansfield and the Origins of Modernist Fiction* (Ithaca, N.Y.: Cornell University Press, 1991).
13. Bridget Orr, "The Māori House of Fiction," in *Cultural Institutions of the Novel* (Durham, N.C.: Duke University Press, 1995), 49–50.
14. Ibid., 50.
15. For a comprehensive literary account of this struggle, see Chadwick Allen, *Blood Narratives: Indigenous Identity in American Indian and Māori Literary and Activist Texts* (Durham, N.C.: Duke University Press, 2002).
16. Orr, "Māori House of Fiction," 78.
17. Ihimaera, *Dear Miss Mansfield*, 9.
18. Elsdon Best, *The Māori as He Was* (Wellington: R. E. Owen, 1954), 66.
19. Elsdon Best, *Spiritual and Mental Concepts of the Māori* (Wellington: R. E. Owen, 1954), 56.
20. James Clifford, *On the Edges of Anthropology* (Chicago: Prickly Paradigm Press, 2003), 2.
21. Ian Gordon, "Katherine Mansfield: The Wellington Years, a Reassessment," in *Critical Essays on Katherine Mansfield*, ed. Rhoda B. Nathan (Boston: G. K. Hall, 1993), 70.
22. Katherine Mansfield, *The Urewera Notebook*, ed. Ian A. Gordon (Oxford: Oxford University Press, 1978), 59, 86, 37.
23. Katherine Mansfield, *The Katherine Mansfield Notebooks*, 2 vols., ed. Margaret Scott (Canterbury: Lincoln University Press, 1997), 136.
24. The story from which the quotation in this section's title comes. Mansfield, "Prelude," 103.
25. Patricia Meyer Spacks, *Boredom: A Literary History of a State of Mind* (Chicago: University of Chicago Press, 1995), 62.
26. Ibid., 82.
27. By the term *vita activa*, or the active life, Arendt proposes "to designate three fundamental human activities: labor, work and action." Hannah Arendt, *The Human Condition* (Chicago: University of Chicago Press, 1998), 7. "They are fundamental," she writes, "because each corresponds to one of the basic conditions under which life on earth has been given to man" (7). Arendt, however, does not read labor as a specifically gendered activity; according to her, in classical antiquity, labor was the activity that primarily defined the slave. Labor was to be hidden in the privacy of the household, as opposed to action, which proclaimed itself in the public realm. Analyzing labor, she writes: "The differentiation between the private household and the public political realm, between the household inmate who was a slave and the household head who was a citizen, between activities which should be hidden in privacy and those which were worth being seen, heard, and remembered, overshadowed and predetermined all other distinctions until one criterion was left: is the greater amount of time and effort spent in private or in public?" (85).
28. Agamben finds the bored subject as being in "closest proximity" to "animal captivation," though he does not relate such captivation to a gendered identity. "For this reason," he writes, "the man who becomes bored finds himself in the 'closest proximity'—even if it is only apparent—to animal captivation." Giorgio Agamben, *The Open: Man and Animal*, trans. Kevin Attell (Stanford, Calif.: Stanford University Press, 2004), 265.

29. Perhaps the most well known of these systems of medical surveillance is Dr. Weir Mitchell's "rest cure," which claimed as its victims both Charlotte Perkins Gilman and Virginia Woolf, the nightmarish psychological consequences of which are hauntingly chronicled in Gilman's "The Yellow Wallpaper."
30. Lydia Wevers, "The Short Story," in *The Oxford Handbook of New Zealand Literature in English*, 2nd ed., ed. Terry Strum (Auckland: Oxford University Press, 1998), 249.
31. Andrew Bennett, *Katherine Mansfield* (Plymouth: Northcote House, 2004), 37.
32. Mansfield, *Urewera Notebook*, 86.
33. Mansfield, *The Katherine Mansfield Notebooks*, 1:139.
34. Ibid., 1:140.
35. Kate Fullbrook, *Katherine Mansfield* (Bloomington: Indiana University Press, 1986), 43.
36. Fullbrook, *Katherine Mansfield*, 43. Emphasis in the original.
37. James Clifford, *The Predicament of Culture: Twentieth-Century Ethnography, Literature, and Art* (Cambridge, Mass.: Harvard University Press, 1988), 145–146.

3. The Dailiness of Trauma and Liberation in Zoë Wicomb

1. In an interview with Clifford in the spring of 2002, the Japanese anthropologist Yoshinobu Ota discussed the possibility of whether *The Predicament of Culture* might signal the "literary turn" in anthropology. While acknowledging that the book is partly about such a "literary turn" or textualization, Clifford expresses his preference for the term "discourse" as the primary subject of the book, which he identifies as "a concept that has much broader, 'cultural' application, both institutionally and politically, than writing as usually understood." James Clifford, *On the Edges of Anthropology* (Chicago: Prickly Paradigm Press, 2003), 105–106.
2. James Clifford and George E. Marcus, eds., *Writing Culture: The Poetics and Politics of Ethnography* (Berkeley: University of California Press, 1986), 3–4.
3. James Clifford, *The Predicament of Culture: Twentieth-Century Ethnography, Literature, and Art* (Cambridge, Mass.: Harvard University Press, 1988), 122.
4. Much of recent literary criticism's interest in the ethical implication of relating to otherness or the alien is inflected through the writings of Emmanuel Levinas. For notable instances of this model of ethical relation as foregrounded in literary criticism, see Derek Attridge's *The Singularity of Literature* (London: Routledge, 2004) and *J. M. Coetzee and the Ethics of Reading: Literature in the Event* (Chicago: University of Chicago Press, 2004); Andrew Gibson's *Postmodernity, Ethics, and the Novel* (New York: Routledge, 1999); and Jill Robbins's *Altered Reading: Levinas and Literature* (Chicago: University of Chicago Press, 1999).
5. Vincent Crapanzano, "Hermes' Dilemma: The Masking of Subversion in Ethnographic Description," in *Writing Culture: The Poetics and Politics of Ethnography*, ed. James Clifford and George E. Marcus (Berkeley: University of California Press, 1986), 52.
6. Patricia Meyer Spacks, *Boredom: A Literary History of a State of Mind* (Chicago: University of Chicago Press, 1995), 1.

7. Bronislaw Malinowski, *Argonauts of the Western Pacific: An Account of Native Enterprise and Adventure in the Archipelagoes of Melanesian New Guinea* (New York: Dutton, 1961), 18.
8. Peter Pels, "The Anthropology of Colonialism: Culture, History, and the Emergence of Western Governmentality," *Annual Review of Anthropology* 26 (1997): 164.
9. Mary Louise Pratt, *Imperial Eyes: Travel Writing and Transculturation* (London: Routledge, 1993), 6.
10. Ibid., 7.
11. Kelwyn Sole, "'The Deep Thoughts the One in Need Falls Into': Quotidian Experience and the Perspectives of Poetry in Postliberation South Africa," in *Postcolonial Studies and Beyond*, ed. Ania Loomba et al. (Durham, N.C.: Duke University Press, 2006), 182.
12. Ibid.
13. Sol Plaatje, *Mhudi*, ed. Stephen Gray (London: Heineman, 1978); Lewis Nkosi, *Mating Birds* (Cape Town: Kwela Books, 2004); Lewis Nkosi, *The Rhythm of Violence* (London: Oxford University Press, 1964); Miriam Tlali, *Muriel at Metropolitan* (Harlow: Longman, 1987).
14. Elleke Boehmer, "Endings and New Beginning: South African Fiction in Transition," in *Writing South Africa: Literature, Apartheid, and Democracy, 1970–1995*, ed. Derek Attridge and Rosemary Jolly (Cambridge: Cambridge University Press, 1998), 43–56.
15. Brian MacAskill, "Inside Out: Jeremy Cronin's Lyrical Politics," in *Writing South Africa: Literature, Apartheid, and Democracy, 1970–1995*, ed. Derek Attridge and Rosemary Jolly (Cambridge: Cambridge University Press, 1998), 187.
16. Ndebele, *South African Literature and Culture: Rediscovery of the Ordinary* (Scottsville, South Africa: University of KwaZulu Natal Press, 2006), 31.
17. Sole, "Quotidian Experience," 182.
18. Ndebele, *South African Literature and Culture*, 61.
19. Ibid., 41, 31.
20. I am aware of the ethicopolitical complications in the use the apartheid-era classification "coloured" to describe Wicomb as well as her protagonist Frieda Shenton. At times, Wicomb herself, like other progressive antiapartheid activists, has declared her preference for the term "black," following the consolidation of all races classified as "nonwhite" under apartheid—including indigenous peoples, Asians, and coloureds. This consolidation has especially been asserted by the United Democratic Front, which brought together all these racial groups in the struggle against apartheid, protesting, significantly, the Tricameral Parliament of 1983, which gave a separate legislative chamber to the so-called coloured and Asians but withheld such rights from the indigenous black peoples. I have, however, chosen to use the term "coloured" here to distinguish Wicomb as a writer with a racially hybrid background from a black writer like Ndebele. Also, in spite of the campaign of solidarity by the United Democratic Front, it has been noted (by Carol Sicherman, for instance) that there are essential differences between the problems faced by Ndebele's black protagonist in *Fools* and those encountered by Frieda Shenton—as Frieda herself comments on, in her discussion with her friend Myra in the story "Ash on My Sleeve," noted below.

21. Carol Sicherman, "Literary Afterword," in *You Can't Get Lost in Cape Town*, by Zoë Wicomb (New York: Feminist Press at CUNY, 2000), 197.
22. Graham Pechey, "The Post-Apartheid Sublime: Rediscovering the Extraordinary," in *Writing South Africa: Literature, Apartheid and Democracy, 1970–1995*, eds. Derek Attridge and Rosemary Jolly (Cambridge: Cambridge University Press, 1998), 57.
23. The title essay in the collection, to which I specifically refer, was presented as the keynote address at the "New Writing in Africa: Continuity and Change" conference held at the Commonwealth Institute, London, November 1984.
24. Zoë Wicomb, *You Can't Get Lost in Cape Town* (New York: Feminist Press at CUNY, 2000), 1; further references to this work will be cited in the text.
25. James Buzard, "Culture and the Critics of *Dubliners*," *James Joyce Quarterly* 37, nos. 1–2 (2000): 55.
26. Johannes Fabian, *Time and the Other: How Anthropology Makes Its Object* (New York: Columbia University Press, 1983), 17.
27. Daniel Mains, "Desire and Opportunity Among Urban Youth in Ethiopia" (PhD diss., Emory University, 2007), 660, 667, 669.
28. Naomi Schor, *Reading in Detail: Aesthetics and the Feminine* (London: Routledge, 1989), 4. Emphasis in the original.
29. Ibid., 7.
30. Pechey, "Post-Apartheid Sublime," 57.
31. Ndebele, *South African Literature and Culture*, 49.
32. Quoted in Carol Sicherman's afterword to Wicomb, *You Can't Get Lost in Cape Town*, 201.
33. Pechey, "Post-Apartheid Sublime," 57.
34. Wicomb, "Shame and Identity: The Case of the Colored in South Africa," in *Writing South Africa: Literature, Apartheid, and Democracy, 1970–1995*, ed. Derek Attridge and Rosemary Jolly (Cambridge: Cambridge University Press, 1998), 101.
35. Ibid., 92.
36. Lewis Nkosi, "Postmodernism and Black Writing in South Africa," in *Writing South Africa: Literature, Apartheid, and Democracy, 1970–1995*, ed. Derek Attridge and Rosemary Jane Jolly (Cambridge: Cambridge University Press, 1998), 75.

4. Amit Chaudhuri and the Materiality of the Mundane

1. Aijaz Ahmad, quoted in Michael Sprinker, "The National Question: Said, Ahmad, Jameson," *Public Culture* 6 (1993): 9.
2. Ibid., 6.
3. Imre Szeman, "Who's Afraid of National Allegory? Jameson, Literary Criticism, Globalization," *South Atlantic Quarterly* 100, no. 3 (Summer 2001): 806–807.
4. Ibid., 805.
5. Nicholas Brown, *Utopian Generations: The Political Horizons of Twentieth-Century Literature* (Princeton: Princeton University Press, 2005), 8.

6. Ibid.
7. Geeta Kapur, "Globalisation and Culture," *Third Text* 11, no. 39 (1997): 23–25.
8. Chinua Achebe, "The African Writer and the English Language," in *Colonial Discourse and Post-Colonial Theory: A Reader*, ed. Patrick Williams and Laura Chrisman (New York: Columbia University Press, 1994), 429.
9. Amit Chaudhuri, "Modernity and the Vernacular," in *The Picador Book of Modern Indian Literature*, ed. Amit Chaudhuri (London: Picador, 2001), xix.
10. See Jürgen Habermas, *The Structural Transformation of the Public Sphere: An Inquiry Into a Category of Bourgeois Society*, trans. Thomas Burger (Cambridge, Mass.: MIT Press, 1991).
11. See Hannah Arendt, *The Human Condition* (Chicago: University of Chicago Press, 1998), especially "The Public and the Private Realm."
12. It should be noted that Jameson's distinction of the public and the private as one "between the poetic and the political, between . . . the domain of sexuality and the unconscious and that of the public world of classes, of the economic, and of secular political power: in other words, between Freud and Marx" (Fredric Jameson, "Third World Literature in the Era of Multinational Capitalism," *Social Text*, no. 15 [Autumn 1986]: 69), perhaps intuitive to us today, contrasts significantly with both the Habermasian and the Arendtian conceptions of the public-private duality. Both Habermas and Arendt have been criticized for their elitist and exclusive notions of public agency; for a collection of these critiques, see Craig Calhoun, ed., *Habermas and the Public Sphere* (Cambridge, Mass.: MIT Press, 1993). For the most significant conception of the proletarian public sphere, see Oskar Negt and Alexander Kluge, *Public Sphere and Experience: Toward an Analysis of the Bourgeois and Proletarian Public Sphere*, trans. Peter Labanyi, Jamie Owen Daniel, and Assenka Oksiloff (Minneapolis: University of Minnesota Press, 1993).
13. See Indrani Chatterjee, ed., *Unfamiliar Relations: Family and History in South Asia* (New Delhi: Permanent Black, 2004).
14. Partha Chatterjee, *The Nation and Its Fragments* (Princeton, N.J.: Princeton University Press, 1993).
15. "The material is the domain of the 'outside,' of the economy and of statecraft, of science and technology, a domain where the West had proved its superiority and the East had succumbed. . . . The spiritual, on the other hand, is an 'inner' domain bearing the essential marks of cultural identity." Ibid., 147.
16. Ibid., 147.
17. Ibid., 9, 147.
18. Ibid., 9.
19. Ibid., 147.
20. Szeman, "National Allegory," 808.
21. C. Nadia Seremetakis, *The Senses Still: Perception and Memory as Material Culture in Modernity* (Boulder, Colo.: Westview, 1994), 19.
22. Sara Suleri, *The Rhetoric of English India* (Chicago: University of Chicago Press, 1992), 12–13.
23. It might be of some relevance here to mention that many of these novelists have varying degrees of professional training in history and the neighboring social sciences, which they

have possibly brought to bear upon their fictional vision. Rushdie's undergraduate degree in Cambridge was in history, and Kesavan is a professor of history in Jamia Milia Islamia University in Delhi. Tharoor, whose Ph.D. is in political science, has probably had the most active and direct professional role in the global and domestic public sphere, first in his long career as a UN diplomat. Following the parliamentary elections in May 2009, he served for a period as an elected member of parliament for the Indian National Congress and the deputy minister of external affairs in the National Cabinet.

24. Significantly, this was also the first occasion since independence when the continuous, indeed dynastic rule of the Gandhi Nehru family-led Indian National Congress was disrupted, following Indira Gandhi's declaration of emergency in 1975, chronicled in Rohinton Mistry's *A Fine Balance*. The declaration of emergency was something of a dictatorial act on Mrs. Gandhi's part, which eventually led to the loss of her popularity, a fact that was reflected in the following parliamentary elections, the first ever that the Indian National Congress lost.
25. Chaudhuri, "Modernity and the Vernacular," xxv.
26. Jon Mee, "After Midnight: The Novel in the 1980s and 1990s," in *A History of Indian Literature in English*, ed. Arvind Krishna Mehrotra (New York: Columbia University Press, 2003), 318–319.
27. Rajeshwari Sunder Rajan, quoted in Priya Joshi, *In Another Country: Colonialism, Culture and the English Novel in India* (New York: Columbia University Press, 2002), 230.
28. Bishupriya Ghosh, "An Invitation to Indian Postmodernity: Rushdie's English Vernacular as Situated Cultural Hybridity," in *Critical Essays on Salman Rushdie*, ed. M. Keith Booker (New York: G. K. Hall, 1999), 30.
29. Chaudhuri, "Modernity and the Vernacular," xxiv.
30. Published in the United States as *The Vintage Book of Modern Indian Literature* (New York: Vintage, 2004).
31. Terry Eagleton, "Anti-Humanism," review of *D. H. Lawrence and 'Difference': Post-Coloniality and the Poetry of the Present* by Amit Chaudhuri, *London Review of Books* 26, no. 3 (February 3, 2004): 16–18.
32. Ibid.
33. Amit Chaudhuri, *D. H. Lawrence and Difference* (Oxford: Oxford University Press, 2003), vii.
34. Chaudhuri, "Modernity and the Vernacular," xvi.
35. Amit Chaudhuri, *Clearing a Space: Reflections on India, Literature, and Culture* (Oxford: Peter Lang, 2008), 14.
36. Chaudhuri, "Modernity and the Vernacular," xxx.
37. Amit Chaudhuri, *A Strange and Sublime Address*, in *Freedom Song: Three Novels* (New York: Knopf, 1999), 74.
38. Indrani Chatterjee, *Unfamiliar Relations*, 3.
39. Chaudhuri, *A Strange and Sublime Address*, 7.
40. Ibid., 80.

41. James Joyce, *A Portrait of the Artist as a Young Man* (New York: Garland, 1993), 28.
42. Amit Chaudhuri, *Real Time* (New York: Farrar, Straus, and Giroux, 2002), 6.
43. Ibid., 7.
44. Ibid., 14.
45. Amit Chaudhuri, *Afternoon Raag*, in *Freedom Song: Three Novels* (New York: Knopf, 1999), 181.
46. Ibid., 173.
47. Eagleton, "Anti-Humanism," 2.
48. Chaudhuri, *Strange and Sublime Address*, 53–54.
49. Michael Taussig, *The Nervous System* (London: Routledge, 1992), 141.
50. Ibid., 143.
51. Vinayek Chaturvedi, introduction to *Mapping Subaltern Studies and the Postcolonial*, ed. Vinayak Chaturvedi (London: Verso, 2000), vii.
52. Dipesh Chakrabarty, *Provincializing Europe*, 112.
53. Dipesh Chakrabarty, "Radical Histories and Question of Enlightenment Rationalism: Some Recent Critiques of Subaltern Studies," *Economic and Political Weekly* 30, no. 14 (April 8, 1995): 757.
54. Naomi Segal, *The Banal Object: Theme and Thematics in Proust, Rilke, Hofmannsthal, and Sartre* (London: University of London Press, 1981), 14.
55. Chaudhuri, *Real Time*, 46.
56. Chaudhuri, *A Strange and Sublime Address*, 20.
57. Ibid., 27.
58. Ibid., 106.
59. Ibid., 66.
60. Amit Chaudhuri, *The Immortals* (London: Picador, 2009), 67.
61. Ibid.
62. Chaudhuri, *Afternoon Raag*, 188.
63. Amit Chaudhuri, *A New World* (New York: Knopf, 2000), 50.
64. See chapter 2 for a discussion of Duffy and Bowlby's reading of modernist flânerie.
65. Amit Chaudhuri, "In the Waiting Room of History," review of *Provincialising Europe: Postcolonial Thought and Historical Difference*, by Dipesh Chakrabarty, *London Review of Books* 26, no. 12 (June 24, 2004): 3.
66. Walter Benjamin, quoted in Amit Chaudhuri, introduction to *Jejuri*, by Aruna Kolatkar (New York: NYRB, 2005), xxiv–xxv.
67. Ibid., xxv.
68. Chaudhuri, *Freedom Song* in *Freedom Song*, 303.
69. James Buzard, "Culture and the Critics of *Dubliners*," *James Joyce Quarterly* 37, nos. 1–2 (2000): 57.
70. Ibid., 55.
71. "One has to convey in a language that is not one's own the spirit that is one's own. One has to convey the various shades and omissions of a certain thought-movement that looks

maltreated in an alien language. I use the word 'alien,' yet English is not really an alien language to us. It is the language of our intellectual make-up—like Sanskrit or Persian was before— but not of our emotional make up." Raja Rao, *Kanthapura* (Westport, Conn.: Greenwood Press, 1977), vii.

72. Amit Chaudhuri, "The Construction of the Indian Novel in English," xxviii.
73. Ibid.

Epilogue. The Uneventful

1. Franco Moretti, *The Way of the World: The Bildungsroman in European Culture*, trans. Albert Sbragia (London: Verso, 2000), 7.
2. The generic difference between prose fiction and poetry is in fact crucial to the way the ordinary is played out in different texts. Two important recent theorists of the literary significance of the everyday in modern Anglo-American literature, Bryony Randall and Siobhan Phillips, both foreground temporality as a crucial epistemological category around which the everyday is embodied. The everyday, at the most fundamental level, is what we experience every day, the day, as Randall points out, being the temporal unit whose structure is most immediately tangible to our senses. Bryony Randall, *Modernism, Daily Time, and Everyday Life* (Cambridge: Cambridge University Press, 2007), 1. The ordinary, in this analysis, emerges as a temporal experience, that which is repeated as part of the physical pattern of the day or the psychological iteration of habit and the inescapable structure of one's daily life. If narrative prose delineates a linear progression through time, poetry is better suited to capture the cyclical, iterative temporality of the everyday. "Poetic time," Phillips argues, "dramatizes the repeated manifestation of an ongoing rhythm rather than the steady advance of an oncoming climax. . . . Verse can even help to articulate the discrete properties of this dailiness—nonnarrative yet temporal, unplotted yet contextual." Siobhan Phillips, *The Poetics of the Everyday: Creative Repetition in Modern American Verse* (New York: Columbia University Press, 2010), 22–23. A poetics of the everyday offers the poet a creative free will within this larger pattern of dailiness— "difference-in-sameness" or a "changing sameness," in Phillips's evocative vocabulary. Every morning is the same yet not quite; every action, performed out of habit or daily need, in such poetics, carries the submerged promise of newness, as the poets of her archive, Frost, Stevens, Bishop, and Merrill, reveal. In effect, such poetics of the everyday translates in temporal terms the duality of the public and the private, the mundane and the transcendental as "in their work, daily practice can maintain effective subjective freedom within an objective necessity" (4), and, accordingly, these writers "aspire to neither the potential solipsism of a private time nor the potential self-effacement of an external order" (10).
3. Liesl Olson, *Modernism and the Ordinary* (Oxford: Oxford University Press, 2009), 75.
4. Thomas L. Dumm, *A Politics of the Ordinary* (New York: New York University Press, 1999), 17.

5. C. Nadia Seremetakis, ed., *The Senses Still: Perception and Memory as Material Culture in Modernity* (Boulder, Colo.: Westview, 1994), 19.
6. Ibid.
7. Such a misconstruction would have to overlook the fact that the most celebrated imagination of banality in the twentieth century has been an aestheticization of the political. In Hannah Arendt's *Eichmann in Jerusalem: A Report on the Banality of Evil*, the motif of banal emerges not only as politically depraved and ethically bankrupt but, perhaps more strikingly, as a force of aesthetic impoverishment. In fact, it might be more accurate to say that in Arendt's reading, the ethical and political depravity of Eichmann's actions derive some of their most damning force from the sheer banality of their aesthetic.
8. Fernand Braudel, *The Mediterranean and the Mediterranean World in the Age of Philip II*, trans. Sian Reynolds (New York: Harper & Row. 1972), 1:21, 1:20.
9. Seremetakis, *The Senses Still*, 20.
10. Braudel, *Mediterranean*, 2:900, 2:903, 2:901.
11. Paul Ricoeur, *Time and Narrative*, 2 vols., trans. Kathleen McLaughlin and David Pellauer, 2 vols. (Chicago: University of Chicago Press, 1984), 102. Emphasis in the original.
12. Ibid., 3, 52, 102.
13. In this essay, Cavell refers to the paper Ricoeur delivered as one of the Lionel Trilling Seminars at Columbia University on November 13, 1980. Cavell's own essay was published shortly before the English translation of *Time and Narrative* appeared in print, and he refers to and quotes from, therefore, not Ricoeur's published volumes but the paper as it was delivered. Since I have not been able to find citation information for these papers (Cavell does not provide any), I have used quotations from Ricoeur's paper as provided in Cavell's own essay.
14. Paul Ricoeur, quoted in Stanley Cavell, *Themes out of School: Effects and Causes* (San Francisco: North Point Press, 1984), 185.
15. Ibid., 190.
16. Ibid.
17. Ibid. My emphasis.
18. Ibid., 190–191.
19. Ralph Waldo Emerson, quoted in ibid., 193.
20. Ibid., 193.
21. Dumm, *Politics of the Ordinary*, 21.
22. Cavell, *Themes out of School*, 193.
23. Chaudhuri, "The Construction of the Indian Novel in English," in *The Picador Book of Modern Indian Literature*, ed. Amit Chaudhuri (London: Picador, 2001), xxvi.
24. Guy Debord, "Perspectives for Conscious Alterations in Everyday Life," in *The Everyday Life Reader*, ed. Ben Highmore (London: Routledge, 2002), 244.
25. Jacques Rancière, *The Nights of Labor: The Worker's Dream in Nineteenth-Century France*, trans. John Drury (Philadelphia: Temple University Press, 1989), vii.
26. Henri Lefebvre, "Towards a Leftist Cultural Politics," in *Marxism and the Interpretation of Culture*, eds. Cary Nelson and Lawrence Grossberg (Chicago: University of Illinois Press, 1988), 80.

27. Sonali Perera, "'All That Is Present and Moving . . .': Thinking Working-Class Writing at the Limits" (PhD diss., Columbia University, 2003).
28. Njabulo Ndebele, *South African Literature and Culture: Rediscovery of the Ordinary* (Scottsville, South Africa: University of KwaZulu Natal Press, 2006), 66.
29. Michael Herzfeld, *The Social Production of Indifference* (Chicago: University of Chicago Press, 1993), 184.
30. Ibid.
31. Mbembe opens his discussion of governmentality in the decolonized states of sub-Saharan Africa with a promise to explore "the banality of power in the postcolony." Achille Mbembe, *On the Postcolony* (Berkeley: University of California Press, 2001), 102. His exploration of governmentality in decolonized sub-Saharan African states relates to his understanding of the aesthetic diffusion of state power (and resistance to such power) in the micropolitics of the everyday. State power, in either its colonial or postcolonial phase, produces itself around "institutions, knowledges, norms, and practices" that shape the mundane everyday. Probably the most natural habitat of such governmental power in the recesses of the everyday in the life of the citizen is the institution that Mbembe acknowledges at the very outset of his chapter "The Aesthetics of Vulgarity" but that he also moves considerably beyond: state bureaucracy, which is an essential and inescapable venue of everyday reality in the private and public lives of citizens of the modern state across the globe. Instead, in this chapter, he primarily seeks to address the crude "belly politics" of African dictators, of which, as he points out, the bureaucratic forms only a limited part. And as it becomes clear from subsequent passages in his writing, "vulgarity" rather than "banality" is the better term for addressing the political implications of his work. Even so, his use of the notion of the "banality of power" in relation to colonial governmentality is intriguing. Inasmuch as such governmentality hinges on structures of bureaucracy, power is produced not only in the cruder space of the vulgar and the directly oppressive but also through mechanisms whose necessary affective consequence is that of banality, monotony, and the oppressive tedium of iterative temporality.

Bibliography

Achebe, Chinua. "The African Writer and the English Language." In *Colonial Discourse and Post-Colonial Theory: A Reader*, ed. Patrick Williams and Laura Chrisman, 428–434. New York: Columbia University Press, 1994.
Adams, Robert Martin. *Surface and Symbol: The Consistency of James Joyce's Ulysses*. New York: Oxford University Press, 1962.
Agamben, Giorgio. *The Open: Man and Animal*. Trans. Kevin Attell. Stanford, Calif.: Stanford University Press, 2004.
Allen, Chadwick. *Blood Narratives: Indigenous Identity in American Indian and Māori Literary and Activist Texts*. Durham, N.C.: Duke University Press, 2002.
Alpers, Antony. *The Life of Katherine Mansfield*. New York: Viking, 1980.
Althusser, Louis. "Ideology and Ideological State Apparatuses (Notes Towards an Investigation)." In *Lenin and Philosophy, and Other Essays*, trans. Ben Brewster, 121–186. London: New Left Books, 1971.
Anderson, Benedict. *Imagined Communities: Reflections on the Origin and Spread of Nationalism*. Rev. ed. London: Verso, 1991.
Appadurai, Arjun. *Modernity at Large: Cultural Dimensions of Globalization*. Minneapolis: University of Minnesota Press, 1996.
——. "The Production of Locality." In *Counterworks: Managing the Diversity of Knowledge*, ed. Richard Fardon, 206–227. London: Routledge, 1995.
Arendt, Hannah. *Eichmann in Jerusalem: A Report on the Banality of Evil*. New York: Penguin, 1992.

———. *The Human Condition*. Chicago: University of Chicago Press, 1998.
Armstrong, Nancy. "A Political History of the Novel." In *Theory of The Novel: A Historical Approach*, ed. Michael McKeon, 467–475. Baltimore, Md.: Johns Hopkins University Press, 2000.
Attridge, Derek. *J. M. Coetzee and the Ethics of Reading: Literature in the Event*. Chicago: University of Chicago Press, 2004.
Attridge, Derek, and Marjorie Howes, eds. *Semicolonial Joyce*. Cambridge: Cambridge University Press, 2000.
Attridge, Derek, and Rosemary Jane Jolly. Introduction to *Writing South Africa: Literature, Apartheid, and Democracy, 1970–1995*, ed. Derek Attridge and Rosemary Jane Jolly, 1–13. Cambridge: Cambridge University Press, 1998.
Auerbach, Erich. *Mimesis: The Representation of Reality in Western Literature*. Trans. Willard R. Trask. Princeton, N.J.: Princeton University Press, 1971.
Auerbach, Jeffrey. "Imperial Boredom." *Common Knowledge* 11, no. 2 (Spring 2005): 283–305.
Austen, Jane. *Northanger Abbey*. Ed. R. W. Chapman. Oxford: Oxford University Press, 1988.
Barber, Benjamin R. *Jihad vs. McWorld: Terrorism's Challenge to Democracy*. New York: Ballantine, 1996.
Barthes, Roland. "Myth Today." In *Mythologies*, ed. and trans. Annette Lavers. New York: Hill and Wang, 1972.
Bauman, Zygmunt. *Modernity and Ambivalence*. Cambridge: Polity Press, 1991.
———. *Modernity and the Holocaust*. Ithaca, N.Y.: Cornell University Press, 1989.
Begam, Richard, and Michael Valdez Moses, eds. *Modernism and Colonialism: British and Irish Literature, 1899–1939*. Durham, N.C.: Duke University Press, 2007.
Benjamin, Walter. *The Arcades Project*. Trans. Howard Eiland and Kevin McLaughlin. Cambridge, Mass.: Belknap Press, 1999.
———. *Illuminations*. Ed. Hannah Arendt. Trans. Harry Zohn. New York: Schocken, 1973.
Bennett, Andrew. *Katherine Mansfield*. Plymouth: Northcote House, 2004.
Berlant, Lauren. "Ordinariness: An Introduction." Description of graduate course, Autumn 2006, at the Department of English, University of Chicago. http://english.uchicago.edu/courses/grad_autumn06.shtml.
Berman, Jessica. *Modernist Fiction, Cosmopolitanism, and the Politics of Community*. Cambridge: Cambridge University Press, 2001.
Berman, Marshall. *All That Is Solid Melts Into Air: The Experience of Modernity*. London: Verso, 1999.
Best, Elsdon. *The Maori as He Was: A Brief Account of Maori Life as It Was in Pre-European Days*. Wellington: R. E. Owen, Government Printer, 1952.
———. *Spiritual and Mental Concepts of the Maori*. Dominion Museum Monograph 2. New ed. Wellington: R. E. Owen, Government Printer, 1954.
Bishop, John. "The Banal, the Boring, and Ulysses." Paper presented at the Nineteenth International James Joyce Symposium, Dublin, June 12–19, 2004.
Blamires, Harry. *The New Bloomsday Book*. 3rd ed. London: Routledge, 1996.

Blanchot, Maurice. *The Infinite Conversation*. Trans. Susan Hanson. Minneapolis: University of Minnesota Press, 1993.
Bloch, Ernst. *Heritage of Our Times*. Trans. Neville and Stephen Plaice. Cambridge: Polity Press, 1991.
Boehmer, Elleke. "Endings and New Beginning: South African Fiction in Transition." In *Writing South Africa: Literature, Apartheid, and Democracy, 1970–1995*, ed. Derek Attridge and Rosemary Jolly, 43–56. Cambridge: Cambridge University Press, 1998.
——. "Katherine Mansfield as Colonial Modernist." In *Celebrating Katherine Mansfield: A Centenary Volume of Essays*, ed. Gerri Kimber and Janet Wilson, 57–71. Basingstoke: Palgrave, 2011.
——. "The Worlding of the Jingo Poem." In "Nineteenth Century Globalization," ed. Pablo Mukherjee, special issue, *Yearbook of English Studies* 41, no. 2 (July 2011): 41–57. Extended version published as "Circulating Forms: The Jingo Poem at the Height of Empire," in "Transnational Ethics," ed. Laura Winkiel, special issue, *English Language Notes* 49, no. 1 (forthcoming).
Bowlby, Rachel. *Feminist Destinations and Further Essays on Virginia Woolf*. Edinburgh: Edinburgh University Press, 1997.
Braudel, Fernand. *The Mediterranean and the Mediterranean World in the Age of Philip II*. Trans. Siân Reynolds. 2 vols. New York: Harper & Row, 1972–1973.
——. *On History*. Trans. Sarah Matthews. Chicago: University of Chicago Press, 1980.
Brown, Bill. "The Secret Life of Things: Virginia Woolf and the Matter of Modernism." *Modernism/Modernity* 6, no. 2 (1999): 1–28.
——. "Thing Theory." In "Things," ed. Bill Brown, special issue, *Critical Inquiry* 28, no. 1 (Autumn 2001): 1–22.
Brown, Nicholas. *Utopian Generations: The Political Horizons of Twentieth-Century Literature*. Princeton, N.J.: Princeton University Press, 2005.
Buzard, James. *The Beaten Track: European Tourism, Literature, and the Ways to Culture, 1880–1918*. Oxford: Clarendon Press, 1993.
——. "Culture and the Critics of *Dubliners*." *James Joyce Quarterly* 37, nos. 1–2 (2000): 43–62.
Byrd, Max. "Two or Three Things I Know About Setting." *Eighteenth-Century Fiction* 12, nos. 2–3 (January–April 2000): 185–192.
Calhoun, Craig, ed. *Habermas and the Public Sphere*. Cambridge, Mass.: The MIT Press, 1993.
Casanova, Pascale. *The World Republic of Letters*. Translated by M. B. DeBevoise. Cambridge, Mass.: Harvard University Press, 2005.
Cavell, Stanley. *Conditions Handsome and Unhandsome: The Constitution of Emersonian Perfectionism*. Chicago: University of Chicago Press, 1988.
——. *In Quest of the Ordinary: Lines of Skepticism and Romanticism*. Chicago: University of Chicago Press, 1988.
——. *Themes out of School: Effects and Causes*. San Francisco: North Point Press, 1984.
Chakrabarty, Dipesh. *Habitations of Modernity: Essays in the Wake of Subaltern Studies*. Chicago: University of Chicago Press, 2002.

———. *Provincializing Europe: Postcolonial Thought and Historical Difference.* Princeton, N.J.: Princeton University Press, 2000.

———. "Radical Histories and Question of Enlightenment Rationalism: Some Recent Critiques of *Subaltern Studies*." *Economic and Political Weekly* 30, no. 14 (April 8, 1995): 751–759.

Chatterjee, Indrani. Introduction to *Unfamiliar Relations: Family and History in South Asia*, ed. Indrani Chatterjee, 1–59. New Delhi: Permanent Black, 2004.

Chatterjee, Partha. *The Nation and Its Fragments: Colonial and Postcolonial Histories.* Princeton, N.J.: Princeton University Press, 1993.

Chaturvedi, Vinayak, ed. *Mapping Subaltern Studies and the Postcolonial.* London: Verso, 2000.

Chaudhuri, Amit. *Afternoon Raag.* In *Freedom Song: Three Novels.* New York: Knopf, 1999.

———. *Clearing a Space: Reflections on India, Literature, and Culture.* Oxford: Peter Lang, 2008.

———. *D. H. Lawrence and Difference.* Oxford: Oxford University Press, 2003.

———. *Freedom Song.* In *Freedom Song: Three Novels.* New York: Knopf, 1999.

———. *The Immortals.* London: Picador, 2009.

———. "In the Waiting-Room of History." Review of *Provincialising Europe: Postcolonial Thought and Historical Difference*, by Dipesh Chakrabarty. *London Review of Books* 26, no. 12 (June 24, 2004): 3–5.

———. Introduction to *Jejuri*, by Aruna Kolatkar. New York: NYRB, 2005.

———. *A New World.* New York: Knopf, 2000.

———, ed. *The Picador Book of Modern Indian Literature.* London: Picador, 2001.

———. *Real Time: Stories and a Memoir.* New York: Farrar, Straus and Giroux, 2002.

———. *A Strange and Sublime Address.* In *Freedom Song: Three Novels.* New York: Knopf, 1999.

Clifford, James. *On the Edges of Anthropology.* Chicago: Prickly Paradigm Press, 2003.

———. *The Predicament of Culture: Twentieth-Century Ethnography, Literature, and Art.* Cambridge, Mass.: Harvard University Press, 1988.

Clifford, James, and George E. Marcus, eds. *Writing Culture: The Poetics and Politics of Ethnography.* Berkeley: University of California Press, 1986.

Cohn, Bernard. *An Anthropologist Among the Historians and Other Essays.* Delhi: Oxford University Press, 1987.

Crangle, Sarah. "The Time Being: On Woolf and Boredom." *MFS Modern Fiction Studies* 54, no. 2 (Summer 2008): 209–232.

Crapanzano, Vincent. "Hermes' Dilemma: The Masking of Subversion in Ethnographic Description." In *Writing Culture: The Poetics and Politics of Ethnography*, ed. James Clifford and George E. Marcus, 51–76. Berkeley: University of California Press, 1986.

Deane, Seamus. *Strange Country: Modernity and Nationhood in Irish Writing Since 1790.* Oxford: Clarendon Press, 1997.

Debord, Guy. "Perspectives for Conscious Alterations in Everyday Life." In *The Everyday Life Reader*, ed. Ben Highmore. London: Routledge, 2002.

de Certeau, Michel. *The Practice of Everyday Life.* Berkeley: University of California Press, 1984.

Deming, Robert, ed. *James Joyce: The Critical Heritage.* 2 vols. London: Routledge, 1970.

Duffy, Enda. "Disappearing Dublin: Ulysses, Postcoloniality, and the Politics of Space." In *Semicolonial Joyce*, ed. Derek Attridge and Marjorie Howes, 37–57. Cambridge: Cambridge University Press, 2000.
———. *The Subaltern* Ulysses. Minneapolis: University of Minnesota Press, 1996.
Dumm, Thomas L. *A Politics of the Ordinary*. New York: New York University Press, 1999.
Eagleton, Terry. "Anti-Humanism." Review of *D.H. Lawrence and "Difference": Post-Coloniality and the Poetry of the Present* by Amit Chaudhuri. *London Review of Books* 26, no. 3 (February 3, 2004): 16–18.
Edgeworth, Maria. *Ennui*. Ed. Robert Lee Wolff. New York: Garland, 1978.
Ellman, Richard. *James Joyce*. 2nd ed. Oxford: Oxford University Press, 1982.
Esty, Jed. *A Shrinking Island: Modernism and National Culture in England*. Princeton, N.J.: Princeton University Press, 2004.
Fabian, Johannes. *Time and the Other: How Anthropology Makes Its Object*. New York: Columbia University Press, 1983.
Felski, Rita. "The Invention of Everyday Life." *New Formations* 39, no. 4 (2002): 607–622.
Ferguson, James, and Akhil Gupta. "Spatializing States: Toward an Ethnography of Neoliberal Governmentality." *American Ethnologist* 29, no. 4 (November 2002): 981–1002.
Fisher, Philip. *The Vehement Passions*. Princeton, N.J.: Princeton University Press, 2002.
Frow, John. "A Pebble, a Camera, a Man Who Turns Into a Telegraph Pole," in "Things," ed. Bill Brown, special issue, *Critical Inquiry* 28, no. 1 (Autumn 2001): 270–285.
Fullbrook, Kate. *Katherine Mansfield*. Bloomington: Indiana University Press, 1986.
Gallagher, Catherine, and Stephen Greenblatt. *Practicing New Historicism*. Chicago: University of Chicago Press, 2001.
Gibson, Andrew. *Joyce's Revenge: History, Politics, and Aesthetics in* Ulysses. Oxford: Oxford University Press, 2002.
———. *Postmodernity, ethics and the novel*. New York: Routledge, 1999.
Giddens, Anthony. *The Consequences of Modernity*. Stanford, Calif.: Stanford University Press, 1990.
———. *Conversations with Anthony Giddens: Making Sense of Modernity*. With Christopher Pierson. Stanford, Calif.: Stanford University Press, 1998.
Gikandi, Simon. *Writing in Limbo: Modernism and Caribbean Literature*. Ithaca, N.Y.: Cornell University Press, 1992
Ghosh, Bishnupriya. "An Invitation to Indian Postmodernity: Rushdie's English Vernacular as Situated Cultural Hybridity." In *Critical Essays on Salman Rushdie*, ed. M. Keith Booker, 129–153. New York: G. K. Hall, 1999.
Gilroy, Paul. "The Black Atlantic as a Counterculture of Modernity." In *The Black Atlantic: Modernity and Double Consciousness*, 1–40. Cambridge, Mass.: Harvard University Press, 1993.
Ginsberg, Michal Peled, and Lorri G. Nandrea. "The Prose of the World." In *The Novel*, ed. Franco Moretti, vol. 2, *Forms and Themes*, 244–273. Princeton, N.J.: Princeton University Press, 2006.

Goodstein, Elizabeth S. *Experience Without Qualities: Boredom and Modernity.* Stanford, Calif.: Stanford University Press, 2005.

Gordon, Ian. "Katherine Mansfield: The Wellington Years, a Reassessment." In *Critical Essays on Katherine Mansfield*, ed. Rhoda B. Nathan, 61–74. Boston: G. K. Hall, 1993.

Habermas, Jürgen. *The Structural Transformation of the Public Sphere: An Inquiry Into a Category of Bourgeois Society.* Trans. Thomas Burger with the assistance of Frederick Lawrence. Cambridge, M.A.: MIT Press, 1991.

Hankin, Cherry. "Fantasy and the Sense of an Ending in the Work of Katherine Mansfield." *Modern Fiction Studies* 24, no. 3 (Autumn 1978): 465–474. Reprinted in *The Critical Response to Katherine Mansfield*, ed. Jan Pilditch, 183–190. Westport, Conn.: Greenwood Press, 1996.

Hansen, Thomas Blom, and Finn Stepputat. *States of Imagination: Ethnographic Explorations of the Postcolonial State.* Durham, N.C.: Duke University Press, 2001.

Hanson, Clare. "Katherine Mansfield." In *The Gender of Modernism: A Critical Anthology*, ed. Bonnie Kime Scott, 298–315. Bloomington: Indiana University Press, 1990.

Hardt, Michael, and Antonio Negri. *Empire.* Cambridge, Mass.: Harvard University Press, 2000.

Harootunian, Harry. *History's Disquiet: Modernity, Cultural Practice and the Question of Everyday Life.* New York: Columbia University Press, 2000.

Hart, Matthew. *Nations of Nothing but Poetry: Modernism, Transnationalism, and Synthetic Vernacular Writing.* New York: Oxford University Press, 2010.

Hegel, G. W. F. *Aesthetics: Lectures on Fine Art.* 2 vols. Trans. T. M. Knox. Oxford: Clarendon, 1975.

Herring, Scott. "Regional Modernism: A Reintroduction." In "Regional Modernism," ed. Scott Herring, special issue, *Modern Fiction Studies* 55, no. 1 (Spring 2009): 1–10.

Highmore, Ben. "Questioning Everyday Life." Introduction to *The Everyday Life Reader*, ed. Ben Highmore. London: Routledge, 2002.

Howes, Marjorie. "Joyce, Colonialism, and Nationalism." In *The New Cambridge Companion to James Joyce*, 2nd ed., ed. Derek Attridge, 254–271. Cambridge: Cambridge University Press, 2004.

Ihimaera, Witi. *Dear Miss Mansfield: A Tribute to Kathleen Mansfield Beauchamp.* Auckland: Viking, 1989.

Ingrassia, Catherine. Introduction to *A Companion to the Eighteenth-Century English Novel and Culture*, ed. Paula R. Backscheider and Catherine Ingrassia, 1–17. Malden, Mass.: Blackwell, 2005.

Jameson, Fredric. "Modernism and Imperialism." In *Nationalism, Colonialism, and Literature*, ed. Terry Eagleton, Fredric Jameson, and Edward W. Said, 43–68. Minneapolis: University of Minnesota Press, 1990.

——. *A Singular Modernity: Essay on the Ontology of the Present.* London: Verso, 2002.

——. "Third World Literature in the Era of Multinational Capitalism." *Social Text* 15 (Autumn 1986): 65–88. Reprinted in *The Jameson Reader*, ed. Michael Hardt and Kathi Weeks, 315–339. Oxford: Blackwell, 2000.

——. "*Ulysses* in History." In *James Joyce and Modern Literature*, ed. W. J. McCormack and Alistair Stead. London: Routledge, 1982.

Joshi, Priya. *In Another Country: Colonialism, Culture, and the English Novel in India.* New York: Columbia University Press, 2002.
Joyce, James. "Drama and Life." In *The Critical Writings of James Joyce*, ed. Ellsworth Mason and Richard Ellmann, 38–46. Ithaca, N.Y.: Cornell University Press, 1989.
——. *Dubliners.* Ed. Shane Weller. New York: Dover, 1991.
——. *Finnegans Wake.* New York: Viking, 1967.
——. *A Portrait of the Artist as a Young Man.* New York: Garland, 1993.
——. *Stephen Hero.* Ed. Theodore Spencer. New York: New Directions, 1963.
——. *Ulysses.* Ed. By Hans Walter Gabler. New York: Vintage Books, 1986.
Kaplan, Sydney Janet. *Katherine Mansfield and the Origins of Modernist Fiction.* Ithaca, N.Y.: Cornell University Press, 1991.
Kapur, Geeta. "Globalisation and Culture." *Third Text* 11, no. 39 (Summer 1997): 21–38.
Kierkegaard, Søren. *Either-Or.* Trans. Howard V. and Edna H. Hong. Princeton, N.J.: Princeton University Press, 1987.
Kincaid, Jamaica. *A Small Place.* New York: Farrar, Straus and Giroux, 1988.
Kirshenblatt-Gimblett, Barbara. *Destination Culture: Tourism, Museums, and Heritage.* Berkeley: University of California Press, 1998.
Kleinberg, Aviad. "What Are the Cultural uses of Boredom?" *Off the Page* blog (February 8, 2008). http://harvardpress.typepad.com/off_the_page/2008/02/what-are-the-cu.html.
Kracauer, Sigfried. *The Mass Ornament: Weimar Essays.* Trans. Thomas Y. Levin. Cambridge, Mass.: Harvard University Press, 1995.
Kristeva, Julia. "Is There a Feminine Genius?" *Critical Inquiry* 30, no. 3 (Spring 2004): 493–504.
Lauter, Paul, ed. *The Heath Anthology of American Literature.* Lexington, Mass.: D. C. Heath, 1990.
Lefebvre, Henri. *Critique of Everyday Life.* Trans. John Moore. London: Verso, 1991.
——. "The Everyday and Everydayness." Trans. Christine Levich, with Alice Kaplan and Christine Ross. *Yale French Studies* 73 (1987): 7–11.
——. "Towards a Leftist Cultural Politics." In *Marxism and the Interpretation of Culture*, ed. Cary Nelson and Lawrence Grossberg, 75–88. Chicago: University of Illinois Press, 1988.
Leonard, Garry. "The History of Now: Commodity Culture and Everyday Life in Joyce." In *Joyce and the Subject of History*, ed. Mark Wollaeger, Victor Luftig, and Robert Spoo, 13–26. Ann Arbor: University of Michigan Press, 1996.
——. "Hystericising Modernism: Modernity in Joyce." In *Cultural Studies of James Joyce*, ed. by R. B. Kershner, 167–188. Amsterdam: Rodopi, 2003.
——. "Joyce and Advertising: Advertising and Commodity Culture in Joyce's Fiction." *James Joyce Quarterly* 30/31, no. 1 (Summer–Fall 1993): 573–592.
Levinas, Emmanuel. *Totality and Infinity.* Trans. Alphonso Lingis. Pittsburgh, Penn.: Duquesne University Press, 1969.
Lewis, Pericles. *Modernism, Nationalism, and the Novel.* Cambridge: Cambridge University Press, 2000.

Love, Heather K. *Feeling Backward: Loss and the Politics of Queer History.* Cambridge, Mass.: Harvard University Press, 2007.

Lukács, Georg. "Realism in the Balance." In *Aesthetics and Politics: The Key Texts of the Classic Debate Within German Marxism,* trans. Rodney Livingstone, 28–59. New York: Verso, 1980.

———. *The Theory of the Novel: A Historico-Philosophical Essay on the Forms of Great Epic Literature.* Trans. Anna Bostock. Cambridge, Mass.: MIT Press, 1971.

MacAskill, Brian. "Inside Out: Jeremy Cronin's Lyrical Politics." In *Writing South Africa: Literature, Apartheid, and Democracy, 1970–1995,* ed. Derek Attridge and Rosemary Jolly, 187–203. Cambridge: Cambridge University Press, 1998.

Malinowski, Bronislaw. *Argonauts of the Western Pacific: An Account of Native Enterprise and Adventure in the Archipelagoes of Melanesian New Guinea.* New York: Dutton, 1961.

Mains, Daniel. "Desire and Opportunity Among Urban Youth in Ethiopia." PhD diss., Emory University, 2007.

Mandela, Nelson. *Long Walk to Freedom: The Autobiography of Nelson Mandela.* Boston: Little, Brown, 1994.

Manganaro, Marc. *Culture, 1922: The Emergence of a Concept.* Princeton, N.J.: Princeton University Press, 2002.

Mansfield, Katherine. *The Katherine Mansfield Notebooks.* 2 vols. Ed. Margaret Scott. Canterbury: Lincoln University Press, 1997.

———. *Selected Stories.* Ed. Angela Smith. Oxford: Oxford University Press, 2002.

———. *Undiscovered Country: The New Zealand Stories of Katherine Mansfield.* Ed. Ian A. Gordon. London: Longman, 1974.

———. *The Urewera Notebook.* Ed. Ian A. Gordon. Oxford: Oxford University Press, 1978.

Mao, Douglas. *Solid Objects: Modernism and the Test of Production.* Princeton, N.J.: Princeton University Press, 1998.

Mao, Douglas, and Rebecca Walkowitz. "The New Modernist Studies." *PMLA* 123, no. 3 (May 2008): 737–748.

Marling, Karal Ann. *As Seen on TV: The Visual Culture of Everyday Life in the 1950s.* Cambridge, Mass.: Harvard University Press, 1994.

Marx, John. *The Modernist Novel and the Decline of Empire.* Cambridge: Cambridge University Press, 2005.

Mbembe, Achille. *On the Postcolony.* Berkeley: University of California Press, 2001.

McKeon, Michael. *The Origins of the English Novel: 1600–1740.* Baltimore, Md.: Johns Hopkins University Press, 1988.

———. "Privacy, Domesticity, Women." In *Theory of The Novel,* ed. Michael McKeon, 435–439. Baltimore, Md.: Johns Hopkins University Press, 2000.

Mee, Jon. "After Midnight: The Novel in the 1980s and 1990s." In *A History of Indian Literature in English,* ed. Arvind Krishna Mehrotra, 318–336. New York: Columbia University Press, 2003.

Miller, D. A. "Discipline in Different Voices: Bureaucracy, Police, Family, and *Bleak House.*" In *Charles Dickens,* ed. Harold Bloom, 123–157. New York: Chelsea House, 2006.

Mofokeng, Boitumelo. "With My Baby on My Back." *Speak* 27 (1990): 21.
Moretti, Franco. "Serious Century." In *The Novel*, ed. Franco Moretti, vol. 1, *History, Geography, and Culture*, 364–400. Princeton, N.J.: Princeton University Press, 2006.
———. *The Way of the World: The Bildungsroman in European Culture*. Trans. Albert Sbragia. London: Verso, 2000.
Moshenberg, Daniel. "A Capital Couple: Speculating in *Ulysses*." *James Joyce Quarterly* 25, no. 3 (Spring 1988): 333–347.
Mufti, Aamir R. *Enlightenment in the Colony: The Jewish Question and the Crisis of Postcolonial Culture*. Princeton, N.J.: Princeton University Press, 2007.
Musharbash, Yasmine. "Boredom, Time, and Modernity: An Example from Aboriginal Australia." *American Anthropologist* 109, no. 2 (June 2007): 307–317.
Ndebele, Njabulo. *South African Literature and Culture: Rediscovery of the Ordinary*. Scottsville, South Africa: University of KwaZulu Natal Press, 2006.
Negt, Oskar, and Alexander Kluge. *Public Sphere and Experience: Toward an Analysis of the Bourgeois and Proletarian Public Sphere*. Trans. Peter Labanyi, Jamie Owen Daniel, and Assenka Oksiloff. Minneapolis: University of Minnesota Press, 1993.
Ngai, Sianne. *Ugly Feelings*. Cambridge, Mass.: Harvard University Press, 2005.
Nkosi, Lewis. *Mating Birds*. Cape Town: Kwela Books, 2004.
———. "Postmodernism and Black Writing in South Africa." In *Writing South Africa: Literature, Apartheid, and Democracy, 1970–1995*, ed. Derek Attridge and Rosemary Jane Jolly, 74–90. Cambridge: Cambridge University Press, 1998.
———. *The Rhythm of Violence*. London: Oxford University Press, 1964.
Nolan, Emer. *James Joyce and Nationalism*. London: Routledge, 1995.
Norris, Margot. *Joyce's Web: The Social Unraveling of Modernism*. Austin: University of Texas Press, 1992.
O'Brien, Flann. *The Third Policeman*. New York: Walker and Company, 1967.
Olson, Liesl. *Modernism and the Ordinary*. Oxford: Oxford University Press, 2009.
O'Neill, Bruce. "Bleak House: Boredom and the Everyday of Bucharest's Homeless Shelters." Draft of PhD diss., Stanford University, work in progress.
Orr, Bridget. "The Maori House of Fiction." In *Cultural Institutions of the Novel*, ed. Deidre Lynch and William Beattie Warner, 73–95. Durham, N.C.: Duke University Press, 1995
Pechey, Graham. "The Post-Apartheid Sublime: Rediscovering the Extraordinary." In *Writing South Africa: Literature, Apartheid, and Democracy, 1970–1995*, ed. Derek Attridge and Rosemary Jane Jolly, 57–74. Cambridge: Cambridge University Press, 1998.
Pels, Peter. "The Anthropology of Colonialism: Culture, History, and the Emergence of Western Governmentality." *Annual Review of Anthropology* 26 (1997): 163–183.
Perera, Sonali. "'—All That Is Present and Moving . . .': Thinking Working-Class Writing at the Limits." PhD Diss., Columbia University, 2003.
Phillips, Siobhan. *The Poetics of the Everyday: Creative Repetition in Modern American Verse*. New York: Columbia University Press, 2010.
Plaatje, Sol. *Mhudi*. Ed. Stephen Gray. London: Heineman, 1978.

Pratt, Mary Louise. *Imperial Eyes: Travel Writing and Transculturation*. London: Routledge, 1993.
Ralph, Michael. "Killing Time." *Social Text* 26, no. 4 (Winter 2008)
Rancière, Jacques. *The Nights of Labor: The Worker's Dream in Nineteenth-Century France*. Trans. John Drury. Philadelphia, Penn.: Temple University Press, 1989.
Randall, Bryony. *Modernism, Daily Time, and Everyday Life*. Cambridge: Cambridge University Press, 2007.
Rao, Raja. *Kanthapura*. Westport, Conn.: Greenwood Press, 1977.
Ricoeur, Paul. *Time and Narrative*. Trans. Kathleen McLaughlin and David Pellauer. 2 vols. Chicago: University of Chicago Press, 1984.
Robbins, Bruce. *Upward Mobility and the Common Good: Toward a Literary History of the Welfare State*. Princeton, N.J.: Princeton University Press, 2007.
Robbins, Jill. *Altered Reading: Levinas and Literature*. Chicago: University of Chicago Press, 1999.
Said, Edward. *Humanism and Democratic Criticism*. New York: Columbia University Press, 2004.
——. *Orientalism*. New York: Pantheon, 1979.
Schor, Naomi. *Breaking the Chain: Women, Theory, and French Realist Fiction*. New York: Columbia University Press, 1985.
——. *Reading in Detail: Aesthetics and the Feminine*. London: Routledge, 1989.
Schwenger, Peter. "Words and the Murder of the Thing," in "Things," ed. Bill Brown, special issue, *Critical Inquiry* 28, no. 1 (Autumn 2001): 99–113.
Sealy, I. Allan. *Trotter-Nama*. New York: Knopf, 1988.
Segal, Naomi. *The Banal Object: Theme and Thematics in Proust, Rilke, Hofmannsthal, and Sartre*. London: University of London Press, 1981.
Seidel, Michael. "The Man Who Came to Dinner: Ian Watt and the Theory of Formal Realism." *Eighteenth-Century Fiction* 12, no. 2 (January–April 2000): 193–212.
Seremetakis, C. Nadia., ed. *The Senses Still: Perception and Memory as Material Culture in Modernity*. Boulder, Colo.: Westview, 1994.
Sicherman, Carol. Literary afterword to *You Can't Get Lost in Cape Town*, by Zoë Wicomb, 187–208. New York: Feminist Press at the City University of New York, 2000.
Sole, Kelwyn. " 'The Deep Thoughts the One in Need Falls Into': Quotidian Experience and the Perspectives of Poetry in Postliberation South Africa." In *Postcolonial Studies and Beyond*, ed. Ania Loomba et al., 182–205. Durham, N.C.: Duke University Press, 2006.
Spacks, Patricia Meyer. *Boredom: A Literary History of a State of Mind*. Chicago: University of Chicago Press, 1995.
Spivak, Gayatri Chakravorty. *A Critique of Postcolonial Reason*. Cambridge, Mass.: Harvard University Press, 1999.
Spoo, Robert. *James Joyce and the Language of History*. New York: Oxford University Press, 1994.
Sprinker, Michael. "The National Question: Said, Ahmad, Jameson." *Public Culture* 6 (1993): 3–29.
Stewart, Susan. *On Longing: Narratives of the Miniature, the Gigantic, the Souvenir, the Collection*. Baltimore, Md.: John Hopkins University Press, 1984.
Suleri, Sara. *The Rhetoric of English India*. Chicago: University of Chicago Press, 1992.

Svendsen, Lars. *A Philosophy of Boredom*. Trans. John Irons. London: Reaktion Books, 2005.
Szeman, Imre. "Who's Afraid of National Allegory? Jameson, Literary Criticism, Globalization." *South Atlantic Quarterly* 100, no. 3 (Summer 2001): 803–827.
Taussig, Michael. *Mimesis and Alterity: A Particular History of the Senses*. London: Routledge, 1993.
———. *The Nervous System*. London: Routledge, 1992.
Tlali, Miriam. *Muriel at Metropolitan*. Harlow: Longman, 1987.
Tomalin, Claire. *Katherine Mansfield: A Secret Life*. New York: Knopf, 1988.
Wagner, Linda Welshimer, ed. *Interviews with William Carlos Williams*. New York: New Directions, 1976.
Walkowitz, Rebecca. *Cosmopolitan Style: Modernism Beyond the Nation*. New York: Columbia University Press, 2006.
Wa Thiong'o, Ngugi. *Petals of Blood*. New York: Dutton, 1978.
Watt, Ian. *The Rise of the Novel: Studies in Defoe, Richardson, and Fielding*. Berkeley: University of California Press, 1957.
Weber, Max. *Economy and Society: An Outline of Interpretative Sociology*. Ed. Guenther Roth and Claus Wittich. Berkeley: University of California Press, 1978.
———. *The Protestant Ethic and the Spirit of Capitalism*. Trans. Talcott Parsons. London: HarperCollins, 1991.
Wevers, Lydia. "The Shot Story." In *The Oxford History of New Zealand Literature in English*, 2nd ed., ed. Terry Sturn, 245–320. Auckland: Oxford University Press, 1998.
Wicke, Jennifer. "Modernity Must Advertise: Aura, Desire, and Decolonization in Joyce." *James Joyce Quarterly* 30/31, no. 1 (Summer–Fall 1993): 593–613.
Wicomb, Zoë. *David's Story*. New York: Feminist Press at the City University of New York, 2001.
———. *The One That Got Away*. New York: The New Press, 2009.
———. *Playing in the Light*. New York: The New Press, 2006.
———. "Shame and Identity: The Case of the Colored in South Africa." In *Writing South Africa: Literature, Apartheid, and Democracy, 1970–1995*, ed. Derek Attridge and Rosemary Jolly, 91–107. Cambridge: Cambridge University Press, 1998.
———. *You Can't Get Lost in Cape Town*. New York: Feminist Press at the City University of New York, 2000.
Williams, Mark. "Mansfield in Maoriland: Biculturalism, Agency, and Misreading." In *Modernism and Empire*, ed. Howard J. Booth and Nigel Rigby, 249–274. Manchester: Manchester University Press, 2000.
Williams, Patrick. "'Simultaneous Uncontemporaneities': Theorising Modernism and Empire." In *Modernism and Empire*, ed. Nigel J. Booth and Howard Rigby, 13–38. Manchester: Manchester University Press. 2000.
Williams, Raymond. *The Politics of Modernism: Against the New Conformists*. London: Verso, 1989.
Wilson, Edmund. *Axel's Castle: A Study of the Imaginative Literature of 1870–1930*. New York: C. Scribner's Sons, 1931.
Woolf, Virginia. "A Letter to a Young Poet." In *Collected Essays*, 2:182–195. New York: Harcourt, Brace, and World, 1967.

———. "Modern Fiction." In *Collected Essays*, 2:103-110. New York: Harcourt, Brace, and World, 1967.
———. "Mr. Bennett and Mrs. Brown." In *Collected Essays*, 1:319–337. New York: Harcourt, Brace, and World, 1967.
———. "The Narrow Bridge of Art." In *Collected Essays*, 2:218–229. New York: Harcourt , Brace, and World, 1967.
Wright, Marcia. Historical introduction to *You Can't Get Lost in Cape Town*, by Zoë Wicomb, vii–xxiv. New York: Feminist Press at the City University of New York, 2000.
Young, Robert. *White Mythologies: Writing History and the West*. London: Routledge, 1990.

Index

Achebe, Chinua, 138–39, 194n73
action, 38, 199n27
Adams, Robert Martin, 56–57
Adiga, Aravind, 138
Adorno, Theodor, 47
advertising, Bloom's response to, 60–61
"Aeolus" (chapter from *Ulysses*), 56
aesthetics, 4; banality and, 5–7, 14, 19–20; boredom and, 6–7, 20–21; deprivation as boredom, 23; embodied through banality, 38–39; Enlightenment modernity and, 8, 16–17; exploration of everyday life, 106; failure of, 103; models, 185n4; modernism, 14, 16–17; of ordinary, 170; politics and, 35; principles of, 8, 42; transcendence, 9; value in Enlightenment culture, 19–20
Afternoon Raag (Chaudhuri), 155–56, 159, 163
Agamben, Giorgio, 186n23, 198n28
Ahmad, Aijaz, 136
Aidoo, Ama Ata, 114
Alice (character from Mansfield), 97
alienness, 103; radical, 45
Anglophone literature, 19–20, 105, 108; banality in, 176; colonial, 3–4; cultural politics of, 175; globalization of, 30; from India, 135–38, 147–48, 150, 168; literary modernism related to, 28–29; postcolonial, 3–4, 35; reading of archives, 6
anthropological humanism, 99, 102–3
anthropology, 99, 168, 191n58, 200n1; boredom and, 26; colonialism and, 104; exploration of ordinary life, 26; functionalist, 191n60; indigenous society and, 83; Joyce and, 62–63, 197n45; literature related to, 27, 101–2; Malinowski and, 62–65; Otherness and, 103–4; poststructuralism and, 191n57; *Ulysses* and, 62–63
anticolonial nationalism, 34, 140
antique principle, 42

apartheid, 108–9, 111–13, 115, 123, 201n20; women and, 131–32
Appadurai, Arjun, 151–52
Aquinas, Thomas (character from Joyce), 42
"Araby" (Joyce), 40, 48–50
Arendt, Hannah, 38, 85, 207n7; *vita activa*, 198n27
Argonauts (Malinowski), 64
"Ash on My Sleeve" (Wicomb), 132
"At the Bay" (Mansfield), 72
Auerbach, Erich, 196n31
Auerbach, Jeffrey, 72–73, 198n7
Aunt Nettie (character from Wicomb), 125
autoethnographicy, 65, 104–5, 118, 167, 191n60
Axel's Castle (Wilson), 53–54

bad detail, 58–59
banality, 103, 169, 179; aesthetics and, 5–7, 14, 19–20; aesthetics embodied through, 38–39; in Anglophone fiction, 176; Chaudhuri and, 28, 35, 162; of colonial life, 3, 40; counternarrative of, 123; critique of historicism, transience and, 41–59; desire, pleasure, and, 8–16; disempowerment of, 33; of empire, 27–36; epiphany of, 48; etymological and cultural histories of, 17–18; everyday life relationship with, 9–10; generic modernity of, 16–27; grandeur and, 41, 115–21; history and, 170–72; Joyce and, 24, 37–40, 62; Mansfield and, 6–8, 11; metropolitan modernity as related to, 12; as motif for colonial and postcolonial literary criticism, 4; as motif for colonial modernity, 27–28; oppositional relationship with literature, 4; of periphery, 40; power of, 49, 148, 178; refuge in, 124–27, 130–31; transcendence and, 13–14; transformation and, 12–13, 128; Wicomb and, 28, 35, 123; Woolf and, 11; youth and, 121–22. *See also* object, common or banal
banal oven, 188n30

Barnacle, Nora, 64
Barthes, Roland, 11, 104
basic needs, 35–36
Baudelaire, Charles, 21, 22
Bauman, Zygmunt, 187n26
Beatrice (character from Wicomb), 131
Beauchamp, Arthur, 76
Beauchamp, Harold, 76
beauty, 42
"Behind the Bougainvillea" (Wicomb), 122, 126
Bengal, 73, 140, 146, 151–54, 164, 167
Benjamin, Walter, 15, 67, 164–65; boredom and, 187n24; sense of fragment, 49
Bennett, Andrew, 94
Bennett, Arnold, 54, 64; Woolf quarrel with, 8–9, 12, 13
Berman, Marshall, 188n27
Best, Elsdon, 81–82, 83
"Beyond Translation" (Chaudhuri), 160
Bhaskar (character from Chaudhuri), 166
Biko, Steve, 132
biographical origin, distance from, 34
Bishop, John, 51
Black Nationalism, 110–11
Bleak House (Dickens), 21
Bloom, Leopold (character from Joyce): advertising and, 60–61; Dedalus and, 57–60, 153; flânerie, 67–68; key, 56–57; pocket of, 54–59, 62; potato, 54–57; soap, 51–57, 59–62; walking, 66
Bloomsbury circle, 1, 6, 31, 77, 80
Boehmer, Elleke, 109
boredom, 5, 67, 120, 178–79; aesthetics and, 6–7, 20–21; as aesthetics deprivation, 23; anthropology and, 26; antithesis of, 103; Barthes on, 11; Benjamin and, 187n24; Chaudhuri and, 162; after contact, 197n5; desire, pleasure, and, 8–16; disempowerment of, 33; domesticity and, 84; Dumm and, 21–22; empire space of, 72; ennui vs.,

22–23, 190n47; ethnographic analyses of, 23–24, 187n25; etymological and cultural histories of, 17, 18–19; evolution of mental state, 22–23; gendered, 75, 84–85; history of thought, 15; Joyce and, 49; Mansfield and, 96–97; modern experience and, 21; as motif for colonial and postcolonial literary criticism, 4; profound, 186n23; psychosis and, 90; Svendsen and, 11; transcendence and, 11. *See also* female boredom

borian, 18

Bowlby, Rachel, 67, 163

"Bowl Like Hole" (Mansfield), 116

Boylan, Blazes (character from Joyce), 55

Braudel, Fernand, 139, 171–75

Miss Brill (character from Mansfield), 84, 88–89

British Commonwealth, 31, 34

British Empire, 27–28, 176; boredom and, 72; decline, 29–30; English-language literature and, 16; inadequacies, 23; literary modernism and, 5–6

Brown, Bill, 62, 186n23

Brown, Nicholas, 136–37

Burnell, Stanley (character from Mansfield), 71–73

Burnell family (characters from Mansfield), 72, 74

Button, Pearl (character from Mansfield), 96, 97

Buzard, James, 26, 63, 118, 166–67

Calcutta, 31, 152–55, 163–65, 167, 198n7

capitalism, 177; consumer, 59, 60; globalized, 165, 187n25; industrial, 50–51; rational, 10

Caribbean writers, 192n61

Casanova, Pascale, 30, 31

Cavell, Stanley, 105, 139, 173, 175, 207n13; view of ordinary, 176

Chakrabarty, Dipesh, 14, 48–49, 119, 158–59, 164

Chandler, Thomas Malone "Little Chandler" (character from Joyce), 37–39

Chandra, Vikram, 141, 145

Chatterjee, Indrani, 140, 152

Chatterjee, Partha, 140

Chaudhuri, Amit, 5, 27, 29, 135; banality and, 28, 35, 162; biographical and imaginative movements of, 31; boredom and, 162; Eagleton on, 157; everyday life and, 150–51; flâneur fictions of, 147–68; Indian narrative, 175; Joyce and, 153–55, 167; on *Midnight's Children*, 144–45; on nation, 146–47; provincial and, 152; works of, 149. *See also specific characters*; *specific works*

"Child in the House" (Pater), 1

"Circe" (chapter from *Ulysses*), 52

classical literature, 4–5

"Clearing in the Bush, A" (Wicomb), 128

Clifford, James, 26–27, 82, 98–99, 101–5, 107; on culture, 197n45; Ota and, 200n1; poststructuralist theory and anthropology, 191n57

colonial desire, 11–12, 91–92; female tedium and, 84–90; unfulfilled, 121

colonial era: Anglophone fiction, 3–4; motifs for literary criticism, 4

colonial history, 94; dynamics of, 7; Mansfield's relationship with, 77; in New Zealand, 92

colonialism, 14, 115; alterity and, 143; anthropology and, 104; banality of, 3, 40; cultural politics of, 35–36; landscape and architecture, 198n7; legacies of, 178; of Mansfield's fiction, 99; narratives of, 36; in New Zealand, 79; politics of, 6–7; social structures, 91; women and, 131–32. *See also* settler colonial population

colonial modernity, 3, 22, 75, 167; banal as motif for, 27–28; disempowerment as condition of, 15; imperial vs., 28

colony: empire vs., 6–7; ethnography of everyday life in, 62–69; genre and narration in, 106–15; modernity in, 3–4, 11–12
commodity misplaced, 59–62
"Construction of the Indian Novel in English, The" (Chaudhuri), 135
consumerism, 24, 50–51, 191n50; satisfaction and, 25
consumption, 32
contact zone, 27, 104, 120
cosmopolitanism, 154
Cranly (character from Joyce), 43–44
Crapanzano, Vincent, 102
Crawford, Robert, 192n65
creative writing, theory and, 149–50
Critical Inquiry, 186n23
cultural hierarchies, 33, 63, 82, 120; imperial, 6
culture: Anglophone literature and politics of, 175; Clifford on, 197n45; construct of, 160; distant, 48; Dublin, 65; Enlightenment, 19–20; left behind, 31–32; Māori, 78; politics of colonialism and, 35–36; postcolonial fiction and politics of, 35–36; spheres, 140–41; tourism and, 32–33; as weapon of struggle, 109. *See also* indigenous culture
Culture, 1922: The Emergence of a Concept (Manganaro), 62–63

dailiness, 62–63, 65; dallying with, 147–68; uneventful, 39–40
Dalloway, Clarissa, 11
Dangarembga, Tsistsi, 113–14
Daniel Deronda (George Eliot), 21
"Daughters of the Late Colonel" (Mansfield), 84
David's Story (Wicomb), 114
Dear Miss Mansfield: A Tribute to Kathleen Mansfield Beauchamp (Ihimaera), 71, 76, 80
Deasy (character from Joyce), 48–49
Debord, Guy, 23–24, 177

De Certeau, Michel, 23–24, 66, 163
decolonization, 7, 16, 31, 141; conflicts of, 36; governmentality and, 208n31; narratives of, 36
Dedalus, Stephen (character from Joyce), 39–41, 50, 65, 67–68; Bloom and, 57–60, 153; Mr. Deasy and, 48–49; theories, 42–45, 49, 59–60
democracy, 25, 50–51
Denison, William, 73
Desai, Kiran, 138
desire, 32; in backwaters of empire, 71–79; banality, boredom, pleasure, and, 8–16; Lefebvre and, 193n71. *See also* colonial desire
Dickens, Charles, 21
Dillon, Leo (character from Joyce), 48
Dirkse, David (character from Wicomb), 114
disempowerment, 23, 33, 34, 73; as condition of colonial modernity, 15
"Doll's House, The" (Mansfield), 72
domesticity, 113; in backwaters of empire, 71–79; boredom and, 84; violence and, 92. *See also* private sphere
"Drama and Life" (Joyce), 37, 41
dramatic, the, 105–6, 115
Dublin, 31–32, 39–40, 56, 64; culture, 65; fiction, 61; narrative, 68–69
Dubliners (Joyce), 38–41, 47, 48, 114. *See also specific short stories*
Duffy, Enda, 29, 67, 163
Dumm, Thomas, 19, 170, 174; on American pursuits of happiness, 24–25; boredom and, 21–22; on everyday life, 25; on ordinary, 25

Eagleton, Terry, 149, 157
Edgeworth, Maria, 190n47
Edwardian fiction, 8–9, 17, 186n23; everyday life represented by, 13; experimental modernism vs., 10–11

Eliot, George, 21
Eliot, T. S., 64
Emerson, Ralph Waldo, 31–32, 173–74
Emmet, Robert, 61
empathy, 9, 102–3
empire: banality of, 27–36; colony vs., 6–7; desire and domesticity in backwaters of, 71–79; Joyce and, 34–35; Mansfield and, 34–35, 71–79; margins of, 3; social structures of, 90; space of boredom, 72. *See also* British Empire
English-language fiction, 5, 6, 29–30, 106; British Empire and, 16; global expansion, 185n5; Indian, 135–38, 146; rise and development of, 20
Enlightenment, 28–29; aesthetic value in, 19–20
Enlightenment modernity, 186n23, 192n61; aesthetic modernism related to, 16–17; aesthetic principles of, 8; literary modernism vs., 16–17, 29–30
ennui, 84–85; boredom vs., 22–23, 190n47; evolution of mental state, 22–23
Ennui (Edgeworth), 190n47
epic, 41
epiphany, 11; banality of, 48; failure of invited, 46; Joycean, 42–45, 49–50, 59–60; object resistant to, 53
ethnic literature, 138–39
ethnographic gaze, 118
ethnography, 99; alienness and, 103; boredom analysis, 23–24, 187n25; of everyday life in colony, 62–69; functionalist, 26–27; Joyce and, 65; Māori and, 82; surrealism and, 102–3, 107
Eveline (character from Joyce), 40
event, 169–75
everyday life, 29, 35–36, 148; aesthetic exploration of, 106; anthropology and, 26; banality and, 9–10; Chaudhuri and, 150–51; in city, 10–11; Dumm on, 25; Edwardian representation of, 13; ethnography of, in colony, 62–69; foreigner, 118; Hegel on, 20; Lefebvre on, 25; local, 118; Mansfield and, 96–97; poetics of, 206n2; rupturing, 90–99; sensory structure of, 170; spatial and temporal experience of, 23–24
excitement, 34, 123
exclusion, 21–22, 34, 197n5
existentialism, 20
Experience Without Qualities: Boredom and Modernity (Goodstein), 21
exteriority discourse, 92

Fabian, Johannes, 119
Fairfield, Beryl (character from Mansfield), 71–75, 84, 89–90, 96–97
family, 152
Famished Road, The (Okrie), 107
fantastic, the, national allegory and fetishization of, 135–47
Father Butler (character from Joyce), 48
female boredom, 14–15, 24, 89; psychosis and, 90
fictionality, 189n35
Fisher, Philip, 185n4
flânerie, 67–68; Chaudhuri and, 147–68
Flaubert, Gustave, 21, 22
Flowers of Evil (Baudelaire), 21, 22
Fools (Ndebele), 110–12, 115
foreignness, 118, 155–56
Foucault, Michel, 25–26
fragment, 49
Frazer, James, 26–27, 62–64, 82
Freedom Song (Chaudhuri), 165, 166
Frow, John, 186n23, 194n13
Fry, Roger, 2
Fullbrook, Kate, 95–96

Gallagher, Catherine, 54–55, 189n35
Gallaher, Ignatius (character from Joyce), 37–39

Galsworthy, John, 8
Gandhi, Mahatma, 141, 151–52, 204n24
gender, 77–79, 81; liberation movements and, 130–31. *See also* male characters; women
gendered boredom, 75, 84–85. *See also* female boredom
Ghosh, Bishnupriya, 146
Gibson, Andrew, 29
Giddens, Anthony, 187n26
Gikandi, Simon, 188n27, 192n61
Gilroy, Paul, 192n61
Ginsburg, Michal Peled, 20
globalization: capitalism and, 165, 187n25; literary, 30, 185n5
Golden Bough, The (Frazer), 63
Goncalves, Jose Reginaldo, 197n45
good detail, 58–59
Goodstein, Elizabeth, 21, 22, 178, 190n47
Gordon, Ian, 82, 91–93
grandeur: banality and, 41, 115–21; ordinary and, 156
Great Indian Novel, The (Tharoor), 141, 142, 145
Greenblatt, Stephen, 54–55
Guha, Ranajit, 192n61
Guha, Sumit, 140

Habermas, Jürgen, 139–40
Hansen, Thomas Blom, 25
Hardt, Michael, 19
Harrison, Johnny (character from Mansfield), 91–92
Harrison, Tom, 63–64
Hart, Matthew, 192n65
Head, Bessie, 113–14
Hegel, G. W. F., 9, 20, 47, 58
Hemingway, Ernest, 124
Herbert, Zbigniew, 194n13
Herzfeld, Michael, 178
Hilda Lessways (Bennett, Arnold), 8–9
"Hills Like White Elephants" (Hemingway), 124

historicism, critique of, 41–59
historiography, 48–49, 123; clashing, 115–21; dominant models of, 106–7; fictional, 114–15; India, 146
history, banality and, 170–72
"Home Sweet Home" (Wicomb), 125–26
Howes, Marjorie, 61
"How Pearl Button Was Kidnapped" (Mansfield), 95
Hyde, Robin, 79

Ibsen, Henrik, 42
Ihimaera, Witi, 71, 76, 78, 80
immigration, 126
Immortals, The (Chaudhuri), 162
imperial administration, 3, 6
"Imperial Boredom" (Auerbach), 72–73
imponderabilia of life, 27, 103
In a German Pension (Mansfield), 77
India, 178; Anglophone literature, 135–38, 147–48, 150, 168; historiography, 146; narrative of, 175. *See also specific places; specific works from India*
indifference, 178
indigenous culture, 36, 73, 94; anthropology and, 83; Mansfield and, 81; Otherness and, 103–4
inner lives, 13, 127
Isabel (character from Mansfield), 98
isolation, 73
"Ithaca" (chapter from *Ulysses*), 52, 57–58, 60

James (character from Wicomb), 128–29
Jameson, Fredric, 135–37, 141, 188n27, 203n12
"Jameson's Rhetoric of Otherness and the 'National Allegory'" (Ahmad), 136
"Jan Klinkies," 125
Jayojit (character from Chaudhuri), 163
Jennings, Humphrey, 63–64
Jolly, Rosemary, 108–9

Joyce, James, 5, 27–28, 41, 163; anthropology and, 62–63, 197n45; artistic duality, 39–40; banality and, 24, 37–40, 62; biographical and imaginative movements of, 30–31; boredom and, 49; capitalism, democratization, consumerism and, 50–51; Chaudhuri and, 153–55, 167; empire and, 34–35; epiphany and, 42–45, 49–50, 59–60; ethnography and, 65; Leonard on fiction of, 47; as modernist, 29; object and, 195n17; as spiritual, 9; use of temporality, 48–49; Wicomb and, 112. *See also Dubliners*; *Ulysses*; *specific characters*; *specific works*

Kapur, Geeta, 137
Kesavan, Mukul, 143, 145–46
key, 56–57
Kezia (character from Mansfield), 98
Kierkegaard, Søren, 15
Kincaid, Jamaica, 32–33, 36, 120–21
Klinkies, Jan (character from Wicomb), 125
knowledge, lack of, 128–29

labor, 38, 86, 88; bureaucratic, 10; feminized, 50, 85; routine and, 96
langweiler, 121
Lawrence, D. H., 149
Lefebvre, Henri, 19, 23–24, 170, 177; desire and, 193n71; on everyday life, 25; on ordinary, 25
le Fleur, Andrew (character from Wicomb), 114
Leonard, Garry, 44, 47, 52, 59–60
"Lestrygonians" (chapter from *Ulysses*), 52, 55, 60
Levinas, Emmanuel, 45, 102, 200n4
"Life of Ma Parker" (Mansfield), 85–88
Linda (character from Mansfield), 72
literary modernism, 83, 99, 115, 185n5; Anglophone literature related to, 28–29;
British Empire and, 5–6; Enlightenment modernity vs., 16–17, 29–30
Little Chandler. *See* Chandler, Thomas Malone "Little Chandler"
"Little Cloud, A" (Joyce), 37–39
"Little Girl, The" (Mansfield), 72
local, 118, 155–56
Long Walk to Freedom (Mandela), 108
Looking Through Glass (Kesavan), 145–46
Lottie (character from Mansfield), 98
Love, Heather, 14, 21
Lukács, Georg, 58–59, 61
Lynch (character from Joyce), 59–60

Maata (Mansfield), 2, 78
Macaskill, Brian, 109
Madame Bovary (Flaubert), 21
Madge, Charles, 63–64
Mahapuku, Martha Grace, 2, 78
Mains, Daniel, 120, 187n25
Malange, Nise, 113
male characters, 85–87
Malinowski, Bronislaw, 26–27, 103, 118, 168; anthropology and, 62–65; coefficient of weirdness and reality, 102, 104, 117; functionalist anthropology and, 191n60
Mandela, Nelson, 108
Mander, Jane, 79
Manganaro, Marc, 62–65
Mansfield, Katherine, 5, 27–28, 116; banality and, 6–8, 11; biographical and imaginative movements of, 31; boredom and, 96–97; colonial history and relationship with, 77; colonial setting in works of, 99; context for work, 2; desire and domesticity, 71–79; diaries, 77–78; diary, December 21, 1908, 1–2, 3; empire and, 34–35, 71–79; everyday life and, 96–97; female boredom, 89–90; gender and sexuality in work of, 77–79, 81; indigenous culture and, 81; male characters, 85–87; as modernist, 29; New

Mansfield, Katherine (*continued*)
Zealand landscape, 78; New Zealand literature development and, 79–80; personal biography, 75–77; travel notebooks, 81; violence and, 92–94, 97, 98; Wicomb and, 113; women in works of, 74–75, 85–87, 96; youth and, 89, 96, 97–98. *See also specific characters*; *specific works*
Mao, Douglas, 46–47
Māori, 78–83, 92–95
Māoritanga, 80
Ma Parker (character from Mansfield), 85–88
Marling, Karal Ann, 191n50
marriage, 86, 140; arranged, 166
Marx, John, 6, 14, 29–30
Marxist theory, 196n34
Mass-Observation project, 63–64
materialism, 13, 136–37
Mbembe, Achille, 208n31
McKeon, Michael, 189n35
Mee, Jon, 144–45
memory, involuntary, 45, 46
metropolitan space, 3, 155; artistic possibilities of, 40; banality and, 12; peripheral space related to, 4, 30–32, 39–41, 192n65
Michael (character from Wicomb), 124–25, 132
Midnight's Children (Rushdie), 107, 113, 135, 141, 146, 150, 164–65; Chaudhuri on, 144–45; publication, 137–38, 143–44, 147
Millie (character from Mansfield), 84–85
"Millie" (Mansfield), 88, 90–94
"Miss Brill" (Mansfield), 84, 88–89
Mr. Mitra (character from Chaudhuri), 162
mobility, 32
mock-heroism, 41
modernism, 6, 158–59, 186n23; aesthetic, 14, 16–17; avant-garde, 28; experimental, 8–11; framework endemic to, 14; high, 11, 16, 26, 104–5, 115; modernity vs., 16–17, 187n26, 187n27; naturalism and, 59. *See also* literary modernism

modernist experimentation, 48
modernist literature, 28, 29–30, 168, 169; object in, 46–47
modernity, 6, 14, 19, 50, 51, 115, 123; banality as related to metropolitan, 12; in colony, 3–4, 11–12; European cultural, 29; generic, 16–27; global, 99; identifying, 187n26; imperial, 28; models of, 5; modernism vs., 16–17, 187n26, 187n27; in New Zealand, 79; philosophical, 28–29; political, 28–29; politicophilosophical, 16. *See also* colonial modernity; Enlightenment modernity
Mofokeng, Boitumelo, 101, 113
Moira (character from Wicomb), 129
Moretti, Franco, 19, 21, 169
Moshenberg, Daniel, 61
"Mr. Bennett and Mrs. Brown" (Woolf), 8
"Mr Reginald Peacock's Day" (Mansfield), 86
Mufti, Aamir R., 192n61
Mukherjee, Meenakshi, 146
Musil, Robert, 21
Myra (character from Wicomb), 128–29, 132

Nandrea, Lorri G., 20
Nan Pym (character from Mansfield), 72
narrative, 5, 172–73, 175; of colonialism, 36; in colony, 106–15; of decolonization, 36; Dublin, 68–69; of India, 175; late-twentieth- and early-twenty-first-century, 176; ordinariness and, 174; prosaic, 10; realism, 10, 17, 29; of spectacle, 179; time and, 169–73
national allegory, 107–9, 133, 175; fetishization of fantastic and, 135–47
national identity, 141
nationhood, 107
native, 33
naturalism, 53–54, 56, 57, 159; binarization of, 58–59; modernism and, 59. *See also* symbolist naturalism
"Nausicaa" (chapter from *Ulysses*), 52

Ndebele, Njabulo, 36, 109–13, 115, 147, 174–77
Negative Dialectics (Adorno), 47
Negri, Antonio, 19
"Nestor" (chapter of *Ulysses*), 48–49
New World, A (Chaudhuri), 163
New Zealand, 2–3; colonial history in, 92; countryside, 71–72, 74, 81–82; literature, 79–82; Mansfield's relationship with landscape of, 78; modernity and colonialism in, 79
Ngai, Sianne, 4–5, 185n4, 186n23
Nietzsche, Friedrich, 15
Nirmalya (character from Chaudhuri), 162
Nkosi, Lewis, 108, 132
Nolan, Emer, 29
noncathartic affects, 4–5, 185n4, 186n23
nonevent, 169–79

object, common or banal, 43, 159, 161–62, 186n23; epistemological opacity of, 46; Joycean studies of, 195n17; lists, 58; in modernist literature, 46–47; resistance to epiphanization, 53; Segal's exploration of, 44–45, 54; in symbolist naturalism, 50–59; in *Ulysses*, 51–59, 60–62. *See also* subject-object relation
object-love, 47
Okrie, Ben, 107
"Ole Underwood" (Mansfield), 94
Olson, Liesl, 13, 28, 57, 169–70; on failure of invited epiphany, 46
Opipi, 82–83, 94
ordinariness, 62–63; cultural construct as, 160; familiar, 163; narrative and, 174
ordinary, the, 23, 148; aesthetics of, 170; Cavell and, 176; dramatic and, 105–6, 115; duality of, 155–56, 166–67; Dumm on, 25; extraordinary and, 118, 166–67; grand and, 156; late-twentieth- and early-twenty-first-century narrative and, 176; Lefebvre on, 25; potential, 174; rediscovery of, 111–13; strange and, 102–3, 168
ordinary details, 53–54, 58, 156, 168
ordinary life. *See* everyday life
Orr, Bridget, 78, 79
Ota, Yoshinobu, 200n1
Other, 16, 82, 102, 103–4, 142; ethics and, 200n4; Self encountering, 45

Pākehā, 79–82, 99
Pater, Walter, 1
Patwardhan, Anand, 137
Peacock, Reginald (character from Mansfield), 86–88
"Pearl Button" (Mansfield), 95–96
Pechey, Graham, 127
Pels, Peter, 104, 191n58
Perera, Sonali, 177
peripheral space: banality within, 40; metropolitan space related to, 4, 30–32, 39–41, 192n65
Phillips, Siobhan, 206n2
Picador Book of Modern Indian Literature (Chaudhuri), 148, 150
Plaatje, Sol, 108
Playing in the Light (Wicomb), 114
pleasure, 32; banality, boredom, desire, and, 8–16
politics, 25; aesthetics and, 35; Anglophone fiction and, 175; of colonialism, 6–7, 35–36; modernity and, 28–29; postcolonial fiction and, 35–36; power, 163; of South African literature, 110; of tourism, 32–33
Politics of Modernism, The (Williams, R.), 30
Politics of the Ordinary, A (Dumm), 25
Portrait of the Artist as a Young Man, A (Joyce), 40–42, 44–45; Walkowitz on, 43
postcolonial era, 178; Anglophone fiction, 3–4, 35; cultural politics of fiction, 35–36; motifs for literary criticism, 4
postcolonial identity, 6, 16, 141–42

poststructuralism, 149–50, 158, 191n57
potato, 54–57
Pound, Ezra, 64
power, 21–22, 107; of banality, 49, 148, 178; hierarchy of, 119; politics, 163; relations, 23, 67
Practice of Everyday Life, The (de Certeau), 66
Pratt, Mary Louise, 26, 27, 104
Predicament of Culture, The (Clifford), 98, 101–2
"Prelude" (Mansfield), 71–72, 84, 88, 97, 98
private sphere, 92, 135, 137–39, 141–44, 172, 198n27; public-, divide, 140, 166, 203n12
progress, 15, 26, 40, 54, 68, 123; evolutionary, 104; expectations of, 120–21; hierarchies of, 81; lack of, 197n5; measuring, 119
prosaic narrative, 10
prose, 10, 20, 168; poetry and, 206n2
protest literature, 108–10, 133, 147, 174–75
provincialism, 14, 154; Chaudhuri and, 152
Provincializing Europe (Chakrabarty), 48, 119
public sphere, 135, 137–39, 141–48, 151, 172, 177–78, 198n27; private-, divide, 140, 166, 203n12

quotidian. *See* everyday life
"Quotidian Experience and the Perspectives of Poetry in Postliberation South Africa" (Sole), 112–13

racial groups, 131
Rajan, Rajeshwari Sunder, 146
Ranciére, Jacques, 177
Randall, Bryony, 206n2
Ransom, John Crowe, 47
Rao, Raja, 167
rationalism, 10
Ray, Satyajit, 137
realism, 59, 150; magic, 143; narrative, 10, 17, 29; regional, 79

reality: coefficient of, 102, 104, 117; weirdness and, 101–6
realization, 49–50
"Real Time" (Chaudhuri), 162, 165
Red Earth and Pouring Rain (Chandra), 141, 145
"Redefining Relevance" (Ndebele), 110
"Rediscovery of the Ordinary, The" (Ndebele), 110, 147, 175–76
refusal, praxis of, 121–33
"Return of the Flâneurm, The" (Benjamin), 164–65
Ricoeur, Paul, 172, 173, 175, 207n13
Robbins, Bruce, 190n47
role-playing game, 151–52
routine, 3, 96, 178
Roy, Arundhati, 138
Rushdie, Salman, 107, 113, 135, 137–38, 141, 146, 150, 164–65; Chaudhuri on, 144–45; publication of work, 143–44, 147

Sachs, Albie, 109
Said, Edward, 25–26, 119
Sandeep (character from Chaudhuri), 151–53, 157–61
Sargeson, Frank, 78, 79, 99
Schor, Naomi, 50, 58–59, 126–27
Schwenger, Peter, 186n23
Sealy, I. Alan, 141, 145
secular vision, 19
Segal, Naomi, 53–54, 159; exploration of object, 44–45
segregated spaces, 122
self-understanding, 21
sensational events, 175
Seremetakis, Nadia, 142, 170, 172, 175
settler colonial population, 73, 95; boredom after contact with, 197n5; Māori culture and, 78; masculine imagination of, 74, 79; social structures, 91; women, 74
sexuality, 77–78, 81

"Shame and Identity: The Case of the Coloured in South Africa" (Wicomb), 132
Shenton, Frieda (character from Wicomb), 111–15, 117–22, 126–30; abortion, 123–25; racial identities, 132–33
Shobha mami (character from Chaudhuri), 160
Sicherman, Carol, 111, 129
Sinai, Saleem (character from Rushdie), 113
"Sirens" (chapter from *Ulysses*), 52
Skitterboud (character from Wicomb), 127–28
Small Place, A (Kincaid), 32–33, 120–21
soap, 51–57, 59–62
Sole, Kelwyn, 35–36, 107, 112–13, 193n71
Solid Objects: Modernism and the Test of Production (Mao), 46–47
South Africa, 107–15, 123, 147; literature, 108, 110. *See also specific works from South Africa*
South Asian literature, 137
Spacks, Patricia Meyer, 14, 16, 84, 90, 103, 121; ennui vs. boredom and, 22–23
spectacle, 147, 171–72, 174, 177–79, 194n73
spiritual condition, 190n47
Sprinker, Michael, 136
Stead, C. K., 78
Stephen Hero (Joyce), 41–45, 50, 68
Stepputat, Finn, 25
Strange and Sublime Address, A (Chaudhuri), 151–53, 157–60
stream-of-consciousness method, 10
subaltern pasts, 158–59
Subaltern Ulysses, The (Duffy), 67–68
subject-object relation, 44, 46, 66; traditional, 47
Suleri, Sara, 142–43
surrealism, 104–5; ethnography and, 102–3, 107
Svendsen, Lars, 11, 33
symbolism, 53–54, 56, 57, 159; binarization of, 58–59; failure of, 46, 47

symbolist naturalism, 65; banal object in, 50–59
Szeman, Imre, 136, 141

Tagore, Rabindranath, 137
Tamieta (character from Wicomb), 127–28, 130–31
Taussig, Michael, 26, 157–58
temporality, 14, 121, 197n5, 206n2, 208n31; in Joyce's fiction, 48–49
Tharoor, Shashi, 141, 142, 145
thing theory, 186n23, 194n13
Third World literature, 135–37
"Third World Literature in the Era of Multinational Capitalism" (Jameson), 135–37
Thoba (character from Ndebele), 110
time, 169–73
Tlali, Miriam, 108
Tomalin, Claire, 75–76, 78
tourism, 32–33, 120–21
transcendence, 10, 15; aesthetic, 9; banality and, 13–14; boredom and, 11
transformation, 57, 159; banality and, 12–13, 128
transgression, 97
transience, 60; critique of historicism, banality and, 41–59
Treaty of Waitangi of 1840, 2, 79
Trollope, Anthony, 76
Trotternama (Sealy), 141, 145

Ugly Feelings (Ngai), 185n4
Ulysses (Joyce), 38–41, 47–50, 69; R. M. Adams, on, 56–57; anthropology and, 62–63; Auerbach's objections to, 196n31; banal objects, 51–59, 60–62; Bishop on, 51; urban landscape of, 61; walking, 66. *See also specific chapters; specific characters*
Unfamiliar Relations: Family and History in South Asia (Chatterjee, I.), 152
United States, pursuit of happiness in, 24–25

Urewera Notebook, The (Mansfield), 81–84, 91–93, 95

violence, 83–84; Mansfield and, 92–94, 97, 98; South Africa and, 110

waiting, 121–23
walking, 66, 163, 165
Walkowitz, Rebecca, 43
Waste Land, The (Eliot, T. S.), 64
Watt, Ian, 189n35
Weber, Max, 10
Weberian bureaucracy, 10
weirdness: coefficient of, 102, 104, 117; reality and, 101–6
Wells, H. G., 8, 9
Weston, Jessie, 64
Wevers, Lydia, 92
Wicomb, Zoë, 5, 27, 29, 114–21, 124–26, 128–32; banality and, 28, 35, 123; biographical and imaginative movements of, 31; classification, 201n20; interiority celebrated by, 127; Joyce and, 112; Mansfield and, 113; rediscovery of ordinary, 111–13; waiting and, 121–25. *See also specific characters*; *specific works*
Williams, Mark, 81–82
Williams, Patrick, 49
Williams, Raymond, 30, 196n34
Wilson, Edmund, 53–54, 58–59
"With My Baby on My Back" (Mofokeng), 101

Wolseley, Garnet, 72–73
"Woman at the Store, The" (Mansfield), 93–94, 97
women: apartheid identity, 131–32; colonialism and, 131–32; coloured identity, 132–33; female tedium and colonial desire, 84–90; feminized labor, 50, 85; gendered boredom and, 75, 84–85; Mansfield's, 74–75, 85–87, 96; poetry by, 113; power relations and, 67; protagonists, 85; protest movement, 130–31; settler colonial, 74; South Africa, 113. *See also* female boredom; gender
Woolf, Leonard, 3
Woolf, Virginia, 13, 17, 54, 163, 169–70, 186n23; banality and, 11; Arnold Bennett, quarrel with, 8–9, 12, 13; depiction of flânerie, 67; diary of future husband, 3; Edwardian vs. experimental modernism and, 10–11; female boredom and, 14–15; human character and, 1
working class, 24
Writing Culture, 101–2

"You Can't Get Lost in Cape Town" (Wicomb), 123–25
You Can't Get Lost in Cape Town (Wicomb), 111–21, 123–25, 133
Young, Robert, 73
youth, 24, 117; banality and, 121–22; Mansfield and, 89, 96, 97–98; maturing, 115

Zoe (character from Joyce), 55

GPSR Authorized Representative: Easy Access System Europe, Mustamäe tee 50, 10621 Tallinn, Estonia, gpsr.requests@easproject.com